Minnesota Swedes

Volume I

The Emigration from Trolle Ljungby to Goodhue County

1855-1912

Second Edition - Revised

Lilly Setterdahl

Minnesota Swedes

Volume I

The Emigration from Trolle Ljungby to Goodhue County

1855-1912

Second Edition - Revised

First edition published in 1996 by American Friends of the Emigrant Institute of Sweden

Copyright © Lilly Setterdahl 2015

ISBN: 978-1507529560

1507529562

CreateSpace.com

Preface

This volume is a revised edition of my out-of-print and much sought after *Minnesota Swedes: The Emigration from Trolle Ljungby to Goodhue County 1855-1912* published in 1996 by the former American Friends of the Emigrant Institute of Sweden. Vol. II published in 1999 with the subtitle *Trolle Ljungby Families in Goodhue County* is still available online.

The work on my first *Minnesota Swedes* was made possible in part by a research grant from the Swedish Emigrant Institute. Contributions toward the publication were coming from the Petri Fund in Kristianstad, the J. P. Bengtsson Fund in Trolle Ljungby, and several memorial gifts received after my husband's passing in 1995.

Since the files to the first volume were lost, the best way to reproduce the book was to reset it. The result is a smaller second edition in which the statistical tables and most of the footnotes have been omitted along with some of the photographs and illustrations. A few footnotes have been changed to endnotes. In some instances, the text has been rearranged. The photographs formerly on the front cover are now in the interior of the book. Thanks to new technology, it has been possible to improve on the quality of the images. An incorrect photo has been replaced with a correct one. Two additional interviews are included.

The chapter "Comparison with Isanti County Rättvik Settlers" compares the Trolle Ljungby settlement with Swedish settlements in Isanti County as researched by Dr. Robert C. Ostergren, and published in his book, *A Community Transplanted: The Trans-Atlantic Experience of a Swedish Immigrant Settlement in the Upper Middle West)*. Dr. Ostergren researched the emigration from Upper Dalarna, especially Rättvik.

To my knowledge, no other study has been made and published in English about former tenant farmers at Swedish castle estates, and how they fared as homesteaders in America, which is one of the reasons I found it important to republish this title. We all know how the Irish peasants were treated by their landlords, but it is shocking to find out what the masses in Trolle Ljungby had to endure in the mid-1800s. They may not have starved, but they had to take the corporal punishment from the estate inspector. One immigrant, Jonas Wallengren, the son of the parish minister in Trolle Ljungby, wrote of them, "They must like the whip since they stay and rather take more of it than leave Ljungby." (p. 57). One young boy was beaten for no reason by the master (p. 37). In their letters, Trolle Ljungby emigrants wrote that they were glad to be free of the slavery. In contrast, they referred to America as the land of freedom.

Most of the individuals who freely shared their memories with us in the early 1990s have since passed away. My late husband Lennart assisted me with the interviews and encouraged me in my work. I could not have done all the traveling without him. We both visited Trolle Ljungby for the first time in the beginning of my research. I had no previous knowledge of the privileges granted to the estate or the tenant farmers' situation, but I did know that a large group from the parish had settled in Goodhue County. We returned several times to the Trolle Ljungby area to conduct interviews and take photographs while I worked on my project during the summer of 1993 at the Emigrant Institute in Växjö. From our home in Illinois, we made many trips to Goodhue County where I performed research in various archives and met with descendants of the Trolle Ljungby group.

Lennart traveled on his own in Minnesota and Wisconsin for almost two years recording oral histories with individuals of various Swedish origins for the Swedish Emigrant Institute, which houses those interviews and also the recordings with Trolle Ljungby descendants. Unless otherwise noted, the photographs in this book were taken by Lennart or myself.

Lilly Setterdahl

Table of Contents

Endorsement

Lilly Setterdahl's study of the chain migration from the Swedish parish of Trolle Ljungby to Minnesota's Goodhue County is a valuable contribution towards satisfying the need to assemble good and complete studies of trans-Atlantic migration experiences that lend themselves to comparison. Indeed she has even taken up the challenge of comparing her findings with those of other similarly organized studies of Scandinavian trans-Atlantic migrations and offers us a number of useful observations. But her work is valuable in another very important way. This has to do with the richness of material. Through interviews with descendants, analyses of letters, public documents, census materials and parish registers, and a remarkable personal familiarity with the respective histories and landscapes of Trolle Ljungby and Goodhue County, she is also able to weave a resplendent tapestry of detail about the lives of those who left their homes in Sweden to take up the challenge of building a new home in Minnesota. This, as much as anything else, makes this a book of great interest to anyone interested in the Great Atlantic migration.

Robert C. Ostergren

Department of Geography, University of Wisconsin-Madison

Source: Foreword in Minnesota Swedes published in 1996.

Trolle Ljungby

The Setting

Located on the Skåne plains between an inland lake and the Baltic Sea, Trolle Ljungby lies in the Villand district that includes 15 parishes and two towns, Åhus and Bromölla. Before 1830 the parish name was Ljungby and then Vestra Ljungby until 1884. Today it belongs to Kristianstad *kommun*.

Trolle Ljungby Castle

Trolle Ljungby parish covers 18 square miles. Many of the 750 to 800 residents worked at the nearby Nymölla Paper Mill or in Bromölla. The castle farm performed business as Trolle Ljungby AB. It covered almost all the land in the parish, and extended into Gualöv, Ivetofta, Näsum, and other parishes, as well as into the province of Blekinge.

The Trolle Ljungby Castle dates back to 1639. The main two-story brick building has two wings and a tower surrounded by a moat. It is built in typical Skåne-Danish style, the so-called Kristian IV-style. The castle is best known for its legendary artifacts, the Ljungby Horn and Pipe, which have been safely kept there since the 1500s. Every Wednesday when the main gate is open they are on display in one of the castle windows for the tourists to view.

The Saga of Ljungby Horn and Pipe

On the estates of Ljungby there lies a large stone called Maglestone, under which the Trolls in olden times were wont to assemble and with dancing and games celebrate their Christmas. One Christmas night Lady Cissela Ulfstand, sitting in their mansion, listening to the merry-making of the Trolls under the stone and curious to have a better knowledge of these mysterious mountain people, assembled her men servants and promised the best horse in her stables to him who would ride to Maglestone at Vesper hour and bring her a full account of the doings there. One of her swains, a daring young fellow, accepted the offer, and a little later set out on his way. Arriving at the stone, he discovered it lifted from the ground supported on pillars of gold, and under it the Trolls in the midst of their revelry. Upon discovering the horseman, a young Troll woman, leaving the others, approached him bearing a drinking horn and pipe. These, upon reaching his side, she placed in the young man's hand, with directions to first drink from the horn to the health of the Mountain King, then blow three times on the pipe, at the same time whispering some words of caution in his ears, whereupon he threw the contents of the horn over this shoulder and set off at the utmost speed over fields and meadows toward home. The Trolls followed him closely with great clamor, but he flew before them across the drawbridge, which was at once pulled up, and proceeded to place the horn and pipe in the hands of his mistress. Outside across the moat, the Trolls now stood, promising Lady Cissela great happiness and riches if she would return to them their horn and pipe, and declaring that otherwise great misfortune and destruction would overtake her and her family, and that it should go especially hard with the young man who had dared to deprive them of their precious articles. True to the predictions, the young man died on the third day thereafter and the horse which he rode fell dead a day later.

W. H. Myers, translator, in book by Herman Hofberg.

From the 1300s through the 1700s the Trolle Ljungby Estate belonged to the noble families Bille, Ulfstand, Gyllenstierna, and Coyet (the latter between 1662 and 1804). The heirs of Peter Julius Coyet received Ljungby and Årup (a large estate in Ivetofta parish) as entailed estate in trust. Two generations later the name of the fief holder was Sparre. Governor Sparre's daughter married Sweden's last national chancellor Carl Axel Trolle-Wachtmeister (1754-1810), the estate holder to Trolleberg. This privilege was transferred to Ljungby in 1830, later renamed Trolle Ljungby. As a result, the name of the family changed to Trolle-Wachtmeister.

Count Hans Gabriel Trolle-Wachtmeister took over the estate after his father's death in 1956. From an interview with him August 30, 1993 and additional information from the estate inspector we learned the following about the estate at the time: The total acreage was 11,580 hectares (28,602.6 acres), which included some forest and about 300 hectares that were taken out of production, according to government regulations (One hectare equals 2.47 acres). The old parish lines were of no interest to the count, and he paid no attention to them. He leased out 4,000 hectares of open land and 400 hectares meadow to 46 different farm operators. The Trolle Ljungby AB had about 50 employees. The main crops were potatoes, sugar beets, barley, rye, and rape. The harvest of barley amounted to between 3 and 6 metric ton per acre. The livestock at Trolle Ljungby included about 200 dairy cows. Note that all these facts might have changed.

The Trolle Ljungby Parish Church

The church located next to the castle was originally constructed about 1200. It has been enlarged and restored several times. The altar from 1639 is carved in oak and painted. To the left of the altar is the pastor's seat adorned with pictures of Apostles Paul and Peter. To the left of the pastor's seat is the entrance to a tomb below, where members of the Coyet family are entombed. The front pews are reserved for the count and his family. It reminds us of the time before 1923 when the count selected the parish pastor. The family crests of the noble families Gyllenstierna, Coyet, and other former nobility of the Trolle Ljungby Castle are affixed to the pews. The oil paintings on the gallery walls are from the 1700s and depict the Articles of Faith. Twenty-one of the original 23 paintings remain. The baptismal font in Roman style is from the 12th or 13th century. In 1991 the Museum of History in Lund

returned several wooden sculptures to the church. Three of five smaller sculptures are from the 1400s. Despite its old age, the interior of the church gives a warm impression. The Lutheran faith is preached from its pulpit. In the adjacent cemetery there is a tomb with the inscription, "Here they sleep, replete with wars, tired of civil duty, the ancient lords of Ljungby. May God grant their souls peace."

The Villand Landscape

The landscape in the Villand district varies more than anywhere else in Skåne. Standing on the highest point at Kjuge Kull, one is in the heart of the area. Here the eyes can feast on beautiful hardwood trees and lakes in three directions. In the middle of Ivösjön a cliff formation with steep sides and a flat top (Ivö Klack) breaks the view of the water. From the road between Råby and Bromölla by Levrasjön's greenish water similar cliffs in Oppmanna, Vånga, and Klagstorp glimmer in pastel colors in the evening haze. Norra Vånga is a world by itself with its forested ridges, narrow fields, and the 175 meter high crest by the lake Grönhultsjön.

Across Ivösjön goes an imagery line east-west, which divides Skåne in two parts. The northeastern part with its forested ridges, lakes, cliffs, and valleys is more reminiscent of Södermanland and Värmland than the genuine Skåne. The landscape south and west of the Villand lakes is part of the Kristianstad plains broken only by hills such as Fjälkinge *backe*, where on a clear day one can see the park, *Stens Huvud,* jutting out into Östersjön.

In Vanneberga, the farmers busy themselves with huge machinery. Near Nymö a former peat bog has been transformed into rich black-soil fields. The land in Trolle Ljungby is free of rocks except in Tosteberga near the sea. Here the cows graze among the boulders in the meadows. The many stone fences seen in this area bear witness of the efforts needed to rid the fields of rocks. Toward Östersjön the landscape changes into Skåne's only archipelago with some 30 islands. The fishing village of Landön at one time had a deep harbor that was very important to the area (From a description in Swedish by Karl Bengtsson). Unless otherwise noted the translations in this book are by the author.

Background History

The Proletarianization of Skåne

The Trollasten in Trolle Ljungby

As a result of a peace treaty with Denmark, Skåne has belonged to Sweden since 1658. At that time the Danish nobility still controlled about half of the land in Skåne. One nobleman managed seven castles surrounded by large estates. When the Swedish king Karl X Gustaf visited Skåne many of the Danish-born noblemen refused to pledge their allegiance to him. Some fled to Denmark and were replaced with Swedish nobility. During *Skånska Kriget* (the Scanian War, 1676-79) the so-called freedom fighters fought on the side of the Danes. The noblemen who could not be trusted to be loyal to Sweden were deprived of their estates. One was executed.

As a lead in making Skåne Swedish, Lund University was founded in 1668, but the re-nationalization process was slow. Gradually, Swedish clergy replaced the Danish-speaking pastors, and people learned to read Swedish. In 1681 and 1682, Swedish laws, courts, and church system were established. During the peace time that followed the Great Nordic War (1700-21) Skåne became fully assimilated with the rest of Sweden.

Sweden has had its own nobility since the reign of Gustav Vasa (1523-60). King Gustav secured 20 percent of all homesteads for the king and the crown. He and his successors traded some of that land for services to the state as for instance military service. The gifts were fiefdoms that could be in the form of temporary ownership of land, income from certain farms, or privileges. The tax-exempt fiefdoms were supposed to last only as long as the king lived, but many were illegally made inheritable. The income from them became taxable about 1900, but then the fief-holder usually took out a corresponding amount from his tenant farmers.

The fief-holder divided the estate into smaller farms that he rented out to tenants who paid the rent by working on the estate. The practice was based on unregulated labor laws. During planting and harvesting time the tenant farmers were often forced to neglect their own crops.

Sweden's first noble estates were established during the reign of Erik XIV (1560-68) and many more were created through the reign of Queen Kristina. The privileged class became even wealthier during the Thirty Years War (1618-48) when the government in dire need of money to carry on the war sold crown land to the nobility. In so doing the government actually reduced its source of future income.

In the beginning of the 1670s the non-privileged farm owners requested lower taxes and a reduction of the nobility-held estates, and as a result the *riksdag* passed a new law in 1680. The estates held by counts and barons and others to the extent that they surpassed 600 *riksdaler* in income were to be reduced to the crown; estates that had been mortgaged or sold were also included. The Trolle Ljungby Estate escaped this "great reduction" by Charles XI, as did most of Skåne.

However, the nearby Bäckaskog Castle Estate, owned by the formerly Danish Ramel family, was taken over by the state.

In exchange for their privileges the castle masters had to provide housing for the king when he traveled outside of Stockholm. School-teacher Ola Lundborg wrote that he remembered when Karl XV anchored at Landön and visited Trolle Ljungby in 1851 and was escorted by the Count of Trolle Ljungby:

Carl was then newly married and arrived with his spouse on the steamer Thor.... The Scandinavian nobility with their fine carriages sparkled in full uniform and livery.... When the travelers went on to Trolle Ljungby for lunch we hurried after on foot. On the steps to the King's parlor, I saw Carl XV ruffle the hair of young Count Hans Wachtmeister.... The boy's grandfather also named Hans laughed and bowed straight forward from the hips every time the King said a word.

The Beginning of Protest

The peasants' struggle for fair treatment by the large landholders began in 1772-76 among tenant farmers in Skåne and Halland against the unlimited workdays on the estates. Showing great solidarity the farmers protested in writing, took part in strikes, and went to court, but it only resulted in eviction and fines. The leaders of the movement received jail sentences.

After the war with Russia in 1808-09 the general population of Sweden was destitute. The nobility agreed that the king and his ministers were to be blamed. The farmers argued that the peasants had to carry the heaviest burden in time of war. When Sweden was forced by France to declare war with England in 1810, 15,000 additional military men were needed. The law left it up to the parish council to decide whether the conscription should be by lottery or otherwise. Most settled on the lottery. Those without representation in the council had no say in the selection. The fact that the drawing preceded the extra call-up of soldiers from each ward added to the dissatisfaction. The results were uprisings not only in Skåne, but also in Uppland and Södermanland. The punishment of the protesters was severe in Södermanland. Many death sentences were issued, but these were later reduced so that the lives of all but one were spared. Count Carl-Axel Trolle Wachtmeister of Trolle Ljungby was the attorney general at the time. The tenant farmers were upset because in the past they had served in the military only half as often as the peasants on crown land or freeholds.

Uprisings in Skåne

The peasants in Skåne began their protest in the area of Ystad. On May 26, 1811, a group of hired men gathered at Krageholm Estate and demanded to see the count, Mr. Piper. When he informed the protesters about the necessity of obeying the law, he was told that if one of them had to go (to serve in the military), they would all go, and from that day they would not obey any orders to work on the estate. As a result troops were called in to keep order.

A young farmer, Ola Persson in Esperöd, Luggude, was selected to peacefully present a written protest to the governor Count von Rosen at a meeting in Helsingborg, asking that the peasants be spared until the trained forces needed help. He was accompanied by a large crowd of supporters. Having accomplished the task of delivering the message, the young farmer was held against his will in the city. The 'bloodthirsty' troops advanced so quickly toward the crowd that few had time to escape. Many protesters were injured. During the trial that followed it became known that the author of the formal protest was a radical retired military pastor and teacher. When this man was sentenced to one year of prison, the protesters became even more despondent and demanding. The government ordered the police in Skåne to disperse the rowdy crowds. Skåne was under siege. Not surprisingly, the farmers were afraid that the government would side with the nobility. The landless masses wanted the landowners to recruit soldiers from their own families rather than among those who worked on the farms.

To demonstrate their case, 1200 angry men marched to Klågerup Castle in Malmöhus län. Equipped with hayforks, scythes, clubs, and a few fire arms, they created great fear. The crowds were difficult to control and property was destroyed and looted. Forcing their way into storage buildings and cellars, the aggravated men refreshed themselves with strong drink. "It was not a happy day for the inspector at Klågerup…. Every lifted club reminded him of the many times he had used the club on the workers…. The inspector's prayers were answered when the troops came to the aid of the beleaguered Klågerup. The grounds surrounding the estate became a battlefield. Fighting bravely with their primitive weapons, the farm workers were overpowered.

Swedish weapons made Swedish blood flow on Swedish land. No one knew how many peasants died on this awful night. The official report stated 30, but many of the bodies had been removed by friends and relatives before they could be counted.

Two hundred prisoners were taken to Malmö Castle Prison at once. The total number of arrests came to 395. The severely injured captives were forced to perform hard labor. Of the 274 who were tried, 14 were freed. There were 20 death sentences. Three men were actually executed. Forty-three received 6-year-prison sentences plus 40 lashes. Others were sentenced to 28 days on water and bread or just 40 lashes. Most of the survivors also became the subject of military service, which was what they had protested in the first place. All foreigners in Skåne were ordered to leave the country within 24 hours. The power of the nobility was intact, but the peasants won the last round when the *riksdag* of 1812 annulled the law of military recruitment and the lottery was cancelled. The protests recurred in the mid-1860s when there was a conflict between the master at Råbelöf Estate and his peasant farmers (Alfred Kämpe and Uno Röndahl).

Kristianstad-bladet commented on the situation on February 10, 1866:

The question whether the master of Råbelöf really has legal ownership to the estate, land as well as income from the same, or if the crown and the farmers have more rights to it, is the cardinal point, and we can honestly say that we are not convinced that the estate master has the legal papers. It is an undisputed and highly remarkable fact that the counts in the past transferred titles on farmers' land to large estates.

The newspaper had researched one nobleman's estate from the 1830s and found that although he could not prove ownership, he nevertheless was granted the income from the property.

The reason for the confusion about ownership can partly be explained by the fact that in the 1500s the farmers paid their taxes to the government by doing workdays on castle constructions. As long as the farmer continued to pay his taxes by doing workdays and did not rent out his land he remained the owner of his land. Otherwise, the crown could confiscate his farm. The nobility could then buy the land from the crown, or the king could give it away (Wallentin).

When Gustav III wished to strengthen his power he was opposed by the nobility. The king then sought support from the burghers, clergy, and tax-paying farmers. With their help, the king managed to pass a law in 1789 that gave non-nobility the right to buy smaller farms from the nobility. Operators of crown land were also given the opportunity to buy the farms they leased from the government (Kämpe).

Inga Ljungquist of Valje explained how one crown-farmer lost his land to the Count of Trolle Ljungby:

Inga Ljungquist

The count bought several crown farms because those who rented them did not understand that they could buy them, so the count beat them to it. He paid only an insignificant amount. A boy driver once overheard the count saying as they drove by some farms, 'This one, I'm going to have, and this one I'm going to have.' The boy told some people about it, and the crown-farmers then went to Stockholm and bought out their tenant farms. This was during the reign of Gustav III. It was supposed to be advertized in all of Sweden's newspapers that the crown's tenant farmers had the first priority to buy, but it was written up only in the capital city papers.... When the count's lawman came out with some papers and presented to them, they thought it was better to belong to the almighty count than to Stockholm. They could not read or write. They did not know the meaning of what they signed.

As a result of the representation reform of 1866 the nobility's seats in the *riksdag* were reduced from one-third to one-fourth. In 1869 it was expected that the 77 tax-paying farmers in the lower chamber would support their suffering brothers in Skåne, the tenant farmers, in their fight for land ownership, but they did not. The leader of the Farmers' Party, Count Arvid Fredriksson Posse, known as one of the worst peasant tormentors in Skåne, sided with the nobility (Kämpe).

The Tullberg Movement

Beginning in 1867 the tenant farmers in Skåne received advice from a former corporal, Samuel Tullberg. As a young man, he had enlisted in the Skåne Hussars. Having finished his time of duty, he became the owner of a farm in Oderljunga parish, but lost it. He then opened an office in Kärrstorp employing several able assistants, among them Eskil Larsson, the son of the bailiff in the area. Having become known as an able advocate, Tullberg was consulted night and day by help-seeking tenant farmers.

Tullberg held his informational meetings at night. With the help of assistants, he convincingly argued that the crown and not the estate masters were the rightful owners of the land operated by the tenant farmers. He was willing to represent them if they paid the court cost. Tullberg used the evidence he had on hand to try to have the farms declared crown land. The advantage of leasing taxable crown land was that it could be purchased.

When Tullberg began to assist the nobility's tenant farmers, the authorities searched for other reasons to arrest him. Having found an old loan paper in Tullberg's name for 4,000 crowns, they arrested him because they thought the loan had not been paid. On the day of the hearing, however, it was discovered that Tullberg had surrendered property in lieu of cash to pay the grantors. The prisoner was immediately released.

Tullberg brought several cases to court demanding that the tenant farmers be relieved from paying taxes to the main estate and that full ownership be granted to the tenant farmers. Most of them could prove that their forefathers had owned the property. When the court learned that Tullberg in that regard had a winning case, it stated that the transfer of ownership had happened so long ago that the statute of limitations had expired.

On February 16, 1866, the case between Major Kennedy at Råbelöf in Kristianstad *län* and his tenant farmers was decided. The result was that the peasants who had refused to show up for workdays were evicted based on their signed contracts. They also lost their crops. *Kristianstad-bladet* wrote on February 17, 1866: "There is no doubt that it will result in terrible hardship; neither is there any doubt that such an awful event will result in an entire parish immigrating to America next summer."

Sharpshooters assisted during the evictions pushing out the residents with drawn bayonets. All their belongings were thrown in the dirt outside. The authorities removed windows and doors and destroyed fireplaces. They chopped up the beds with axes, so the people would not return. The un-threshed grain was removed from the barns. But when the soldiers and other authorities had left, the people began to move back in, repairing what had been destroyed. The count issued new evictions that were followed by two months of hard labor. Meanwhile, the opinion against the excessive abuse grew. In 1868, the paper, *Helsingborgs Tidning*, which earlier had been on the side of the wealthy landholders, admitted that it could hardly be worse in Russia. Other papers wrote that the tenant farmers' situation was not much better than that of the thralls.

When the nobility learned that the farmers planned to bring the question before the *riksdag,* the authorities agreed that Tullberg had to be stopped. A reward of 500 *riksdaler* posted by the masters of the castle farms naturally was an incentive for his capture. Both Tullberg and his wife were hunted like wild animals in the woods. One can guess that they planned to join the emigrant stream to America. It did not take long to capture Tullberg. Chained from head to foot, he was brought to the jail in Helsingborg. For security reasons he was quickly moved to Malmö in the cover of darkness. The public was told that he was very dangerous. Eskil Larsson and his brother Bengt were also captured. Chained together they were taken to the prison in Malmö. When the case came up at Åkarp on March 12, between 500 and 600 people had gathered. After a few hours, all the accused walked out as free men. Many gave up and immigrated to America.

Kristianstad-bladet reported on one emigrant who left because he had been evicted by the count of Råbelöf:

Among the several hundred persons who have reported to the emigration agents in the city that they intend to move to the United States a group of 20 persons left for Göteborg last Tuesday to continue with the first available transport to America. Among them was the well-known Råbelöf farmer Swen Larsson. After a judgment by the district court for Skåne and Blekinge and eviction from his home under the Råbelöf estate, he went to Stockholm to ask his Majesty the King to appoint a committee to investigate the dispute between the estate owner and the farmers. Financially, Swen Larson is secure and is likely to do well in the new world. The desire to emigrate is spreading among the people and it seems that the emigration from this area will be of significant proportions.

While *Kristianstad-bladet* seems to have sided with the farmers and their advocate Mr. Tullberg, most historians pay little attention to this ugly chapter in Sweden's past. Ingvar Andersson and Jörgen Weibull write that the nobility's large landholdings were justified:

These farmers who had become subjects to the nobles and paid their taxes to them obviously had difficulty in maintaining any measure of independence, especially since the lords in question that acquired on the Continent a purely feudal attitude toward subordinates. Enormous as the growth was in respect to wealth and political influence on the part of the nobles, it had its justification in the brilliant contributions made by them during the war period. Nevertheless, it became a source of danger to the existence of free husbandmen as well as to the central government authorities.

In *Bonden i Svensk Historia*, Professor Sten Carlsson describes Tullberg as an opportunist:

No less than 256 castle tenant farmers applied in 1867-68 for the right to become crown farmers and to be able to buy their farms. They then received an acquisition receipt from the Treasury Board noting that the documents had been received. Tullberg convinced the farmers that these receipts were receipts which released them from all their duties toward the estate owners. Consequently, they refused to pay their fees and to show up for workdays. The estate owners then answered by threatening to evict. The authorities sided with the estate owners, but asked them to be lenient. Tullberg and his coworkers were jailed, but freed after a short time (1869). The tenant-farmers movement versus the nobility contributed to the demise of workdays and the introduction of regular lease contracts.

It is a common misconception that the demise of the workdays also meant the demise of workdays on the estates. At Årup's Estate regular lease contracts were not in use until about 1925. One day's participation in the hunt was still written into the contracts.

The Tenant Contracts

Through 1853 the contracts issued by Årup's Estate, held by Count Wachtmeister, stated that the workdays had to be performed as needed. In 1837, two workdays per week were stipulated in addition to the 52 required "whenever requested." From 1857 the latter clause was omitted. Instead, a certain number of workdays were required without saying when. In 1876, the contracts requested a specific number of male workdays "on days to be determined in advance for each year." However, female workdays were to be performed during the summer and as called for. In 1891, one contract specified two workdays per week on days to be determined by the estate office.

Two contracts for tenant farmers under Trolle Ljungby are indicative of the freedom the count had in deciding on which days the tenants were to work. One contract, dated Trolle Ljungby in December of 1880 and signed by Trolle Wachtmeister, stated that 50 male workdays had to be performed on days which for each year will be decided by the "owner." Paragraph 10 stated:

Should the tenant become legally tied to any crime expiated with a fine or become bankrupt, arrested, or found to be in neglect of fulfilling the stipulations of this contract, he will lose the tenant right and will be required to immediately vacate the property, which cannot under any circumstances be passed on to any other person without permission.

The other contract for a tenant farm under Trolle Ljungby, dated March 3, 1902, states that the crofter should perform 90 male workdays, but no more than three per week. As usual, he had to bring his own food and tools. For each day he was absent, he had to perform two workdays. In addition he had to repair the buildings that he occupied, dig ditches, repair roads and fences, and see that the chimney, the baking oven, and the fireplaces were kept according to the law to prevent fires. The crofter had to insure the buildings to a value determined by the count. Should the crofter erect any new buildings during the contract period, the same would become the property of the "landowner" at the end of the period. No hunting or fishing was allowed by the tenant farmer. He could not take in any boarders. The contract did not state how large the farm was. The wording was basically the same in the above contract for 1880.

After the 1907 farm-leasing law the landowner had no right to order work which was not contracted and the workdays had to be more evenly divided throughout the year. The worker should be given one day's notice before he was expected to show up for work. The same year, a revaluation was made regarding the profitability of the crofts and tenant farms under Trolle Ljungby and Årup, both administered by the Wachtmeister family.

The use of one *tunnland* (a land unit equal to 1.21 acre) of good land was valued at 20 crowns, while work and benefits were valued as follows: one male workday 2.30; one female workday 1.50; one horse-load of brush for firewood 3.00; one cartload of peat 2.00; doctor's care per family 5.00. The real estate tax was also counted as a benefit (20 crowns for 12 *tunnland*). Other benefits listed for Åby under Årup usually included fire insurance for buildings and crops. The soil at Åby was sandy with rocks and, in places, also swampy. The evaluation included the buildings. The report was dated Trolle Ljungby February 10, 1908, and signed by H. Th. Borgstrom (the inspector). He recommended that new contracts be issued for Årup's Estate for ten years from March 14, 1908 and suggested a ten percent decrease in workdays for the crofts under Trolle Ljungby compared to Årup, except those contracts that were already lower than recommended at the time.

What follows are a few samples from the inventory of rented farms at Åby under Årup owned by Trolle-Wachtmeister, Åby No. 4, 11 *tunnland,* lifetime contract against 104 workdays a year; Åby no. 7, 11 *tunnland*, operated by a widow, 104 male workdays; Åby No. 31-32, 2 *tunnland*, 36 female workdays. All the labor had to be carried out "on own meals." Most of the land in the area was wet and rocky.

The contracts under Årup issued March 14, 1908 show that the number of workdays had increased by ten for one of the crofters and decreased by 17 for another. The preprinted contracts still carried the clause, "the dates for the workdays to be determined by the employer." In the fall, if surrendering the lease, the crofter had to plant certain acres of land. When all the requirements had been fulfilled, the proprietor had to pay the operator 15 crowns cash annually for firewood expenses.

It was not until 1925 that the farm rent was paid in cash at the Årup Estate and the situation was probably the same under Trolle Ljungby. A handwritten paragraph in one contract outlined the duties of the tenant farmer in case the direction of a road should change. In 1933, one workday was requested during the annual hunt. The landholder paid the fire insurance premium, but at the end of the contract period, the tenant farmer was required to reimburse him (Landsarkivet, Lund).

Peaceful Protest in Trolle Ljungby

The tenant farmers in Trolle Ljungby protested peacefully in 1867. Several persons had signed a petition which questioned the count's ownership of the farms that they operated. One tenant farmer and one hired man were sent to Stockholm to present the petition to the King. *Kristianstad-bladet* published various views in four issues in February and March 1867. The first reported that the delegates had been personally received by his Royal Highness, who had promised to influence the decision.

An anonymous writer refuted the report in a letter to the editor published on February 13th, stating that the petition had not been delivered:

Having arrived in Stockholm, they asked for audience on one of the regular audience days before His Royal Highness, but the chamberlain on duty informed them that they could not be admitted and that they were running around with rubbish. If they believed they were in the right, they should use the legal way through the court system, he said, adding that it would be best for them to return home and mind their own business.

The letter-writer insisted that not one of the protesting tenant farmers had any reason to complain since they were cared for in all regards by their master, but unfortunately, he noted, they have come to believe that they can become owners of their farms by petitioning.

On February 20, a third writer identified by initials only blamed the inspector at Trolle Ljungby:

We want to believe that Governor W. is a good master... but one regrets all the more the fact that his nearest employees are not happy to merely serve their master, but raise above their fellow servants to become masters and tormentors themselves, thereby hindering the estate master from doing all the good and useful which otherwise, no doubt, would be beneficial....

A fourth contributor commented that certain tenant farmers have gotten the idea they can become owners of the farms they operate by making trouble. The lengthy petition, which was brought to Stockholm, has been preserved. It says in part:

We are tenant farmers at the Trolle Ljungby Estate in Skåne, but according to tradition which can be proven by circumstances, our forefathers have for a long time in the past occupied our farms as crown farmers under the King and Crown as farm-owners, or other tax-paying farmers. Our situation in many respects is worse than that of our forefathers. To be a tax-paying farmer is to be a free man.

The petition ends with an appeal to the king to proposition the next *riksdag* to appoint a committee to closely examine the tenant farmers' demands and the ownership to the land, etc. No doubt, there was dissatisfaction among the tenant farmers in Trolle Ljungby.

Mrs. Ljungquist said she knew about a place in Tosteberga that had never paid any rent to the Trolle Ljungby Estate because it was a soldier's croft and belonged to the Crown. "During the time of Inspector Borgström at the turn of the century, they began to write contracts…. If one could not prove otherwise, the estate considered the farm its own…. They [the peasants] could read but they were humble," Mrs. Lindquist said.

The Farm workers' Organization

The first Swedish farm workers union was organized in 1899, and in 1904 the Scanian Farm Workers Union became a reality. From the beginning, the estate holders were dead set against the new ideas and refused to negotiate with the union. This resulted in a farm workers strike in Skåne in 1907-09. Once again, the Råbelöf Estate became the center of action. Its *patron*, James Kennedy, a member of the parliament, refused to accept a collective agreement in April of 1907, the union answered with a strike. Kennedy then imported Polish workers, hired strike-breakers, and ordered police and military men to establish order on his estate. But that was not all. Without mercy, he emptied his farm workers' family dwellings. In all, 28 families were thrown out, some headed by men who had been crofters at Råbelöf for 30-40 years.

The conflict escalated during the summer. When the estate holders in northwestern Skåne refused to sign an agreement with the Farm Workers Union, 250 workers went out on strike. At the end of October a compromise was reached. The right to organize and to carry on collective bargaining was acknowledged, but the hated servant law remained unchanged for another 20 years. A version of this law was in effect until 1926. In reality it meant that many sons and daughters who could have been supported at home were obliged to work elsewhere.

On October 2, 1907, Trolle Ljungby Farm Workers Union No. 82 was organized. Its prime mover and chairman was Willy Oskar Nielsen, born in 1877 in Odense, Denmark. Nielsen was a carpenter and wood handler at Trolle Ljungby Castle Farm. Under the name of Mjölner, he gave out a handwritten paper called "Revy" (Revue), in which he ridiculed Count Hans Trolle-Wachtmeister and the hated inspector Borgström at Trolle Ljungby as traitors and strike-breakers. Needless to say, it was not long before Nielsen was fired and evicted from his wretched dwelling at Trolle Ljungby.

On May 5, 1908, the farm-workers union at Årup and Trolle Ljungby issued a blockade. It read:

Workers, do not become traitors!

Blockade

Since repeated efforts by the Scanian Farm-workers union have convinced us that it is impossible through negotiations to get Count Trolle-Wachtmeister to grant the crofters negotiation rights, and since his administration has tried to fire persons who have done nothing but defended their rights, we hereby declare all the crofts under Årup, Trolle-Ljungby and Vanneberga farms in blockade, and this blockade includes all workdays and work contracted by the estate administration. For the leased Ljungby farm, the blockade applies to the crofts and not to work.

Anyone who breaks this blockade will be considered a strike-breaker.

Trolle-Ljungby and Årup, May 5, 1908

On behalf of the Scanian Farm Workers Union locals in Årup and Trolle-Ljungby

The Boards

Red blockade posters were pasted to all crofts. These were still very much in evidence when the evictions were carried out one year later.

Evictions at Trolle Ljungby

In 1909, the same year as the great labor strike occurred in Sweden, the crofters under Trolle Ljungby requested that they be allowed to pay cash rent instead of doing two to three workdays per week in exchange for farming ten to twenty acres of land. As a result, 19 families were evicted.

Kristianstad-bladet's photographer was present although press coverage was forbidden. Sixty years later the paper reviewed the eviction (March 29, 1969):

Today, the photographer's pictures are unique. They show the crofter families humbly waiting for the unavoidable and uneven fight with the estate owner. Their dispute was about the workdays on the estate. They preferred to pay cash rent for the land they operated. The master of Trolle Ljungby was not agreeable. Seven policemen carried out the crofters' belongings. Beds, chairs, tables, weaving-loom parts, spinning wheels, and all kinds of smaller household articles were carried out of the simply furnished cottages and placed in a pile on the dirty stone-covered ground. To make the misery worse, the crofter had to pay one hundred crowns in eviction cost. If he did not remove his belongings from the grounds the same night, everything was heaved out on the road, because nothing could remain on the estate property.

Some of the 19 evicted families found a roof over their heads at the newly constructed *Folkets Hus* (Public Hall) in Vanneberga.

The first evictions took place at Magletorp located by the famous Trollasten under which the trolls sang and danced in the saga of the horn and pipe. The three who were evicted from their crofts at Magletorp were Per Jönsson, Sven Eriksson, and Nils Ljung. Ljung had worked the land of the estate for 27 years.

A periodical by the same name as the public hall (*Folkets Hus*) explains how funds were procured for the building: "The dissatisfaction with the crofters' working conditions and their contracts probably explains why so many bought shares and showed such eagerness in the building of the new hall."

Many members of the union were blacklisted said Hilding Krona, who remembered that one of them immigrated to Canada. Most of the evicted crofters were too old to emigrate. Ernst Svensson said most of them became day laborers for crown farmers. He remembered when his grandfather was evicted from a croft at Sjötorp in Trolle Ljungby. From Lennart Olsson we learned that many of the evicted crofters moved to Nymö, where most of the farms were freeholds. The count of Trolle Ljungby administered most of the land in Gualöv, Ivetofta, and Näsum, but in Nymö and Fjälkinge only a few farms, Olsson said. Signe Andersson recalled that the crofts were located in Espetorp, Magletorp, and Vanneberga. After the evictions, the land was farmed by the main estate, she said.

The Cotters (*Statare*)

It has been said that the miserable conditions the tenant farmers and crofters had to endure were followed by the cotter misery. The system was a way to secure farm workers who would work for one farm owner only. By providing family dwellings, the owner could also request that the cotter's wife worked on the farm. Usually, it was her duty to milk several cows. She was then allowed to take home a certain amount of milk to her children. Other staples could also be included in the 'allowance.'

"I don't know how my parents could stand it," said one woman as she looked back at her childhood years. Her parents worked as *statare* for 18 years at various farms. She described the living quarters that one farm owner provided in 1928 as follows:

The house was located at the edge of a swamp without a basement, so it was damp and cold. There were four 2-room apartments and no kitchen. Mother had to cook on a small stove that stood on four legs and had room for two pots. The baking oven was located at the other end of the house.... The house was built in the late 1800s.... Water sometimes covered the dirt floor in the shack that was used as a barn. Her father had to build a shelf for the pig to lie on. Her parents got up between 3 and 4 o'clock in the morning to do the milking. When the cows grazed at a distant location, it was necessary to get up even earlier.

Gunnar Rosquist gave a man's view of his parents' 25 years as *statare* (cotters) beginning in 1901. One of the farms they served was Råbelöf. The threshing took several days. The grain was carried across the yard to a storage bin. "It was a long way to walk with sacks on your back that weighed one-hundred kilos. Sometimes the grain had to be carried all the way to the third floor. When the men began to work the second day, they had no skin left on their shoulders, but it would be many days before all the grain was threshed," Gunnar said.

He allowed that during World War I, the cotters had more food than the factory workers. The cotters' rows of apartments were still standing in the 1990s in Trolle Ljungby although they had been remodeled and were used for other purposes.

Life Styles

The Buildings

Carl Linnaeus (later von Linnaeus) described the Skåne farms in 1749: "The farm buildings for each household are usually built in a fort-like fashion facing a yard in the center. The clay walls are white-washed and the roofs straw-covered…." Linnaeus continued:

The buildings in the cities were traditionally constructed of brick. The farmers began to use brick as building material at the end of the 1700s. The living quarters and the outbuildings were still connected. The low family dwellings were usually built of brick with or without a wood frame. The cock-loft had a room at each end. Simpler shacks were usually built of clay mixed with straw which were sundried after being constructed. Such shacks could be made in one day at a work party. The adobe dwellings kept well in good weather, but following a long period of rain or flooding, the shack could float away in a stream of clay.

The peasant houses of the 1830s have been described by C. Forsell and Kurt Genrup:

The cottages on the Skåne plains usually have clay floors. The walls are constructed of cement and wood. One enters through the brewing house and kitchen, where the stove always is placed by the far wall. The next room is the main living room, where the table is nailed to the floor on sturdy legs next to one wall. The bed which is made of rough timber… stands in one corner…. The chickens are often kept inside and even the geese at the time of the hatching would get a place in a closed box.

The traditional Skåne building style, also common in Denmark and in nearby communities in Halland and Blekinge can still be seen in historic parks. Many long, low farmhouses have been remodeled for today's modern living. Straw-covered roofs presented a fire hazard. Both Edith Bjerstedt and Ola Lundborg mention fires in their writings. Lundborg was instrumental in the founding of a fire insurance association September 30, 1887.

Klara Persson told us that her family's rented farm had a thatched barn roof. Lighting struck in 1961, and the fire spread quickly through the connected buildings. The family lost everything. Count Trolle Wachtmeister decided not to rebuild. He collected the insurance money and built a small house for the family. Klara's brothers, who had done the farming, had to find other work. After that, the land was farmed by the main estate.

Some farmers living close to Blekinge where rocks are plentiful constructed their barns of field stone. Many such outbuildings remain in the area. Timber was especially scarce before the pine forests had developed. The growth was helped along by people spreading out branches to prevent the soil from blowing away. When there were cones on the branches, the seeds dispersed on the ground and began to grow. Eventually, the ridges that were formed by blowing sand became covered with pine trees.

Outbuildings made of timber were usually painted red, but the family dwellings were white-washed. Edith Bjerstedt described her parents' home in the early 1900s, starting with the main room. A table with four chairs stood in the middle of the floor on a piece of linoleum. Four rag-rug runners were placed around the outer edge of the linoleum. The parents' bed stood by one wall, made up during the day. The bed clothes from other beds were piled on top. Extra beds were brought in at night. Other furnishings included a writing desk and a sewing machine. The room had a ceramic fireplace. In the brick-floored kitchen there was a bench for doing dishes, a stove, a big baking oven, and a pantry. The house also had a maid's room and a room called *lillestuga*. A weaving loom was always in use during the winter months. This farm was relatively large, more than 100 acres of both tilled land and grazing land. The house was lit with five gas lights powered by carbide from the basement.

Edit Bjerstedt

Most homes had a brewing house. Grain was often stored on the second floor. Mrs. Bjerstedt's father built a new building for storing grain and hay and paid for everything himself because the count refused. "When it was finished, they came from the estate and inspected it because it was on their land," Mrs. Bjerstedt said. Her father owned the farm machinery jointly together with another farmer.

Mrs. Bjerstedt also described a cottage situated close to the road, but a little lower. When there was a big gusher the rainwater would wash down into the dwelling. The occupant had bored a hole in the floor to get rid of the water. The 'kitchen' had a dirt floor, a baking oven, and an open hearth where the cooking was done in a three-legged kettle. One poor woman had no kitchen at all. She washed her dishes on a wooden bench in a shed. She still kept her home clean, Mrs. Bjerstedt said.

The Farms

When the old village structure was broken up in Trolle Ljungby around 1850, the crofters' cottages in Vestra Ljungby were moved to the outskirts of the castle farm. The simple shacks were taken down, moved, and put up again on a piece of land which was unbroken and often swampy. The buildings that were not worth moving were torn down and the crofter dismissed.

Dr. Bodil Persson

Although some were satisfied with the move, the process left many disgruntled. Dr. Bodil Persson of Bromölla, who has studied the history of the area, suggests that perhaps the break-up of the villages was one of the reasons why the emigration from the parish to America was so significant in the late 1850s. The villages in Östra Ljungby and Tosteberga were "moved out" between 1848 and 1851.

The public schoolteacher Ola Jönsson Lundborg described some of the difficulties involved:

It was not easy to exchange good old fields, which one had enjoyed taking good care of... and receive other land that one of the neighbors had mistreated, or to exchange meadows for heather and tarn. By lottery, my father was assigned a farm in Norre Vång.... While he used to harvest 20 horse-loads of hay he can now hardly get one armful, and the grain reaching only to the partition in the bin.

The development was a continuation of the *enskifte* introduced in Skåne in 1803 for those who wished to concentrate their holdings to one connected farm unit. The first to carry out the reform was Rutger MacLean at Svaneholm in Malmöhus län. This redistribution of land was followed by a more encompassing land law in 1827. The noblemen who controlled the land on which the village enclaves were located were certain to request the break-up of the villages, especially if they were located close to their manor or castle. In the beginning it was difficult to convince the farmers, whether freeholders or renters, about the value of the reform. They were used to the old village structures. Tenant farmers had no choice, and they were often the ones who suffered the negative effects of the reform. When their farms were combined into one or more larger units, some of the tenants were no longer needed.

Gösta Persson related that his mother's father was lucky to get what he wanted when the various farm lots were drawn in a lottery. He was not so happy when the count told him and other tenant farmers to go to a place between Bromölla and Sölvesborg to get field stone with which to build fences 500 meters long. There were no rocks and no other suitable material for fences on their farms. Each trip took one whole day. Persson later buried the rocks.

In Mrs. Bjerstedt's description of the farms in Tosteberga we find that most of the rented farms were about 25 acres in size in the early 1900s. A farm of that size normally fed two horses and four to five cows in addition to sheep, hogs, and chickens. A few farms were larger than 60 acres, but there were holdings as small as 2.5 acre. If a farm was 50 acres, the operator usually had eight to ten cows. He also employed two hired men and two female servants. Bee-keeping and fishing supplemented the income in Tosteberga. Able-bodied men and women worked as day-laborers for farmers.

Gyetorp, a small area of 20 acres, was divided into four crofts. Somehow this village escaped the land reforms of the 1800s. Until 1936 the crofters' fields and meadows were scattered. Yet, one of the four crofters managed to feed one horse, three cows, two to three hogs, and a few chickens. To support his six children he had to work in a factory in the wintertime.

The Crops

The largest production of tobacco in the country could be found in Åhus, Fjälkinge, and Nymö. The plants were cultivated primarily by women and children. The growing of tobacco could bring in from 500 to 750 crowns a year, and was well worth the work.

Edith Bjerstedt said that just about every home in Tosteberga grew tobacco in the early 1900s. Many women made extra money by rolling cigars in their homes until the fabrication became monopolized in 1918. A returning emigrant, Per Johansson, introduced corn to the area.

The main crops grown in Trolle Ljungby, 1870-1890 (in order of quantities) were potatoes, oats, barley, wheat, and rye. As the harvest of potatoes increased, processing plants were needed. At the turn of the century, many distilleries and starch factories were built in Villand to make use of the abundance of potatoes. At harvest time the school children had 14 days off to pick potatoes. The waste product from the distilleries was fed to the cattle. Tobacco was commonly grown in the Villand District.

In the 1850s, Count Axel Wachtmeister recommended fodder carrots as a crop. He grew them on the vacated cottage lots formerly well cultivated by the crofters in the village of Vestra Ljungby. Sugar beets were introduced at the end of the 1800s. Men and women from Småland came and harvested the beets, which were then delivered to the railroad stations and taken to the sugar refinery in Karpalund (Färlöv parish).

Anna Magnusson's parents had lived in the United States and returned. Anna was seven years old when her parents bought a farm in Östra Ljungby. She said:

My father was a forerunner in getting machinery for the farm. He was very progressive. There were islands in the Baltic Sea where they had animals during the summer. They had lots of sheep and took them out in a motorboat. Their crops were rye, wheat, lots of potatoes, and also beets. Four brothers worked on the farm and two hired men. One took care of the animals. They raised riding horses which they sold to the military.

The nobility, as well as returning Swedish Americans, were often fore-runners in introducing new crops and machinery.

The People

According to the household registers for Trolle Ljungby 1871-1875, the occupations were: 85 tenant farmers, 65 crofters, 674 servants (of which 73 lived at the castle farm), 46 day-laborers and at least 300 boarders. Other occupations found in the registers include teacher, miller, saddle-maker, shoemaker, mason, forester, soldier, dragoon, smith, grocer, tailor, weaver, fisherman, inspector, bookkeeper, gardener, bailiff, midwife, and boats people. In the 1870s, the castle farm was headed by Countess Sofie Louisa Wachtmeister, born in 1825. She was the widow of *Hovmarskalken* (the Master of the Royal household) Count Axel Knut Wachtmeister. They had three sons and two daughters.

Through the middle of the 19th century people did not wander far to find work. They walked or traveled by horse. The first railroad in Skåne was built between Malmö and Lund in 1856. Those living close to the shores had access to water transportation and fishing. The only processing plant in Trolle Ljungby in 1878 was a flour mill in Vestra Ljungby owned by the count. There were stores in Vanneberga, Toste-berga, and Vestra Ljungby. These variety stores stocked just about everything. In addition to food items and candy for the children, they sold work clothes, stockings, fabric, spades, pitchforks, and other smaller implements, as well as kerosene.

Olof Peter Wallengren served as parish pastor from 1845 until 1865. The bishop once said that people in Ljungby and Gualöv had been half barbarians, but that Wallengren converted them. In one of his reports, Wallengren wrote, "The young people's parties are still too many and have such bad influence on morals, health, and well-being that I believe they should be categorized as one of the worst nuisances and sins."

Wallengren fought hard for temperance. He was a friend of Peter Wieselgren and the count at Årup. While Wallengren was the organist and preacher in Ivetofta in 1840, he took the initiative to start a sugar refinery to stimulate the production of sugar beets and decrease the crops that were made into liquor. He also persuaded Trolle-Wacht-meister to close the distillery at Årup. Wallengren was married to Petronella Agritz. They had ten children. One of them, Jonas, immi-grated to America.

A local lodge of IOGT was founded in Vanneberga in 1883 and one in Tosteberga in 1905. Edith Bjerstedt joined the youth lodge when she was 16 years old. She said she had kept her temperance oath ever since. Older people like her grandfather also joined. The lodge hall was the gathering place for young and old. She never saw anybody drunk, but noted "It was a big change for many who were used to drinking. Nearly all the drinkers signed up," she said.

From a biography written by Stephen Rosenquist we learn how the deplorable conditions in the mid-19th century also affected the child-ren:

Of the very early life of my grandfather very little is known except that when he was seven years old, his father died. When his dad died, his mother 'rented out' all the brothers and sisters... to the neighbors as helpers or to learn various trades. However, my grandfather was 'rented out' to the very cruel Baron of Trolle-Ljungby, which is the name of a castle....

My grandfather's meals were nothing to speak of.... He would eat what was left after the older people ate. He would eat out of the egg shells and off the plates when people were through eating. He never got anything else to eat, except on very, very special occasions and holidays.

When the Baron was drunk, he would come staggering out of the castle with the familiar stick, wake up Bengt Per, who was sleeping in the barn, and beat him for no reason. Bengt Per always swore to himself that he would come back and kill the Baron. He was nearing the age of 16 when he finally let out on his own. Freedom at last!

In a personal interview, Stephen Rosenquist added that when his grandfather's mother found out how her son was treated by the baron, she went to the castle and asked to have the boy released. "She was kicked out," she said (Interview by the author in Sweden in 1993).

Ola Lundborg related how his mother as a young girl of 8 or 9 kept watch over the cows at the castle farm while they were grazing. At one time, when Mr. Wachtmeister was scared by a bull, he called on the little girl, who was able to drive the beast away. As she became older she served as a bricklayer assistant several times and even helped with chimney sweeping. She then had to climb with equipment on her back up to the highest point of the castle. In the wintertime she worked as a laundry maid at the castle.

In 1884, Lundborg wrote about a scarlet fever epidemic. "We have scarlet fever in the area and there are families who have lost several children. May our little ones be spared...." It was not to be. Lundborg could not bear to write about it until some time later, but then he used ten pages to vent his grief. He does not seem to think that the doctor came soon enough and that enough was done to save the little ones. The two boys, Viktor and Axel, were buried on the same day, March 6, 1885. Four white doves, which Lundborg had bought for his children earlier, flew above the funeral cortege. Meanwhile the third child was ill and not expected to survive, but he did. He was in bed for six weeks and when he tried to stand up his legs would not carry him. The next two sons were named after their two departed brothers.

The winter of 1887-88 was severe. Ola Lundborg wrote that school-teacher Blom walked to Åhus to pick up his quarterly salary, and one day later he was found frozen to death in a sheep shack.... "His near-sightedness without glasses probably caused him to get lost. He was married, had a boy, 9-10 years old, and a girl, about 2 years old. Blom had lost four sons in one week.... They died of scarlet fever and diphtheria, and got the same horrible end as my two boys," Lundborg wrote.

Edith Bjerstedt's *morfar* (mother's father) was sent out to beg when he was ten years old. He learned to read but not to write. Her other grandparents learned both. Her father did not sleep in a house until he was married at age 30. He slept in the hay in the barn. When he did workdays at the castle farm, he had to get up at 2 a.m. and keep on working until sundown. He brought his own food and tools. Edith slept in an unheated room with the window open to prevent tuberculosis even when it was -25 Celsius (2 below F). They heated bricks to place in the bed. Her sisters had died of the disease.

The Food

Skåne is famous for its *spettkaka*, a high cone-shaped torte that got its name from the *spett* (pole) which is part of the equipment needed to make the cake. It has always been a specialty made by trained bakers. The recipe in about 1880 called for 60 eggs, 1 1/2 kilos sugar, 1 ½ kilos potato flour, and 100 grams of butter to grease the paper with. The recipe was so large that two different batches had to be prepared. Each was whipped for one hour. The batter was applied to the pole through a paper cone, one layer at the time. The pole stood on a plate that could be rotated in front of an open fire. While the first batter was applied the second batch was made. The procedure for half of the cake took 1 ½ hours. A total of 12 hours was needed to finish the cake. The glazing took one hour. One basket of beech wood was needed for the fire. How much did the baker charge for this work of art? The price was 6 crowns, which came out to half a crown per hour of work for two people. Mother Sissa had a *spettkaka* bakery in her home in Barum. Her husband, Jöns Persson, was a fisherman. Signe Andersson in Ostra Ljungby told us that *spettkaka* was ordered for parties celebrating even birthdays, such as the 50th, 60th, and 70th birthday.

Another Skåne specialty is goose. Ole Brodd, Kenyon, Minnesota, remembered that his family in Nymö kept geese in the early part of the century. The feathers were used for mattresses, and the goose fat was made into sandwich spread, which he said tasted much better than lard.

Edith Bjerstedt in Tosteberga mentioned geese only in one context. Her mother used to be treated to sandwiches spread with goose fat at one place in Tosteberga. The hostess spread it out with her thumb, but it still tasted good. Signe Andersson confirmed that families in the area had geese. They celebrated *Mårten Gås* Day on November 11. That was the time the geese were ready to be slaughtered. *Lutfisk* was one of many party dishes through the year in Skåne in the 1800s. The staples were potatoes and bread. Mrs. Bjerstedt described the baking of 27 loaves that weighed about 4-5 kilos each:

In the morning we put the flour in the trough, boiled water and added cumin. Next we poured the water over the flour, stirred, and pounded the batter with a long dough paddle for half an hour. After that the dough rested until evening when we added more flour and kneaded it for one hour before covering it and letting it rest until the next morning. At 4:30 a.m. it was kneaded again before we went out to the barn to milk. After breakfast we made it into both regular and round loaves that we placed on floured wooden benches to raise. Before we put them in the oven we brushed them with water. The loaves baked for 2 to 3 hours. When they were done we wiped them with a pork rind to make the crust softer. Finally, we carried them down to the basement and placed them on long wooden shelves hanging at a distance from the ceiling.

The big baking oven was fired up with dry pieces of sticks and wood. When the bread was served the foreman of the male servants had the honor of slicing it. There was a difference in rank also among the servants. Ole Brodd, Kenyon, Minnesota, who emigrated with his family in 1903, remembered his mother slicing the bread herself. She made the rye bread into big loaves, which she held against her chest while she sliced it, he said. Other staples included bacon and fish. In the winter time, it was popular to go out on the ice and bob for eel. Some people supplemented their meager income by peddling fish.

The Schools

In the 1880s construction of school buildings was the biggest expense for the parishes. A school house cost between 15,000 and 20,000 crowns to build. Many parishes rented a building for the lower grades. Trolle Ljungby rented four of the seven schools in the 1870s. Each school had one teacher. In 1876, there were 342 school-aged children in the parish. Twenty-one attended schools outside the parish and 53 were taught at home. One of the teachers cared for the parish library containing 342 volumes, which was founded in 1858.

In Kristianstad in 1856, public school was taught in the poorhouse. The city fathers planned to build an addition to accommodate both a school for small children, and a day-care center, where younger children would receive needed care while their parents worked, or had to be away from home for other reasons.

Fjälkinge, located next to Trolle Ljungby, got its first school in 1836. The teacher, Sven Rosenberg, received 7 ½ barrels of rye, 100 *riks- daler banko* cash, housing, and firewood for nine months of teaching school. During the summer he gave private lessons and wrote for a judge to make ends meet. The teacher was a friend of the temperance promoter Peter Wieselgren of Västerstad. A temperance lodge was formed in Fjälkinge as early as 1837.

The new schoolhouse in Vanneberga was finished in 1866 when Ola Lundborg became the teacher. He continued to teach there for over 40 years, seven more years than required for retirement. The reason he stayed on was that he wanted to benefit from an expected increase in salary and pension. His pension thus came to 1,013 crowns a year. His starting salary was 600 crowns. He also received benefits in kind. In 1884 Lundberg wrote, "This year the school board will cause me a decrease in salary by cancelling the ninth month of school for which we have had 75 crowns the last few years.

On his final day of school, he tested his pupils by asking them to figure both the circumference and inside volume of a cylinder; the third grade had to figure the side of a house in four different ways, average, parallelogram, one triangle, and three triangles.

The Emigration

The Swedish Trailblazers

Among the best known Swedish trailblazers in America are the Hedstrom brothers from Nottebäck in Kronoberg's län. Olof Hedstrom came to the United States as a sailor in 1826 and settled in New York. Having been converted to Methodism, he preached his faith on the "Bethel Ship" in the harbor. His brother Jonas Hedstrom arrived in 1833 and came to Victoria, Illinois, in 1839, where he founded the first Swedish Methodist Church in America in 1846. One of the first financially successful early Swedish emigrants was Swen Magnus Swenson of Barkeryd, Småland, who left Sweden in 1836 and founded a Swedish settlement in Texas. In 1838, the Freeman brothers from the area of Skara in Västergötland became farmers in Wisconsin.

After 1840 Sweden's liberalized emigration law made it easier for more citizens to leave the country. Among them were Gustaf Unonius of Uppsala and members of his household, all heading for Wisconsin in 1841. In 1845, Peter Cassel and a group of farmers from Kisa, Östergötland, founded a Swedish settlement in southeastern Iowa. The mass exodus of the first emigration period began in 1846 when several hundred religious dissenters of the Eric Jansson sect fled north central Sweden and founded the Swedish colony of Bishop Hill in Henry County, Illinois. Pastor Lars P. Esbjorn emigrated from Hille, Hälsingland and established a Swedish Lutheran settlement at Andover, Illinois. He was followed by many Lutheran pastors, among them T. N. Hasselquist from Skåne and Erland Carlsson from Småland, as well as Lutheran pastors-to-be, such as Eric Norelius from Hassela in Hälsingland. These pioneer pastors became important leaders for the Swedes in America.

When the liberal newspaper *Aftonbladet* in Stockholm and other papers began to publish letters from Swedish emigrants in the early 1940s, the first-hand descriptions stimulated people's interest in America. An uncertain future in the new world often seemed more attractive than the prospects in Sweden. The push and pull factors were regulated by the conditions on both sides.

The Push Factors

The social discontent and economic crisis—the results of the nobility's proletarianization of Skåne and the population explosion of the 1800s—became important push factors for the emigration from Skåne.

Despite efforts by the government to bring some of the land acquired by the noblemen into the hands of the peasants, the Swedish nobility still owned one-third of the arable land in the late 1700s. About 80 percent of that land was worked by tenant farmers who paid their rent by performing workdays on the main estate. In Skåne and Halland that system required the tenant farmers to take care of the main estate as well as the land they rented. Each tenant farmer was responsible for a certain portion of the main farm. He had to work that land regardless of the time it required. The tenant farmers also had to provide conveyance for their masters. When a new law in 1789 gave the peasants the right to buy farms owned by the state, the nobility took advantage of the law and bought farms owned by the state. Meanwhile, most peasants were unaware of the new law.

As the discontent of the tenant farmers at the noble estates grew they began to protest. Between 1772 and 1776 they protested against the unlimited workdays. In 1811, it was the lottery system for military service that prompted uprisings. In the 1860s the peasants began to question how the nobility had acquired their land. Funds were collected in 46 parishes in Skåne to pay the court cost to pursue the matter. All over Skåne, tenant farmers started court cases which they rarely won. Even those who won did not always get to keep their farms. Sometimes the legal decision was overturned by the *riksdag*, where the nobility had a strong voice. The tenant farmers' fight for independence from the nobility could be summed up as follows:

The operators of many farms which were recorded on the books as tenant farms under the castle or freeholds handed down from father to son from time immemorial against the duty to fulfill certain workdays at the main estate, argued that they had the right to full ownership; consequently they wanted to avoid entering into new contracts carrying burdens dictated by the head of the main estate. Many who were convinced about their rights—and in the beginning some court cases actually were won by peasants—refused to fulfill the obligations listed in their contracts, and as a result they were evicted from their homes with the help of executive powers. (Rune Persson)

When the peasants marched on the large estates, protesting what they considered to be unfair treatment, the nobles answered by bringing in the troops to disperse the crowds. The leaders of the protests were arrested while others were fired or evicted.

Following the uprisings, it was not likely that the Count of Trolle Ljungby looked favorably on the possibility that his servants would obtain weapons to practice target shooting. In the 1860s, Swedish newspapers reported on activities of the target practice corps. The 64-men corps in Ivetofta led by public school teachers Pettersson and Svensson was in danger of being dissolved because the parish pastor had requested that the corps refrain from practicing on Sundays. Pastor Johansson declared that he was not against the corps, only the blaspheming of the Sabbath. *Kristianstad-bladet* argued that Sunday was the only time the servants had time to practice. The article-writer suggested that the pastor had been influenced by Count Trolle-Wachtmeister, the head of the Valje Farm in Ivetofta. It was strange, the paper said, that not one servant at Valje Farm belonged to the corps. It was also surprising that the count would want to work against the government's defense efforts. The paper asked, "Who should be more interested in that the people of Ivetofta and Trolle Ljungby would be able to defend property and life, not to mention freedom and independence, than the noble owner of Trolle Ljungby, Årup, and Valje Estates?" A letter to the editor protested the article, saying it had insinuated that the chairman of Ljungby parish council, Count Axel Trolle Wachtmeister, had forbidden his servants to join the corps. The paper had obtained a copy of the minutes of the paragraph in the parish council minutes in which the corps was discussed. It read in part: "Resolved that people could sign up for the corps at Trolle Ljungby Estate office on the 17th, but that it was considered less appropriate for servants to become active members." The chairman had already joined the corps.

In the petition to the king in 1867, the Trolle Ljungby tenant farmers claimed that the land they farmed had been either crown land or freeholds in the past, and that a third alternative did not exist. It is not known whether the king ever saw the petition.

In Trolle Ljungby almost all the land was administered by the count. Out of 28 larger farms in the parish in the 1870s, 23 were 'owned' by the count, two by the state, and only one was a freehold. The tenant farmers paid their taxes to the count.

The uprisings among the peasants throughout Skåne and in other parts of Sweden are examples of how dangerous the situation had become in the 1860s. In 1869, a member of the Farmers Party proposed that the *riksdag* appoint a committee to investigate the ownership of the land. However, Count Arvid Posse argued that if the proposal was approved it would lead to civil war in Sweden. Consequently, the motion was defeated.

Kristianstad-bladet often quoted from other newspapers. An article taken from *Öresundsposten* stated that Sweden did not have laws to protect tenant farmers on noble estate like Denmark had:

The emigration from Skåne continues at a fast pace. From Göinge, and many other areas, large groups of people head for America to seek their fortune. The movement has grown strong at the noble estates, in some cases perhaps due to the disputes about the ownership to certain farms under the estates.... When many large landowners in Skåne and other provinces began to deprive tenant farmers, crofters, and workers of the land which their forefathers had farmed, break up entire villages, and tear down the buildings, it turned the farmers into "statare" (farm workers) many of whom soon became dependents of the parish. Their circumstances made them into welfare cases, because no humane and fair law existed to protect tenant farmers like in Denmark. It was easy to see that this absolute arbitrariness and heartless egotism would soon become self-defeating. However, we had not assumed that it would happen so soon. Now, it seems that the poor downtrodden and impoverished people at some estates have begun to think about saving themselves from their misery and ominous future. One can feel pity, but one is not surprised. (Aug. 24, 1869)

The article went on to say that many large landowners did not care what happened to the poor servants and their families after their work had made themselves rich.... "He reasons like the first brother-murders, "Shall I take care of my brother? Thousands believe that their situation cannot get any worse. What rebuke for the motherland!"

The unrest continued well into the 20th century. In 1909, the Count of Trolle Ljungby evicted nineteen crofters (small-farm tenants). Encouraged by membership in the Farm Workers Union, the crofters tried to exchange their workdays for cash rent. When they went out on strike, they were evicted for breach of contract.

The Economic Hardships of the Landless

Sweden remained an agricultural society until the last quarter of the 19th century. In 1850, 90 percent of the population lived in the countryside and was wholly dependent on the soil. The shifting of land and breakup of the old village structures had both positive and negative results. More land was tilled and the production rose, but many villagers disliked having to move, and some were left without any land at all.

In Skåne as a whole the shifting of land resulted in more acreage. Between 1805 and 1833 new arable land increased at an annual average of 4,450 hectares in Malmöhus län and 2,000 hectares in Kristianstad län. However, while the number of farm owners increased, the number of tenant farmers decreased at a high rate in both counties, from 4,673 to 2,998 in Malmöhus län and from 3,532 to 2,059 in Kristianstad län. The number of small lots climbed, thus adding to the proletarianization.

Kristianstad-bladet claimed that the tendency was to merge the smaller units into bigger ones, thus displacing its occupants:

A new time has arrived with new circumstances. When plots of land are combined to form larger units, many crofters are turned into statare (farm workers) *and these are no better off than serfs or thralls. Possibly they have their freedom, as it is called, to move if they want to, but this freedom is an illusion because what parish or individual will receive a servant who is destitute and accompanied by a flock of children?* (August 26, 1869)

Like the cotters, the tenant farmers and crofters had many children, and only one could continue renting the farm. Many crofts had disappeared. In Skåne; the farms were not divided to the extent they were in other parts of Sweden. There were no large forests that could be cleared and used for farming. The masses of children who grew to man-and womanhood generally had no choice but to hire out as farmhands and maid servants. They could not expect their standard of living to improve as long as there were hordes of other peasants who were willing to take their places. More people than ever wanted a piece of the common cake, but the cake was no bigger than before.

Although the proletarianization was more severe in Skåne than elsewhere in Sweden, the national figures show that it was a problem in the rest of the country as well. Between 1780 and 1855 the lower class grew from 51 to 74 percent, while the middle class decreased from 48 percent to 25 percent. The upper class remained the same or one percent. The lower class was divided into "half-proletarians, "proletarians, and "rag-proletarians."

Kristianstad-bladet commented on the emigration of the landless on April 11, 1866. "A large number of people are presumed to immigrate to America this summer. For the most part they come from farm families, who are subjects/servants of the large estates. About 60 persons are leaving from Trolle Ljungby.

The Population Explosion

In 1815 the population of Sweden was less than 2,500,000. In 1850, it had grown to 3,500,000. In Trolle Ljungby the population increased from 1,327 in 1805 to 1,887 in 1850 (42 percent), which was less than in Skåne as a whole (63 percent). The national average was 44 percent. In 1865, 2,104 individuals lived in Trolle Ljungby. In the decades that followed the population decreased somewhat due to emigration, so that in 1886 it was 1,831. The population explosion has been attributed to three factors, peace, potatoes, and vaccine.

The enormous increase in the population of the 19th century was first of all due to a decrease in mortality, which in turn was the result of peace, better nourishment—especially thanks to the increased cultivation of potatoes—and improved medical and sanitary amenities, including vaccination against smallpox (Ingvar Andersson and Jörgen Weibull).

While the population of Trolle Ljungby grew, the number of farms in the parish increased by only two from 1810 to 1840 and these were small holdings between 1/8 and 1/16 of a *mantal* (assessment unit of land). In the 1850s, a lake southwest of the castle was partly drained, which added some land area, but it consisted mostly of swamps. Between 1840 and 1865 an additional nine small farms were operated separately, two of which were smaller than 1/64th of a *mantal*. It is easy to understand that these few additional farms could not compensate for the population increase.

The prices of wheat, rye, barley, and oats did not fluctuate a great deal in Villand, Gärd, and Albo districts in 1853-1856. The price of oats remained constant and barley rose. Wheat and rye went up in 1853, but fell the next year. In 1855, however, those prices increased significantly, but fell back again in 1856. The city of Kristianstad showed higher prices overall.

Jonas Wallengren, who emigrated in 1856 from Trolle Ljungby, wrote home to his father in 1857 and commented about the high prices of cattle and the low grain prices in Sweden. He wondered why the emigration from Ljungby had ceased, but did not mention the economic crisis in the United States which was a deterring factor.

On August 25, 1866, *Kristianstad-bladet* reported that the reason for the depressed economy was large quantities of unsold liquor. In just one village in the area about 20,000 cans were in storage.

Due to the situation in the financial market the banks are forced to keep considerable funds on hand as security for ominous circumstances and are thereby hindered to assist the populous in need of loans other than short-term loans at a high rate. Such loans may be feasible for a few businessmen, but sooner or later they become ruinous for the farmers.

Although the emigration increased significantly from Trolle Ljungby in 1868-1869, *Kristianstad-bladet* did not report any crop failures or famine in 1867 and 1868 like the ones occurring in certain other provinces. However, on July 1, 1868, the paper wrote about the drought: "After a long wait we have finally received some rain although it is hardly enough to soften the ground." On August 2, the paper quoted *Christianstads Läns Tidning* saying: "The export of cattle from Gothenburg has decreased significantly due to the present recession in England. Also, the shipping of dairy products has decreased due to the hot weather which makes it very difficult to preserve the products."

The Farm Bureau *(Hushållningssällskapet)* reported in 1869 that the lack of rain during the summer had affected the crops in Villand, but that the harvest of wheat and rye was good. Other crops were either average or below average. In 1870, the Farm Bureau recommended the use of commercial fertilizers to prevent the shortage of fodder following crop failures.

While Hans Mattson was in Sweden in 1869 he wrote a letter to the Swedish-American Press which said in part:

Despite the considerable progress the country and even the people as individuals have made, regretfully, it has to be admitted that at this time [the situation] *is highly deplorable. In certain provinces, especially in Småland, Dalsland, parts of Halland and Westergöthland the supply of bread is already depleted. I have been there my self and seen large crowds with thin, pale faces beg for bread.... In one house that I recently visited, no less than thirteen beggars arrived while we had dinner. (Svenska Amerikanaren, Chicago, April 6, 1869)*

Mattson blamed the situation mostly on oppression by the upper classes. "Here is grain in abundance at low prices. If they only had work, no one would have to suffer, but there is no work and why? There is a lack of enterprising efforts. And the fault lies with the rich and with the government." He also criticized the prevalent scorn of physical labor and laborers, which he said leads to the emigration of the working class.

At the end of the 1860s a male workday was valued at 58 *öre* (about 16 cents), a female workday at 37 *öre*, a child's at *33 öre*, and a day laborer's at one *riksdaler* in southwestern Skåne. (One crown equals 100 *öre*) The annual wage for a hired man, including food and a place to sleep, was 350 to 400 *riksdaler* a year. However, one man who had worked as a hired man said that his cash pay was 100 *riksdaler* for one year. (One US dollar was worth approximately 3.25 *riksdaler* at the time.)

There is no evidence of religious oppression being a deciding factor in the emigration from Trolle Ljungby. The only dissent mentioned by Ola Lundborg came from one or two Swedenborgian. Pastor Wallengren and Pastor Braun disputed with one Swedenborgian in Östra Ljungby for an entire day without being able to change his views.

According to an article published in *Hemlandet,* Galesburg, April 15, 1856, a religious awakening took place in the area in the fall of 1855, but it occurred within the framework of the Lutheran Church. Prayer meetings were held in Vanneberga and in the large church in Vinslöv. People came from Småland, Blekinge, and Halland from as far away as ten Swedish *mil.* "When the Lord's Prayer was said in the church the worshippers kneeled...."

The Baptists began to proselytize in Skåne in 1857. A letter to Pastor P. G. Ahnfeldt asked "What can be done about Anabaptists who are tenant farmers, who cannot be treated as vagrants?" From Jonas Wallengren's America letters we learn he had been informed about the progress of the Baptists. "I saw in Father's letter that the Baptists can practice their faith without interference and that many already have joined the sect," he wrote. This does not necessarily mean that there were Baptists in Trolle Ljungby because the same day, Wallengren penned a letter to his brother saying, "You wrote that everything is the same in Ljungby as when I left.... I can imagine that all the sects that are started in Sweden attract quite a bit of attention." (May 23, 1857)

Another letter from Sweden written by Hans Mattson was published in *Svenska Amerikanaren*, Chicago, April 20, 1869, saying in part, "It is supposed to be religious freedom here, but in reality dissenters have no freedom. They are often the objects of harassment of various kinds. The ministers still persecute laymen preachers of other denominations than the official state church."

Christian Jonsson of Åkarp was the first America emigrant from northeastern Skåne. When he, accompanied by a son, left Sweden in 1848, he knew of only one Swede in America, the Methodist preacher O. G. Hedstrom in New York. Hedstrom advised Jonsson to continue to Knox County, Illinois, which he did. Jonsson had been enticed by glowing accounts in the newspapers about the free and fertile country in the West. Having lived in Galesburg a year and a half, he visited Sweden and gathered an emigrant party of 40, among them his wife and eight children, Nils Eliasson, and Per Bodelsson. All were from northern Skåne.

The initial emigrants from an area often gave the impulse to further emigration when they visited Sweden. In about 1849, a well-to-do family in Ignaberga had an unusual visit by an American lady and her

Swedish maid. The maid told some of the young men about the new land, and they decided to emigrate. Among them was a carpenter by the name of Lofgren.

One of the young men who emigrated at the same time as Hans Mattson was Ola Nilson from Önnestad. He was well acquainted with Pastor T. N. Hasselquist, then a pastor at the Åkarp church. Nilson recommended Hasselquist to Pastor Lars Paul Esbjorn in Andover as a suitable pastor for the Swedes in Knox County. When Pastor Hasselquist left in 1852 he brought a party of 60 emigrants from the area.

Also in 1852, Nils Hokanson from Hjersås, who had lived in California, visited Sweden and returned the same year with a group of 60 emigrants, including 44 from Skåne and six from Blekinge, a neighboring province.

Two Early Emigrants from Northeastern Skåne

Among the emigrants from northwestern Skåne in 1851 were Hans Mattson and Trued Pearson, both of whom were to settle in Vasa, Minnesota. Pearson remained there most of his life, but Mattson soon left the colony and lived in many different places. Hans Mattson was born on December 23, 1832 in Önnestad. Having advanced to the rank of colonel in the Union Army during the Civil War, he became an agent for American railroad companies and ocean liners, a member of the Minnesota Board of Immigration, Secretary of State, and ambassador to India. He was a remarkable example of what a farmer's son could accomplish in America. No early letters from Mattson have been preserved, but from his published autobiography we learn that during his first year in America he experienced many difficulties that he did not write home about. He said he refrained from complaining, but neither did he advise his parents to come to America, which he had promised to do if he thought it would be a good idea. He said that the letters recommending emigration had come from his travel companions who settled in Galesburg and Moline, Illinois, where they considered the prospect to be good. When Mattson's father and brother arrived in 1852, he accompanied them to western Illinois. Mattson says that his father liked the "big west" very much.

The father, Matts Hansson, descended from respected farm owners in the Villand district. He was born in Fjälkinge in 1805. Before his marriage he received an inheritance that enabled him to buy a farm at Skoglösa in Önnestad. His wife, Elna, was born on the island of Ivö. Both had roots going back to Hovgården in Ivö. Before Hans was 14 years old, the family had moved twice, first to another farm of their own at Önnestad, and then to Kellsagården, a larger farm which his parents rented. The farm was located near the church in Önnestad.

Hans received his first schooling at the age of six from an itinerant teacher, who went from farm to farm to teach. He started public school at the age of eight. When it was time for him to begin his confirmation classes he added private lessons in writing and mathematics. His tutor was his future brother-in-law S. J. Willard. Later he, too, became a pioneer in Vasa. Hans Mattson was confirmed in Önnestad by Pastor T. N. Hasselquist, who became a well-known pioneer pastor and educator in western Illinois.

When Hans began his studies at the Latin School in Kristianstad, he had already received a better education than most of his peers. During his second year, the Danish-German War broke out. As soon as the Swedish government decided to send troops to help Denmark, Hans besieged his parents to let him become a volunteer in the Artillery. His mother gave in when he threatened to join without her permission. What Hans did not know was that his mother had spoken to the regiment physician, who was also their family doctor. To prevent Hans from joining the forces in Denmark, the doctor sent him to the hospital for a slight cold.

Having entered military school in the fall of 1849, Hans soon realized that as a farmer's son, he had no chance of advancement in the Swedish Army like the young noblemen. Together with his friend, Hans Enström (later Eustrom), Hans Mattson decided to immigrate to America, where "inherited names and titles were not a prerequisite for promotion," Mattson wrote in his autobiography, *Minnen*:

America in those days was not very well known in the parts of Sweden where I lived, because only a few persons from the whole härad (Göinge district) had emigrated thus far. However, we knew it was a new land with a free and independent people, and that it had a 'free' constitution and huge natural resources, and these were reasons enough for us to go there. It was not difficult to get my parents' per-

mission. They were interested in finding out more about the new country, and if the news was good, they also planned to emigrate.

Mattson received his discharge as constable cadet from the Royal Wendes Regiment in April of 1851. His father hitched up his horses and drove him and Hans Enström to Helsingborg where the two young men joined other emigrants on the first leg of the journey on board a schooner to Gothenburg. From that city, they sailed on top of iron cargo on the brig *Ambrosia*, which arrived in Boston on June 29, 1851.

When Mattson tried to make a living by working in the forest in the dead of winter without mittens, his hands became so severely frostbitten that he almost lost them. Being completely helpless, he had to be fed, dressed, and washed like a baby for three months. After he was well he worked for food only in order to pay for his care. When springtime came, he worked as a hired man for $5.00 per month, starting his day at 5 a.m. and working until dark. The pay was less than he would have received in Sweden.

One year after his arrival in America, Hans Mattson learned that his father and brother were on their way to Boston. While he waited for them in New York for one month, he became ill, but survived thanks to his friend Hans Eustrom who was living in New York at the time. With the arrival of family members and some much needed money, Hans Mattson got a new start. He spent one year with his father and a brother in Galesburg and Moline, where all three worked at various temporary jobs until his mother and sister landed in Boston in the summer of 1852. Sister Anna and her husband Sven Willard had taken out their exit papers in 1852, but did not emigrate until 1853. The parents soon bought a farm in Moline with money that the mother had brought from Sweden. Those who did not have any money were determined to go to Minnesota, where land was cheaper. Hans Mattson, his father, sister, and brother-in-law Sven Willard joined them, and the party arrived in St. Paul in August 1853. Matson wrote:

We had heard that a number of Swedes lived at Chisago Lake and some near Carver, but all of them had settled on timbered land. We also learned that near Red Wing in Goodhue County there were places with both woods and prairie land and a good water supply.

One of Hans Mattson's travel companions on the journey to America was Trued Pearson, who at first settled in Knoxville, near Galesburg,

Illinois. He might very well have written letters to Sweden telling about the good prospects in western Illinois. Pearson was born July, 1827 in Läreda, Stoby, Skåne, where his father owned a farm. Pearson wrote an autobiography in which he relates why he chose Illinois as his destination:

There was much talk about America. Some people whom I knew had actually gone there and stayed in Illinois, and they had written home to friends and acquaintances about the magnificence over there on the other side of the Atlantic. I saw a couple of those letters and seriously began to think about checking it out.

Trued Pearson had a brother who was an inspector at an estate in Skåne considered attending an institute so that he too could become an inspector. His brother then told him that it was a difficult job. If he didn't tyrannize the workers, he got in trouble with the master. When Trued decided to emigrate, he received 100 *riksdaler* from his brother in travel money.

Upon his arrival in Knox County, Illinois, Trued Pearson immediately got a job working for a farmer and was paid $18.00 a month. In his autobiography he described how impressed he was with the vastness of the land. While being out in the countryside hunting prairie chickens together with a friend, he had a chance to evaluate the land. He wrote:

We drove straight out on the prairie. When the [prairie] chickens popped up their heads above the grass, we could stand in the wagon and shoot as many as we wanted. We were a couple of miles outside the city, and no matter how far we went we saw only the sky and the grass. I understood from the look of the grass that this was the richest farmland I had ever seen, unless the plains of southern Skåne could possibly measure up to the same fertility. But oh, how small the Scanian fields were compared to these enormous plains that seemed to be endless as we rode around all day. I will never forget the impressions of this day. It seemed to me that there would be room for all impoverished farmers on this land and that they would receive plenty in return for their work.

Having seen the plows which the farmers used, Pearson sought work at a plow shop in Knoxville and was paid $20.00 per month, plus food and lodging. After his marriage to a Swedish woman in 1854, Trued Pearson decided to fulfill his dream of a farm of his own somewhere in the 'West.' "Being born a free Skåne farmer's son, it was below my dignity to always work for Yankees or others. At this time, there was much talk about Minnesota as being the right place in all respects for healthy sons from the North to make it as independent farmers," he wrote in his autobiography. He first went to Carver, but in 1856 he settled in Vasa with his family. He remained on the same farm for 40 years.

As we have seen, the influential trailblazers from the area were young farmers' sons. They were soon to be followed by the landless masses, young men and women, who did not have a well-to-do father with means of support as was the case with Hans Mattson. Trued Pearson said that the captain on the boat had advised those with families to go west and take land. Those who had money were told to forget they had it until they had lived in America for two years. To us, who lacked funds, he said, "You are the luckiest because you are forced to work and to learn the language. You will know the value of the money before you can lose it." Later, Pearson would verify the captain's words. He had noticed on several occasions that even a small starting capital could be more harmful than helpful to newly-arrived immigrants.

The America Letters

The news about the so-called Mattson settlement in Minnesota, later named Vasa, must have reached Trolle Ljungby because Vasa became the destination for many who left in 1855. Once the first group was settled, letters were exchanged between the pioneers on the prairie and the parents and brothers and sisters at home in Sweden. As we will see, these letters resulted in a chain migration from Trolle Ljungby to Vasa. Swen Olson, a former hired man at the Trolle Ljungby Castle Farm, wrote what was probably his second letter home before Christmas in 1855:

Here are very good plains, which have neither stones nor trees, but here is a shortage of woodland because it is taken, and it is difficult to get water out on the prairie, but I have a good spring on my land. I don't have as much woodland as my friends, but much better farmland and a water spring by the east end. It is a good place for cattle. You ought to come soon if you plan to come. There is still room for a few next to us. Members of my family can build on my land.

You brother-in-law, Ola Andersson, come here and take my brother Ola with you. You should be able to find a suitable place. Then we will help one another as best as we can with oxen so that we can farm ourselves. If you want to and have the desire, it is better here than in Sweden because this is the land of freedom, but one has to work. But our work benefits no one else. If you come here, there is enough food and work on the land that I have and the rent is free.

Olson also wrote that a pastor had visited them and that he might return to stay. "If one considers the future, the prospects are good since one can become a landowner. Here, one is free from all fees and taxes except on what one owns...." It is likely that Olson answered questions that the relatives had asked in their letters.

A letter from Sweden to Bengt Anderson, who also arrived in 1855, has been preserved. The father in Sweden acknowledged a letter received on August 10, 1856:

"You write that your new house is finished so that you moved in on June 7 and that you have enough room to house two families who have arrived from "Hisby" (?) Slott. [Norelius mentions settlers from Bosjö Kloster.] We also find that you have made a real-estate deal.... We thank you so much for the American gold coin...."

In a letter dated January 12, 1857, Swen Olson wrote that the land had increased so much in price in Vasa that his farm was worth 1,600 dollars (or $10.00 an acre). He then goes on to tell that there was a place by Geneva, 80 English miles southwest of Red Wing where land could be had for $5.00 an acre. A new settlement was being founded in Geneva and many in the area planned to move there in the spring. "If you... should desire to come here, then I will sell and accompany you to the new area, where land can be had for the government price." For anyone who cannot afford to buy land, Olson said, it was possible to rent land.

On July 12, 1861, Olson wrote about the Civil War, comforting his parents-in-law by saying that it rages far away from where they live. To his brother-in-law who had married in Sweden, he wrote that he was not against the marriage, but added, "I am sorry you will stay in Sweden and take on the bondage which will weigh you down forever, because you could have been a free from it."

In a letter dated October 26, 1865, Swen Olson mentioned that un-broken land was valued at about $10.00 per acre. "Two hundred miles west of here there is virgin land as it was here when I arrived. Every man who has reached the age of 21 can take 160 acres for nothing and only pay for the papers [deeds], but the provisions are that one has to live on it [the land] and improve it as soon as possible. When they have lived on it for five years, they get their deeds, whether they have tilled ten or 100 acres does not matter." He did not want to advise anyone to come because "some think that large buildings and complete farm-steads are available the same as at home, ready to move into, but it's not like that. Here one builds one's own house according to one's assets," he wrote.

Swen Olson's brother-in-law Ola Anderson settled in Vasa in 1856. He wrote a letter to Sweden dated January 12, 1857, in which he thanked his parents for helping him to come to "this land of freedom. I like it so well here that you could not have given me a better gift in Sweden...." He said he had worked in a flour mill for 6 weeks and received one dollar a day. He asked his brother Anders if he planned to become a soldier or come to the land of freedom. He sent greetings to a friend asking if he planned to rent a farm or if he wished to come to America and be free from the slavery. Then he added that the trip to America was not as difficult as one might think. "There were no questions about the passports in Göteborg. They didn't ask us or the soldiers for their passports. We bought the small slip of paper and then we were Ame-ricans and free men there in Göteborg."

The next time Ola Anderson wrote home to his relatives he had visited Baileytown, Indiana, together with relatives and friends. On the way back to Minnesota, he had stopped in Chicago for five days to see the big city. He described in detail the marble buildings and the churches of various denominations. He also visited the Swedish Lutheran's educational institution Augustana Theological Seminary, since he was acquainted with some of the students. He offered to come to Sweden to accompany his relatives to America. To show that there was no class distinction in America, he told the story of how Abraham Lincoln had worked as a hired man for farmers. "He has tilled and fenced 160 acres land by himself... and now he has advanced to the highest post in the land and sits in the president's chair."

A woman who arrived from Trolle Ljungby in 1875 wrote to her sister in 1878 saying:

I want to answer your question about coming to America.... Both Nels and I want you to come. It would be a much better future for you than going at home as a slave. I want to tell you truthfully, my dear sister that I would never go to Sweden ...because here I live in much happiness and freedom.

Jonas Wallengren, who emigrated from Trolle Ljungby in 1857, wrote a letter from New York saying: "Here is the finest view you could find.... Everything is built with taste. The harbor is so filled with vessels that if Sweden's whole merchant fleet was in one place it would not come to so many ships. Every house is a palace." From Moline, Illinois, he wrote: "I am more satisfied with America than I thought I would be when I left home...." He added, "Everyone usually thinks that the beginning is the hardest, and that is true, but it soon passes, because not too many years are needed to become independent. If they wanted to slave all their lives in Sweden, they could not reach that point." Wallengren spent three weeks in Bishop Hill assisting bricklayers. He compared the colony with the Trolle Ljungby Estate:

The Swedes have it good at Bishop Hill; they are unbelievably rich. Their buildings are so huge that in comparison Ljungby estate would look like a peasant farm. They have 11,000 acres of land, hundreds of cattle, nearly 150 pair of oxen, almost 100 horses and mules, as well as countless chickens and other fowls. They have a steam mill, a tannery, and many other shops. They have one store there and one in Galva. Besides the many cattle they sell every year, they sell much wheat flour and broom corn alone for over 100,000 dollars.

In another letter Wallengren wrote, "Here are good opportunities for a laborer to live as well as a millionaire, and he can walk as straight as one who has one-thousand dollars in his pocket." Having received a letter from Jöns Olson, who criticized the slavery in the United States, Wallengren became passionate. His reflections were: "Either they forget or don't want to remember what goes on in Sweden." Referring to a certain *usling* (wretch) he wrote: "If he were to receive as many beatings as he has dispensed, he would surely be ripped apart. [Likely referred to the inspector at the castle farm] They must like the whip since they stay and rather take more of it than leave Ljungby. If they chose to come here, they would be sure of not getting such visits, and also of being treated as brothers." He continued to elaborate on slavery in an undated letter from Lyons, Iowa:

The greatest difference between the slaves in America and in Sweden is the color of their skin. Most of the slaves, at least those who are somewhat manageable, are much better off than many of the so-called free day-laborers at Ljungby. Slaves are necessary because of the burning sun in the South. I think Sweden's noblemen would gladly see slavery introduced in Sweden if only it were in their power.

Signe Anderson, Trolle Ljungby, told us that her uncle, Mons Andersson, who immigrated to New Zealand said, "When I left in 1900, all the workers under Trolle Ljungby were just like thralls." It was unusual that the emigrants looked back on their home community as a harborer of "slaves" and "thralls." It has to be understood that it in this context it referred to the way the Count of Trolle Ljungby ruled over the tenant farmers and workers.

The Newspapers

The local paper *Kristianstad-bladet* was by its own admission, "Liberal without exaggeration, independent without being hypercritical and fearless without presumption…" It published material which in the beginning was mostly against emigration.

The Number 1 issue was published September 20, 1856. The first article about the United States appeared on October 15, 1856 and read in part, "In America the industry makes history. It prepares the way for new inventions and new states; it sets the stage for future players in the human drama; the axe and the saw. Electricity and steam are promising forces, the servants of provenance."

In the spring of 1857, the paper announced many auctions of tenant farms due to "vacating." The real reason was likely the emigration. Few farms gave up their contracts to anyone else than a member of the family. One article headlined, "The experiences of a Swede in America" told of a fire on board a ship from Canada to Chicago and a flood along the Mississippi River, which rendered the immigrant penniless and homesick to the point that he returned to Sweden.

A few years later, the paper reproduced an article from the Swedish-American newspaper, *Hemlandet*. A woman from Rinkaby, Svenborg

Andersdotter, had died in Vasa of injuries received in the Indian mass-acre in New Ulm, Minnesota The Scandinavian Society in New York warned of 'runners' who were being sent out from boarding houses to recommend cheap rooms rented out by countrymen. Once there, the article said, the immigrants are usually robbed and then dragged to the recruiting offices, where they are swindled out of the sum that the United States Government pays everyone who enrolls in the Army. Articles such as these describing fires, floods, Indian massacres, robberies and kidnappings were bound to scare some prospective emigrants; yet, more and more people decided to emigrate (Published April 4, 1863 and March 5, 1864).

The America letters published in the newspapers usually contained both praise and caution. Olof Larsson, who had settled in Burlington, Iowa, wrote a letter to the paper in 1868, saying that during his journey from Wisconsin he had met many Swedes, and "all of them praised America as a good country especially for tradesmen; I didn't hear anyone who wished to return to Sweden to stay." He continued:

I don't want to encourage anyone to emigrate, but I cannot help but say that workers can easily become independent here. Moreover, one is free. Through the universal vote the government acknowledges one's value as a human being. One thing, however, is necessary for anyone who wants to make America his home, temperance. Drinkers cannot gain any confidence here. (October 19, 1868)

A letter from Stockholm, Wisconsin, located on the east side of the Mississippi River opposite Red Wing, told about people who spe-culated in government land. "They buy well-situated land at $1.25 an acre and sometimes sell at a profit of several hundred percent. The homestead seekers then either have to buy from the speculator or move on to the forest or the prairie to take less well-situated homesteads of 160 acres. After they have paid the $15.00 registration fee, they can farm the land tax-free for five years." (September 9, 1868)

Another letter from Stockholm, Wisconsin, probably caused some stir among hardworking maid servants and farm wives in Sweden as it stated: "The woman here is freed from all work outdoors. Yes, she even leaves some of the work inside the house to her husband. She decides with or without her parents' blessings whom she will marry which often happens at age 11 or 12...." (September 9, 1868)

The Emigrant Agents

The first emigration from Trolle Ljungby occurred at about the same time that the Mexican-American War Veteran Otto August Malmborg, a native Swede, began to recruit emigrants in Sweden and Norway for the Illinois Central Railroad. Two Trolle Ljungby emigrants settled in Moline, Illinois, in 1854.

The economic crisis in the United States in 1857 and the outbreak of the Civil War in 1861 curtailed emigration from Sweden for several years. Meanwhile, some observers traveled to the new world to find out first hand what it was like. One of them was M. Rubenson of Gothenburg who made his journey to America in 1863. He reported in detail about the accommodations on board the Allan Line or "Montreal Oceans Steam-Ships-Company," as it was also called. About the travel time, he stated that the ocean journey to Quebec lasted 10 to 12 days (presumably from Liverpool). The train trip between Quebec and Detroit, Michigan, took 48 hours. Following a change of trains in Detroit, the journey continued for 16 hours on the Michigan Central Railroad to Chicago (*Kristianstad-bladet Bihang*, February 24, 1864).

Ads by steamship companies became frequent from 1866. The various lines had agents in the city of Kristianstad. The American Emigrant Company was accused of publishing misleading information in *Götheborgs Handelstidning* when stating that their Liverpool vessels made the journey to New York in 5 to 6 days. *Kristianstad-bladet* tried to set the record straight by publishing a letter from Liverpool on September 19, 1866, saying that it generally takes eleven and one-half day between Liverpool and New York. "No steamship will go faster," the article said.

In 1865, the price for an adult ticket on a steamer between Hamburg and New York was 160 *riksdaler*. On a sailing vessel it was 85 *riksdaler*. The agent was C. F. Holmberg of Kristianstad (September 2, 1865).

In 1868, Skandinaviska Huvudkontoret in Copenhagen advertised tickets via Hull and Liverpool to Boston, New York, or Quebec, Canada, for 135 *riksdaler*; Chicago 172.00; Galesburg, Illinois 182.00; and Red Wing, Minnesota, 206.00. Children under 12 paid half fare. All baggage was transported free. The company, which was authorized by the Danish government, was a general agent for the Cunard Line. It also had an agent in Hässleholm. (July 15, 1858). The Thaysen Expedition offered tickets from Åhus on Skåne's east coast to Malmö, Landskrona, and Helsingborg on the steamer *Götha*, and on to New York via Hamburg (June 8, 1868).

While Hans Mattson was active in the United States recruiting Scandinavian immigrants to Minnesota after they had arrived in the United States, mostly through advertisements in Swedish-American newspapers, Captain M. O. Lindbergh began a campaign in Skåne in 1868. Like Mattson, Lindbergh was born in Skåne and a Civil War veteran. *Kristianstad-bladet* carried a lengthy paid advertisement "Svensk Koloni uti Minnesota, Nord Amerika" signed M. O. Lindbergh. It recommended the formation of a colony where the settlers could assist one another. He said that the Swedes usually do not understand the benefit of cooperation like the Germans do. "It is through the combined abilities and beneficial cooperation of many that economic comfort and the prospect to be heard in the society and the state can easier be achieved." Lindbergh added that he was not a friend of emigration, only of the emigrants, and since the emigration is bound to continue, he feels obliged to be of assistance by founding a colony. He wrote:

During my long residence in the United States, I have come to believe that Minnesota offers the biggest advantage regarding climate and other conditions for Swedish settlers. Therefore, I have decided that the colony should be located in Minnesota, and I have been in contact with residents there—experienced persons whom I know in order to get necessary assistance to carry out the project. Every colonist who has reached the age of 21 or is the head of a household has the right, according to the new homestead law, to select and take a homestead of 160 acres against payment of 50 riksdaler riksmynt for all of it, and if one wishes, one can buy a larger spread at $1.25 per acre. (September 16 and 23, 1868)

At first, Lindbergh planned to sail from Copenhagen. When he advertised that those who had booked tickets with him were to sail from Helsingborg instead on April 15, 1869, the Fredricksen Agency in Copenhagen reacted swiftly. Mr. N. P. Fredricksen claimed that Lindbergh had negotiated a contract with him to carry emigrants via New York to Minnesota for 205 *riksdaler* per person with Lindbergh receiving a 10 *riksdaler* commission. "He has now broken the contract by closing a new one with emigrant agent Horneman for net 112 Swedish *riksdaler* to Portland." Fredricksen promised to honor the tickets until the end of 1869 and asked if Colonel Hans Mattson really could recommend Mr. Lindbergh.

In the same issue, Lindbergh requested that all who had tickets with him via Copenhagen should exchange them for tickets from Helsingborg. From there the group would travel directly to Hull aboard an English steamer and then from Liverpool to Portland, Maine, with the Allan Line. He answered Fredricksen saying that he had never had the contract with him, only an agreement. Since then Mr. Fredricksen had raised the price and limited the travel destination to New York. Lindbergh's statement was followed by one written by Hans Mattson, dated Kristianstad December 31, 1868, in which he verified that Captain Lindbergh is known in the United States as a righteous and honorable man fully competent to lead and establish a larger colony in America and that he has adequate relations over there to be able to prepare new homes for the settlers. "Therefore, it is my pleasure to recommend him as a man whom the emigrants can trust." (January 30, 1869)

Lars Ljungmark found that Lindbergh's expedition had changed when it departed on April 15, 1869. "There were no plans for a homogeneous Swedish colony in Minnesota. Instead, the members formed a travel party around Lindbergh and they were to settle individually or in small groups to a great extent under the auspices of the St. Paul & Pacific Railroad. Lindbergh, the former leader of a colony, had become a travel guide supported by steamboat and railroad companies." According to Ljungmark the main reason for this change was that the criticism in the newspapers had scared many people away from his enterprise. Ljungmark thought that the appearance of Hans Mattson in Sweden was a more significant factor.

On January 13, 1869, an article appeared in *Kristianstad-bladet* warmly recommending the services of Colonel Mattson, who could be reached at Trolle Ljungby. In an undated letter to his wife, probably written on February 15, 1869, Mattson wrote: "Tomorrow I expect a lot of people who want to sign up for the voyage with me. I could get a terribly large group, but do not want to take more than a couple of hundred. It will be enough trouble with them."

In a supplement to the paper dated February 24th, *Kristianstad-bladet* carried a full-page ad by W. Horneman's authorized Steamship Expedition, endorsed by Mattson. The ad said that the distance to Chicago via Quebec was shorter than via New York, and that no runners were encountered in Quebec because the vessels dock close to the railroad station. It seems likely that Mattson took over Lindbergh's passengers who did not wish to switch carrier.

Lars Ljungmark summed up Mattson's method of recruiting emigrants as follows:

Mattson's method ... to let the editorial office of the Kristianstad-bladet handle advertising instead of entering his own advertisements, turned out to be very successful. There was never any controversy as in the case of Lindbergh's expedition which had been advertised more openly. Not even the conservative press reacted to the rather obvious emigration propaganda carried out by Kristianstad-bladet, or to the activity of Mattson. Nor was Mattson accused by any Swedish newspaper of carrying out emigration promotion. (Ljungmark, For Sale—Minnesota)

Working for the St. Paul & Pacific Railroad, Mattson was commissioned before his departure from Sweden to buy land in Minnesota for several Scanian farmers. For their account, he brought a considerable sum of money with him from Sweden. Mattson's group left from Copenhagen May 7, 1869 on the Wilson Liner *Cato* and arrived and arrived in Quebec on May 22nd via Liverpool on the Allan Liner *European*. Of the 441 emigrants, 172 had tickets to Chicago, 119 to Red Wing, 92 to St. Paul, and 58 to other destinations outside Minnesota. The emigrants to Red Wing consisted mostly of wives, children, and others who joined family members already settled in Goodhue County (Ljungmark).

Having arrived in Chicago with his group, Mattson wrote letter to his wife dated May 26, 1869, in which he described the journey:

We had a long voyage due to head winds and fog for several days. I have 400 people in my company, but only a couple of hundred are headed for Minnesota, among them many relatives and friends. I hope there will be housing available for those who stay in Red Wing.... All are in good health, and they have given me a letter of appreciation and look to me as their father, so I want to make them as comfortable as possible at their arrival. (Minnesota State Historical Society)

Kristianstad-bladet printed the letter of appreciation June 26, 1869 from the travelers addressed to Colonel Mattson. Only four of these emigrants are listed as being form Trolle Ljungby (Ola Larsson, Knut Månsson, Jöns Persson, and Swen Nilsson). In his autobiography, Mattson said he had sent one party ahead of himself in the beginning of April. It departed from Helsingborg under the leadership of Captain Lindbergh. Mattson must be referring to the party departing on April 15, which Lindbergh considered to be his group.

In the early 1870s, Mattson became the agent for both the Northern Pacific Railroad Company operating between Duluth and Moorhead and the Lake Superior & Mississippi Railroad Company between St. Paul and Duluth. He arrived in Sweden with his family on June 21, 1871 to promote land in Minnesota, remaining until the spring of 1873. Having returned in the fall of the same year, he stayed in Sweden until January of 1876. The last two years, he lived with his family in Gothenburg. In his autobiography he wrote: "Part of this time I contributed to the colonization of the province of Manitoba in Canada," he wrote in his *Minnen.*

The Lake Superior & Mississippi Railroad Company published a 44-page booklet in Kristianstad in 1872 with H. Mattson listed as land agent. The booklet gave detailed information about the state of Minnesota, its natural resources, products, railroads, schools, laws, taxes, welfare, villages and cities, climate, the land along the railroad, etc. The price of railroad land varied between $3.00 and $7.00 per acre, which could be paid in cash or installments. The daily wage for workers was reported to be between $1.50 and $3.00 for men and from $8.00 to $12.00 a month for maids. The booklet referred to the Swedish settlements of Chisago, North Branch, Cambridge, and Rush City. The gathering point was either St. Paul or Duluth, where Scandinavian agent Mr. Christensen was employed by the company to assist prospective buyers.

The Northern Pacific Railroad Company published a pamphlet in Swedish in New York in 1873. Here it says, the price of land varied between $2.50 and $8.00 per acre depending on the distance from the railroad. It could be paid in installments over a period of eight years.

The pamphlet also pointed out that the railroad could use five to six thousand workers. It assumed that the Swedes who read the pamphlet were already in America. In Sweden, the pamphlet was handed out by the railroad agent Karl Möllersvärd, editor of *Kristianstad-bladet,* was now also an agent for the Allen Line (Ljungmark).

Not only did the emigrants have to weigh the push and pull factors mentioned above, they also had to consider their family circumstances and warnings against emigration. The economic conditions improved in Sweden in the 1870s, and emigration from Trolle Ljungby was relatively low during that decade.

Kristianstad-bladet continued to inform readers about the many difficulties the emigrants might face, but did not correct obvious exaggerations that were sent directly to the paper, or copied from other sources. In 1865, the paper carried an editorial which included the following:

With the knowledge we have about the situation in America, we consider it our duty to caution against rather than for emigration, even express a sincere warning against it.... Unfortunately, most of those who have been smitten by the emigration fever will not listen to warnings or information..... However, we shall continue to print information that we know is reliable.

The letter that followed was dated "Gatsbury" (Galesburg), Knox County, Illinois, Nov. 1, 1865. It was written by an unidentified person who had been in the United States for eleven years and was in good circumstances and said in part:

I know several people who write to Sweden and brag and entice many others to come here. Yes, they even lie right out, writing only about what they can make, but nothing about what it costs to live and reside here. They convert our dollars to riksdaler and believe they can become rich here in a few years. (December 15, 1865)

The writer stated there were Swedes who approached countrymen in New York, enticing them to go to the South "where they are treated worse than slaves." Finally, the letter-writer listed the prices of food and clothes, saying that the food for one person cost one dollar a day or 50 cents for a daily meal, although it was possible to live cheaper.

When he listed some very high prices for clothes, his figures became totally unbelievable.

In 1866, the same paper published two letters from emigrants, which described the ocean travel in horrible terms. One letter was from a person who had traveled to New York via Liverpool. It said that the ship had sailed on May 12, and that neither the food nor the coffee was fit for consumption—only the ship rusks. Water for tea was distilled on board. Cholera broke out and one after the other died and all were buried at sea. Seven people died in one day. After the ship had arrived in New York it was quarantined for six weeks.

The other letter was from an emigrant who had traveled via Scotland. It described the journey between Scotland and New York, complaining about the food and coffee furnished by the line, as well as the accommodations. There were 800 people on board with two to each bunk. "On one occasion, a sick passenger was brought up on deck and treated badly. When Ola Jonson of Ignaberga—brother-in-law of the parsonage farmer in Ignaberga—wanted to help him, he was hand-cuffed and jailed (September 12 and 15, 1866).

The paper *Göteborgs-Posten* called the Swedish farmers' economic situation "worrisome" in 1867, but disliked that the emigrant agents could freely carry on their human trade without the interference of the authorities. A correspondent working for the same paper reported about the taxes in the United States, saying that he had heard from Sweden that the high rate of taxation there was the reason for the emigration. He added: "I can assure you that one has to pay taxes on everything here, whether one is a farmer, tradesman, or merchant... if one owns a watch or a carriage, there is a special tax for that." (As quoted in *Kristianstad-bladet* June 26 and July 10, 1867)

In 1869, *Kristianstad-bladet* wrote an editorial article against the companies formed in America for the purpose of settling groups of immigrants in one place. Agents had arranged for emigrants from Dalarna, Östergötland, and Närke to become part owners of such ventures, and the editor thought that the Swedish diplomats in the United States ought to investigate those companies (July 5, 1869). The reason for the editorial may have been that the editor, Karl Möllersvärd, had been appointed agent for the Allan Line in the spring of 1869. He did not care for the competition. Late in 1871 he became the general agent in

Gothenburg, and one year later was appointed general agent in Sweden and Denmark for the Northern Pacific. Möllersvärd had become an emigration promoter instead of an emigration opponent (Ljungmark).

Many newspaper items were published to discourage emigration. The Swedes who were already established in America may have intentionally written letters to newspapers to try to curtail the influx of new arrivals. Perhaps they were tired of constantly being asked to be of assistance. Usually, it was only during their first year in America that they wrote enthusiastic letters to Sweden. After that, they often expressed the view, "We do not want to advise anyone to come here." It was their way of trying to avoid being blamed if someone they knew experienced difficulties in the new country.

Data about the Emigrants

According to available records in Sweden, a total of 1,086 persons emigrated from Trolle Ljungby between 1850 and 1914. Of these, 1,033 were excerpted from the household examinations rolls through 1901. Since the household rolls were not available after that date, the additional 53 emigrants were added from statistical records for the years 1902-1914. Of the 1,033 emigrants found in the household rolls, 904 had taken out exit papers for America, 119 for Denmark, 8 to Germany, and one to Australia. The Swedish Statistical Bureau reported that 35 emigrants returned to Trolle Ljungby between 1881 and 1920. The re-migration rate of 3 percent was low compared to other parishes in Sweden.

Of the 1,086 emigrants, 243 were farmhands, 140 female servants, 168 children, and 102 wives, 95 sons living at home, 81 daughters living at home, 66 boarders, 20 tenant farmers, and 15 day laborers.

Most of the emigrants were unmarried. Although the civil status is not listed for all, 194 were reported as married and 821 as single from 1854 through 1901. For the same period, 434 emigrated with family members and 599 alone. The greatest family emigration occurred 1855-1857 (79) and 1866-69 (72).

There were four villages in Trolle Ljungby. For two periods with large family emigration, 1855-57 and 1866-69, Vanneberga contributed 43 percent of the emigrants, Västra Ljungby 34 percent, Tosteberga 13 percent, and Östra Ljungby 10 percent.

The Trolle Ljungby Emigrants' Travel Routes and Destinations

For various reasons it has been difficult to trace the travel routes of the Trolle Ljungby emigrants. Apparently, many of them left from either Helsingborg or Copenhagen. The route from Helsingborg was established by Hans Mattson and his travel companions in 1851.

The microfilms of the passenger arrival records in Boston for 1854 list two Trolle Ljungby emigrants, Per Hansson and Berta Månsdotter. They are known to have settled in Moline, Illinois, in 1854. The woman later moved to Vasa, Minnesota. The Boston records do not include the years 1855-56 when many of the emigrants from Trolle Ljungby are likely to have used that port of destination. In 1857, two passengers from Trolle Ljungby are listed, namely, Anders Abrahamson and Pernilla Abrahamsdotter. A search of the Boston arrival records for 1860-66 did not turn up any additional passengers from Trolle Ljungby. Therefore, it can be assumed that they had begun to use routes to New York or ports in Canada. In the excerpted passenger arrival records for New York, 1855-1860, only one (of the Trolle Ljungby emigrants), Jonas Wallengren, could be identified with certainly as having landed in New York. He said in his first letter that other emigrants from Ljungby had sailed on another ship. From Ola Anderson's letter, we know that he, too, sailed from Gothenburg to New York in 1856. The passenger arrivals recorded in Quebec have been microfilmed, but the film copy at Emigrant Institute is illegible or very difficult to read for most of the years that the Trolle Ljungby emigrants may have used this port of entry. In 1863, 13 persons from Trolle Ljungby sailed from Hamburg to New York on board the *Elia*. There may not have been room for all 15 in the group, as Pehr Tufveson sailed on the *Bavaria* and Erik Nilsson on board the *Saxonia*. The only other Trolle Ljungby emigrant found to have traveled via Hamburg is Anders Jonsson who sailed from that city on board the *Germania* to New York in 1865. From 1869 the emigrant agents in Gothenburg had to submit lists of the emigrants to the police department in Gothenburg before departure. Yet, many of the emigrants who are known to have sailed from that city are not listed—probably because their initial place of embarkation was a port in Skåne. For the years 1869-73, none of the emigrants from Trolle Ljungby could be identified with certainty. An attempt to trace them in the computerized passenger records for 1869 at the Emigrant Register in Karlstad was unsuccessful as well. The passenger records for Copenhagen were also consulted. An attempt was made to find listings of families from Trolle Ljungby. In the records for 1869, four such families were found to have departed from Copenhagen. They were headed by Ola Daun, Per Jonsson Wiberg, Jöns Persson Wiberg, and Per Persson (Tosteberga). Single individuals could not be identified with certainty in these records. However, when checking the passengers with destination Red Wing, Minnesota, six names were matched.

Nils Johansson of Hässleholm, who had done much research on the emigration from Skåne, believes that most emigrants from the northern parishes, including the Kristianstad area, chose to travel via Copenhagen and England. In the passenger records for Malmö for 1874, seven Trolle Ljungby emigrants were found to have departed for Galesburg, Illinois. For the period 1880-1896, it was easier to identify Trolle Ljungby emigrants in the departure records for Malmö. The following destinations were found:

Eastern United States: New York 30, New York City 14, New York or Boston 14, Boston 6, and Providence 1; Minnesota: Red Wing 17, Northfield 5, Hastings and St. Paul/Minneapolis 3 each, other Minnesota destinations 10; Illinois: Chicago 23, Paxton 20, Princeton 4, Moline 2, and Peoria 2; Nebraska: Wahoo 2, Hastings, Hooper, and Sutter, one each; Indiana: Peru and La Porte, one each; Kansas: Assaria 3, Unidentified 1; Iowa: Davenport and Red Oak, one each; Cities in the West: Denver, Seattle, and Ft. Worth, one each; Other countries: Canada 12, and Buenos Aires, Argentina 4.

The above has to be viewed as a sampling of the Trolle Ljungby emigrants' destinations during the relatively late emigration period. The passenger records were of very limited value in my study. My own research of other source material, mainly Swedish-American church records, has revealed that more than 300 former Trolle Ljungby residents settled in Goodhue County, Minnesota. About 200 of the passengers departing from Malmö or Göteborg 1880-1928 were emigrants from Trolle Ljungby (*Emigranten Populär*).

Swedes in Goodhue County

Introduction

The beginning of White Settlement

Organized on March 5, 1853, Goodhue County encompasses 764 square miles, or 488,833.84 acres. The county has many streams, but no lake. Lake Pepin is a mere expansion of the Mississippi. The bluffs along the shores of the Mississippi at Red Wing and Lake Pepin reach as high as 350 feet.

When the first land in Minnesota opened up to settlers in August of 1851 the land-seekers poured in. The first settlers were largely of New York and New England extraction. Many of them came directly from the eastern seaboard states, while others had migrated via states west of the Allegheny Mountains.

The early land-seekers traveled north on the Mississippi River to reach Goodhue County. The ferry traffic across the river was established about 1863. Having landed at Red Wing, they staked their claims in the river valleys and along the creeks in the northern and northeastern parts of the county, where the many steep-sided slopes make the land-scape rough and hilly. Here, the settlers found the timber and water that was essential for their survival.

Eric Norelius, who became an important religious leader for the Swedes in the area, gave the following description of the county:

The land is natural prairie, more level in the southwest, but in general hilly and uneven and cut up by streams. Trees line the streams and give material for building, but across the whole prairie around the houses groves have been planted so that that one nowhere sees barren stretches. Clay predominates, but sandy soil forms a small belt from Cannon Falls to the East or Southeast and occasionally comes to the surface. As a rule the earth is fertile, but for many years it suffered from irrational use. (Dr. Bergendoff's translation, 1984)

The First Swedes in Minnesota

The honor of being the first Swede in Minnesota usually goes to Jacob Fahlstrom (1793-1859). As a young boy he sailed the seas on his uncle's ship when he for reasons unknown was left behind in Canada. He found refuge with the Indians and married an Indian woman. Having made his way to Minnesota about 1819, he worked for the American Fur Company. In the 1850s, he lived with his family in Washington County.

When the Swedish author Fredrika Bremer visited St. Paul in October 1850 she wrote, "If I were to live on the Mississippi it would be here. It is a hilly region and on all hands extends beautiful and varying landscapes." Her admiration of America became known in Sweden when her book, *Hemmen i den Nya Världen* (The Homes in the New World), was published.

One of the first Swedish-Americans to call attention to Minnesota was Eric U. Nordberg of Bishop Hill, Illinois. While exploring St. Croix Valley in the winter of 1850-51, he sent a letter and a map to Per Anderson in Moline, resulting in that Anderson, Per Berg, P. Wicklund, and Anders Swenson with families arrived at Chisago Lake and founded a Swedish settlement. Nordberg took a claim at the site of the present Center City.

On September 7, 1851, Per Anderson, who was from Hassela, wrote a letter to Eric Norelius saying, "Here is room for several parishes; the climate is healthy and wonderful…." Later, Norelius noted that many Swedes who were in Illinois 1850-51 longed for the North, and did not care for a farm in Illinois—not even if they were to receive it as a gift!

According to a historical marker in Scandia, Washington County, the first Swedes to settle in Minnesota were Carl A. Fernstrom, Oscar Roos, and Aug. Sandahl, originally from Västergötland. They arrived from Illinois in October of 1850, but did not remain for long in Scandia.

The First Swedish Settlers in Goodhue County

The first Swede in Goodhue County, according to Norelius, was "doctor" Nils Nilson from Östergötland. Having arrived in Red Wing from St. Paul, he worked as a hired man for Dr. Sweeney and belonged to the Swedish Lutheran Church in Red Wing. He also lived in Vasa.

Goodhue County history books describe Hans Mattson as one of the first settlers in Vasa and the only one who could speak English. He and his companions first set up a tent camp in the timber on Belle Creek, adjoining the place later called Jemtland in the southwestern part of Vasa Township. Here, they cut hay and prepared for the winter. In September of 1853, Mattson and his brother-in-law S. J. Willard took claims in Vasa close to where the Lutheran Church now stands. Ch. Roos and A. G. Kempe established their claims in the valley of White Rock, which later became a village with a post office.

Mattson recalled that he and his partner almost froze to death when sleeping outside one night as the temperature plummeted to 40 degrees below zero. While they lived in a shack in the woods, he said, they saw more Indians than white people. A party of Sioux Indians camped nearby for several weeks. The braves brought them game and fish, and the squaws used to stay with Mattson's sister for several hours to help care for her baby.

Trued Pearson described the Indians as kind and easy to get along with. Entering their tents alone, he was always well received. He even smoked the peace pipe with them. "It is true that the American settlers treated the Indians in the most shameful way, while on the other hand, the Swedes always treated them well," he wrote, adding that they were rewarded when no Swedes were killed by Indians, other than by mistake during the Indian uprisings.

In the beginning of 1854, Mattson and Willard returned to their claims and built a small log cabin on Willard's land. Norelius wrote that it was not surprising that the first settlers from northern Skåne chose the area:

One cannot help seeing a certain likeness between Vasa and the area around Kristianstad. Anyone who has stood on Fjelkinge Backe and looked at the landscape, counting the 21 churches that can be seen in all directions, has no difficulty to picture Vasa, except for the waterways, the lakes, and the sea, which we do not have. The ones who came here saw an attractive landscape, highlands changing into prairie, woodlands, crests, and valleys with grass that was heavy but not long, and a large flora of wildflowers. (Vasa Illustrata)

On November 23, 1855, Hans Mattson married Chersti Peterson from Stoby. The following year, the couple moved to Red Wing, where

Mattson became a merchant. In 1857, he was in Geneva, Freeborn County, for the purpose of establishing a Swedish settlement there. His friend Hans Eustrom and his wife, who had arrived from the East, took pre-emption land in Geneva and remained in the area. Mattson speculated in land, and in the banking crisis of 1857 he lost everything and had to sell out what he owned in Vasa. Norelius commented on the speculations that occurred:

1857 was a difficult year, and conditions were severe until the outbreak of the Civil War. They resulted from the intense speculation mania which reached even to the pioneer settlement in Vasa. People borrowed money on their land as security, partly to pay the government land office for the purchase, partly to be able to buy beasts of burden, tools, etc. When the speculation bubble burst the times turned hard and debts were unpaid. One while it looked as if the majority would lose their lands and the settlement totally ruined. Yet with industry and sacrifice in time of need—most fight their way through these difficult days. (Bergendoff's translation, 1984)

Mattson started anew by studying law in Red Wing. After one year, he was considered to be a full-fledged lawyer and was admitted to the bar. While studying to become an attorney, he likely received financial support from either his parents or his wife's parents. His father, Matts Hansson, had assumed his son's last name of Mattson. When he and his wife arrived in May of 1854, they brought a pair of oxen and a milk cow with them from Moline. Mattson's father-in-law Peter Nilson was referred to as the "rich man" in Vasa.

The land records show that Hans Mattson sold many parcels of land to Swedes in 1856 and 1857. In the fall of 1858 he filled a vacancy as county auditor. Eric Norelius had been elected, but due to his move from the area, he could not serve. In October the Republican Party elected Mattson to the post. Mattson later regretted having accepted the duty, because he thought he could have advanced faster and easier in his former occupation—presumably that of the lawyer. But for the time being, the auditor's position resulted in improved financial circumstances for his family. In 1860, Mattson became the lieutenant for a military company in Red Wing. He wrote, "None of us who participated could have imagined or suspected the terrible war which was to engulf the country in blood and fire."

Religion

An important pioneer in the church history of the area was Rev. Eric Norelius. On September 3, 1855, he organized the Vasa Swedish Evangelical Lutheran Church. It was the first time the name of Vasa was used. Earlier the settlement had been referred to as Swede Prairie, the Mattson Settlement, or White Rock, so named after the white cliff in the area that looked like a small Swedish church from a distance. The name Vasa was chosen to honor the Swedish King Gustav Vasa, who reigned from 1523 to 1560, and established the Lutheran faith in Sweden. The Vasa congregation had 88 members, including children. In the afternoon the same day, Norelius organized another Lutheran congregation in Red Wing with 82 members, young and old.

The author near the top of the White Rock

Shortly after visiting Vasa, Norelius received a call to become the pastor of the congregation. He began his duties in May of 1856 by serving the congregations in Vasa and Red Wing. Pastor Norelius married Inga Peterson, the daughter of one of the settlers, and shared the hardships of pioneer life in the wilderness with her and his parishioners. He says that very few settlers had any money when they arrived and neither did he. During the winter of 1855-56, a 16-square foot house was erected on Willard's farm to serve as a church, school, and parsonage. Norelius' salary the first year was one hundred dollars. In 1858 he received payment in kind totaling one barrel of beans and a few bushels of corn. It was all the parishioners could manage.

When the congregation had decided to make an addition (a lean-to) to the log church in Vasa, each member was asked to contribute one board and 50 cents. Trued Pearson had just earned one dollar, so he had the money, but was at a loss about where to find a board. When he heard that another church member had some boards, but no cash he went to him and purchased a board for 50 cents. Then each man could happily bring a board and 50 cents to the church.

In 1856, Norelius bought 160 acres in White Rock for $130.00 from a bachelor who lived in Red Wing and moved there with his wife. He described it as follows:

Here beside a lovely spring was a small so-called claim cabin, 8 ft square with turf roof and earth floor. As an addition I built a shed out of two loads of rough, unplanned boards brought from Red Wing. This was our residence and we moved in before there was floor, roof, windows, or doors, and at night slept on a heap of chips until we had better. Soon we had roof of a kind, for we stretched cloth to form both roof and ceiling, but since it was loose, rain came through, and then we had to sleep under an umbrella. (Bergendoff's translation)

The nearest neighbor to the west was Trued Granville Pearson. Norelius traveled mostly on foot. He says that he had to sell his horse to buy bread. When winter approached, he and his wife moved first to Red Wing and then in 1858 to Chicago, where he became the editor of the Swedish language newspaper *Hemlandet*. A small plaque in a gully in White Rock marks the place where Norelius's first, owned home in the Unites States stood. The lovely spring that he mentioned was bound to swell at times as the land by his cabin was low and prone to flooding. The Norelius farm was located in Section 33 in the vicinity of the White Rock cliff which gave the area its name. The plaque was dedicated in 1958 (See interview with Milton Swenson).

Norelius gave an account of the various Swedes who arrived in Vasa before the Vasa Lutheran Church was founded. About the members from Trolle Ljungby and nearby parishes in Kristianstad län, he wrote, "They were usually excellent farmers and good church people, who in their homeland had benefited from good parish schools." Scanian also arrived from Stoby, Ivetofta, Vånga, V. Karup, Viby, Önnestad, and Fjälkinge in Kristianstad län, as well as from Bosjö Kloster and Munktorp in Malmöhus län. Settlers from other provinces included several from various parishes in Småland, such as Algutsboda, Lönneberga, and Ekeberga. Värmland was represented by Karlskoga, Arvika, and Långbanshyttan. Other settlers hailed form Östergötland, Närke, Halland, and Västergötland.

In addition to the Swedish Lutheran churches founded in Red Wing and Vasa in 1855, sister congregations were organized in Cannon Falls in 1857 (Ansgarius Lutheran Church); in Welch in 1857 (Cannon River Lutheran Church); in Spring Garden in 1858 (Spring Garden Lutheran Church); in the town of Goodhue in 1869 (Zion Lutheran Church); and in Welch in 1873 (Cross of Christ Lutheran Church).

When the foundation of the church building in Cannon Falls had been laid, Norelius walked 17 miles to Hastings to order the lumber and had it delivered. Shortly thereafter, most of the Swedes in Cannon Falls moved to Waseca County. The few who remained were reluctant to finish the work on the church building. Norelius had bought the lumber on time at four percent interest, and was responsible for the payment. People helped themselves to the lumber, and the only compensation Norelius received was a sack of flour which one honest person left in trade.

Despite the hardships Norelius and his wife had endured in Minnesota they returned to Vasa in 1861. Of the two-hundred dollar annual salary he had been promised he received $137.00 the first year. In the years that followed, the parishioners were able to meet the obligations toward their pastor. By 1867 his salary had increased to $500.00.

The second church building in Vasa was not constructed until 1862 because the parishioners could not decide on the site. The only way they could get access to the desirable top of the knoll was to purchase a 40-acre lot. Norelius says that the congregation never used one hundred dollars for a better purpose. The church was 40 feet long, 26 feet wide, with a 12-foot addition on the north side for sacristy. It was also used as a parochial school.

Norelius wrote about the impact of the Civil War on religious activities:

The war years in general brought a spiritual apathy. This was especially the case at the close of the war. Disdain for God's Word, drunkenness and extravagance got the upper hand. I admit that I then almost despaired of the continued existence of the congregation. In the winter of 1865 I called the congregation together for a special meeting and told the members plainly, though not harshly that the church would be ruined if they did not seriously follow the constitution, and exercise a Christian discipline. (Dr. Bergendoff's translation)

A visitor to Vasa in 1872 praised the congregation and the beautiful new church, but expressed surprise about the way the worshipers dressed. The men wore light American suits, and the women wore tulle and silk dresses that could be likened to those worn at gala celebrations in Stockholm. "I did not see any hand-loomed skirts or anything like the Swedish peasants costumes," he wrote in a letter to a newspaper (*Nybyggaren*, St. Paul, Nov. 7, 1872).

Hans Mattson described the change which had taken place in people's attitudes as follows:

When the Swedish farmhand and servant girl, who in the old country had been held down by poverty and without any prospects for the future, came to this country, a new hope and courage were kindled in them. The previously so timid girl gained self-assertion and poise and dared to look people in the face. Sometimes this may have been carried to a degree which in some cases bordered on the ridiculous, especially as it asserted itself in love for finery and gaudy clothes, but on the whole the transition usually brought out the finer qualities of character. The farmhand lost his listlessness and the slouchy carriage, and the new surroundings created a new man out of him. (The Swedish Element in America)

The majority of the Swedes were Lutherans, but Norelius had some competition from Methodists and Baptists, even from his own brother, Anders, who was a Baptist preacher. When the third Vasa Lutheran Church edifice was finished in 1869, the Methodists had built a small church on a hill to the East. Much later, the Mission Covenants had a lot in Vasa, but no church was built. The Baptists built a small church in the village, but it was sold and converted into a creamery. In the area of White Rock, a former schoolteacher and old-fashioned 'reader' preached, baptized, and gave communion to members of his group made up of mostly well-to-do farmers. When the preacher wanted to divorce his wife and marry a young girl who was betrothed to someone else, he and his forgiving wife were forced to sell their farm and move away.

The Vasa Lutheran Church membership increased the most between 1860 and 1870. Many came directly from Sweden, but the largest portion came from Chisago Lake and Illinois, according to Norelius. Meanwhile, Red Wing's Swedish population also increased, which resulted in the organization of a Swedish Covenant Church in 1874 and a Swedish Baptist Church in 1892.

Politics

Vasa became the most Swedish of all the townships in Goodhue County and it was here that many of the Trolle Ljungby emigrants settled. Vasa Township was organized July 5, 1858 shortly after Minnesota had become a state. The township covered an area of 26,193.41 acres and was larger than Trolle Ljungby parish. The following officers were elected to the board: Charles Himmelman (supervisor and chairman), Charles Charlson (supervisor), Nils Peterson (supervisor), Swante John Willard (town clerk), Nils Swanson (assessor), Matts Mattson (overseer of the poor), Nils Johnson (constable), Gustus Carlson (overseer of the roads), and William Fessenden (overseer of the roads). Justices of the peace were Granville Peterson and Franklin Morrison. In addition, Swan P. Peterson was elected as one of the overseers of roads, John Sundell as collector, and Eric Anderson as constable. S. J. Willard was elected county auditor in 1864 and was re-elected at least five times. As we have seen, Hans Mattson served as county auditor, 1858-1860.

The strong representation of Swedes in the township government was unusual before the Civil War. As Robert Ostergren pointed out, "Election of large numbers of immigrants to public office... was relatively rare until the 1880s. Willard had been a school teacher in Sweden and Trued Granville Pearson had lived in Illinois before moving to Minnesota, so evidently, they, as well as other Swedes, felt comfortable with the English language. They were not from Trolle Ljungby, but in later years their descendants held non-political offices as we have learned from interviews in my study group. Betty Bender's father served as mayor of Cannon Falls, and Donald Trulen was a politician in Red Wing for five years.

Trued Pearson, Justice of the peace, had come to Minnesota with the intent of settling in Carver. Having been invited by Mattson to visit Vasa, Pearson decided to remain there... mainly because the settlement had a Swedish Lutheran congregation. In Carver, Pearson said, the Baptists had gotten ahead of the Lutherans. While Pearson walked around to find the best place for his future home, he made some observations:

There were large plains with level land and fertile soil, but these areas lacked timber and water. For new settlers on virgin land, it is necessary to have both woodland and water. This is the reason why the first settlers always leave the best land to those who come later.

Pearson bought 160 acres in Section 32 in White Rock for $25.00 from a bachelor, who worked in Red Wing. Half of the land was arable right away and the other half was timbered. He paid for having five acres plowed, built a cabin, bought some implements and animals, and then his money was gone. Everything was expensive he said. A barrel of flour cost twelve dollars. He lost the hay he had gathered the first summer in a prairie fire, and a neighbor had to feed his oxen over the winter. The following year, Pearson cut down ... linden trees that were between 25 and 30 feet high and built a house which was still standing 40 years later.

The financial panic of 1857 was caused by "booming times," according to Pearson. The wildcat speculations flourished. "We held elections—necessary as well as unnecessary—of officers who received excessive salaries. Almost everybody had at least one official duty." Pearson was elected to one county office and one local office. The taxes were raised to pay for all the debts, but no one had any money to pay. Gold and silver were out of circulation. The so-called wildcat bills were almost worthless. Thanks to his contacts with politicians, he could use otherwise worthless drafts (received as payments for his services) to pay his taxes. Products of all kinds were unsalable.

Later, the Swedish influence must have diminished, because Trued Pearson wrote in his autobiography that the Americans tried to control the Swedes in politics. Pearson and a few other Swedes then decided to outmaneuver the Americans in an election. In Minnesota an immigrant could vote after four months of residency provided he had declared his intention to become a citizen. The "ringleaders" had made up voting ballots listing only their names. The action prompted Pearson and another Swede from Jemtland to make up ballots as well. These were circulated among their friends who were glad to have the opportunity to vote for fellow Swedes. Underhanded methods were used on both sides. At times, the mere presence of a strong-muscled Swede, Store John, was enough to keep the Yankees in check, Pearson recalled.

Perhaps it was this rivalry between the Swedes and the Americans that prompted the Swedes in Vasa to organize a mutual insurance company in 1859 exclusively for Swedes. After a brush fire in 1859, they saw the need for the protection the insurance could provide. The bylaws stated:

Anyone of Swedish nationality can become a member of this society if he lives within a radius of 15 miles of the Vasa Swedish Lutheran Church; if he lives farther away he can become a member upon the recommendation of the president or one of his helpers. (From the 125th Anniversary celebration)

It was not until 1890 that the bylaws were changed to allow non-Swedes to join although the Swedish language prevailed at meetings until 1898. The Swedes in Spring Garden appear to have been a little more liberal from the beginning as they called their mutual company "Scandinavian Union Protection Association for Fire Lightning and Storm" at the time of its founding in 1868. One hundred years later, the two organizations joined.

Meanwhile some rich Americans and Englishmen made a pact not to sell their farms to Swedes. Yet, the Swedes took possession of one beautiful country place after the other in Featherstone Township. Pearson predicted that his countrymen would take over the Americans' farms for the simple reason that they had more and healthier children. Finally, one American admitted, "You were right in your prediction. You have really taken our land and houses. But don't you see that we are as quickly taking your children and then the country is again ours... They are or will soon be ours, not Swedes but Americans." Pearson had to agree that Americanization was unavoidable. However, at the time he wrote his autobiography, 1893-1902, all houses, churches, shops, factories, and post-offices for more than twenty miles from north to south and fifteen miles from east to west were operated by Swedes. "The language, the customs, and habits—were all Swedish."

Isanti County experienced a similarly strong Swedish presence. Ostergren comments, "Americans had become a minority in Isanti County by midway through the settlement era." However, in contrast to Goodhue County, the businesses in the small trade centers in Isanti County were predominantly owned by Americans. According to Ostergren, "the overwhelming 'Swedishness' of the entire Isanti area, which extended into neighboring counties as well, fostered a uniquely deep sense of isolation from the host society." For a period of time, the high concentration of Swedes in one place undoubtedly delayed the Americanization process. However, as amateur historian Trued Pearson acknowledged and as scholars such as Robert Wiebe has observed, the effort "to master an impersonal world through the customs of a personal society" was bound to be an ultimate failure.

The Settlers from Trolle Ljungby

The First Settlers from Trolle Ljungby, 1855-56

In the summer of 1855, Hans Mattson went to Illinois to meet a group of Swedish emigrants who had arrived in the midst of speculation mania. Among them were Swen Olson,[i] Swen Swenson,[ii] Anders Nilson,[iii] and Bengt Anderson[iv] and their families from Trolle Ljungby. The fact that Mattson went to meet them indicates that either he knew them or he had promised to assist them. They settled in an area in Vasa which became known as Skåne.

The various *rotar* (wards) established by the Vasa Lutheran Church were: **Kyrkoroten** (the Church ward), which included Jemtland); **Skåne** to the northeast of the church ward; **Småland** to the north, but east of Belle Creek; **Spring Creek** to the east and northeast; **Göta** south of Skåne and extending into Featherstone Township; **White Rock** to the south, extending into Belle Creek Township; **Vesterbotten** to the south, but west of the Belle Creek; and **Norrbotten** to the northwest.

The Cambridge Lutheran Church also had wards. Ostergren found that some of the wards had a concentration of emigrants from one parish in Sweden although they were not named after that parish. While kinship was evident in the formation of the cluster in the Skåne Ward, the degree of transplantation of the home community went one step further in Cambridge, where the membership of the Northern Ward closely resembled the membership in Rättvik's Ovanhed *fjärding,* and the members of the Western Ward were largely from Västbygge *fjärding* in Rättvik.

In 1856, many new settlers arrived both directly from Sweden and from other places in the United States. From Trolle Ljungby came Lasse Pehrson with his wife, accompanied by their grown children Pehr Larson and Bengta Lassedotter. In the party were also Pehr and Lars Jönson, both of whom had families, two men by the name of Jöns Nilson, one of whom had a family, Nils Jönson, Ola Anderson, Ola Pehrson, Pehr Larson, and other single men and women. Land records indicate that Lasse Pehrson, Pehr Larson (son of Lasse) and Lars Johnson (Jönsson) bought government land the same year. Mattson sold land to men named Ole Pehrson and Nils Johnson in 1856. Families also arrived directly from Kiaby, Fjälkinge, and Viby in Kristianstad län. Other Swedes came to Vasa via Batavia, St. Charles, and Pecatonica, Illinois, Sugar Grove, Pennsylvania, and Wisconsin.

The families of Swen Swenson, Swen Olson, Anders Nilson, Bengt Anderson and his wife, and the single man Ola Swenson all lived in a small cabin during the first winter on the land that was homesteaded by Swen Olson in Section 13. The cabin was located a few hundred feet south of the pond on that farm. This was the only farm along the road (Hwy 19) that had a pond. It still has.

Inside the cabin, there was a bed in each corner. The hired man slept under the rafters. The center of the room was used for cooking and eating. It was common that a small group of emigrants shared the same cabin the first year. In the summer of 1856, they moved to their homesteads. They sectioned the land so that there was prairie on the west side and woods on the east side. Thus, instead of having a square 160 they divided the section so that each family farm was a quarter mile wide and a mile long. That way each family had land for crops and trees for logs and firewood.

Ola Swenson never married. He continued to work as a hired man. The families that located in the following order from north to south in Section 13 were: Swen Swenson, Swen Olson, Anders Nilson, and

Bengt Anderson. Swen Olson later purchased another farm in the south part of the township and rented out his first farm to Nels Johnson for several years.

In 1865, Anders Nilson moved to a farm south of Vasa. In the 1877 plat book, Jacob Anderson from Älvsborg's län is listed as the owner of the former Anders Nilson farm. (From a typed manuscript compiled by Stanley Winford Swanson and Doris Swenson) Lasse Pehrson and his wife Karna came to Vasa in 1856 after their daughter and son-in-law had already taken a claim there. Lasse homesteaded in Section 12 north of the farm owned by Swen and Nilla Swenson.

Hans Mattson wrote in *Hemlandet* in 1856 that the mixed prairie and woodland in Vasa offered advantages compared to the forested land at Chisago Lake. He also considered it unlikely that the settlers in Vasa would have to pay for the land before they had received income from it. The time of payment depended on when the government decided to put it up for sale. Swen Olson wrote in a letter to Sweden in late 1855, "I cannot know when it [the land] has to be paid, whether it will be next fall or not."

The first settlers did not have to starve because game and fish were abundant. Wild strawberries, raspberries, grapes, and plums enriched their diet. One pioneer recalled seeing at least 500 deer crossing the river at Reads Landing in 1849. For other supplies the settlers had to walk to Red Wing and carry their purchases on their backs for ten miles. But where would the people from Trolle Ljungby get ten dollars for a barrel of flour? Well, Swen Olson hired out for 20 days and received one dollar per day. The first year, he plowed four acres of his land. He wrote that it cost between five and six dollars an acre to break the land. Most likely, he had to hire someone to do the work because a pair of oxen could cost as much as one hundred dollars. Three to five yoke of oxen were needed to pull the breaking plow that threw furrows that were from 18 to 24 inches wide. One and a half acre was a good day's work. Once a settler had an ox, he usually made a wagon. The wheels were made by sawing four rounds off the trunk of an oak tree and making a hole in the middle for a wooden axel. When the wagons had been in use for a while they shrieked so it could be heard far and wide, thus the name shriek wagon. Hans Mattson was the first to acquire a team of horses.

The cost of building a cabin was not prohibitive because the settlers usually helped each other with the construction. They equipped their cabins with a stove, which they had to buy. Olson noted that the cost of a stove was between ten and thirty dollars.

"It does not take much to build. We build with large trees and cut them on two sides; then we lay them ... and smear chalk in the cracks. Such houses are the fastest to build and they are warm. We don't have any pine, but oak, aspen, elm. We can buy boards... but they are very expensive," he wrote.

The Land Records

Bengt Anderson and Anders Nilson were the first of the Trolle Ljungby emigrants to buy land according to the Book of Records for the Town of Vasa. The year was 1856. We know that Anderson arrived in Vasa on August 22, 1855. For him, the date of payment apparently was October 4, 1856, because on that date he and his wife took out a mortgage for $412.00 payable in one year for 160 acres. Anderson made sure he would have some funds left for expenses after he had paid for the land. According to the Minnesota Commissioner of Statistics, the cost of starting out as a farmer around 1860 was estimated at $795, including implements, provisions, cows, a team, and a wagon.

Lasse Pehrson bought 160 acres in section 12 in the hills between Vasa and Red Wing in 1856. His son, Per Larson, settled in Section 11 in 1856.

Swen Swenson and Swen Olson purchased their land in 1860. Their "bounty land" papers were signed by Abraham Lincoln in 1861. Olson's name is given as Swan Oleson in the grant paper on file in the Goodhue County Courthouse. It has been copied in its entirety to show what such a document contained:

The United States of America to all to whom these present shall come greeting. Whereas in pursuance of the act of Congress approved March 3, 1855 entitled "An addition to certain acts granting bounty Land to certain Officers and Soldiers who have been engaged in the Military Service of the United States" there has been deposited in the General Land office Warrant No. 71206 for 160 acres in favor of Tally S. Doudge, Mary I. Doudge, and Sarah Ann Doudge, Minor Children of Tally Doudge deceased. Musician Captain S... Company, Virginia Militia War 1812 with evidence that the same has been duly located upon the South half of the North East quarter and the South half of the North West quarter of Section thirteen in Township One hundred and Twelve North of Range Sixteen west in the district of Lands Subject to sale at Henderson Minnesota containing one hundred and sixty acres according to the official plat of the survey of the said Land returned to the general Land Office by the Surveyor general, the said warrant having been assigned by Tally S. Doudge and by Melichi Naney, Guardian of the said Mary I. Doudge and Sarah Ann Doudge, to Swan Oleson in whose favor said tract has been located. Now know ye that there is therefore granted by the United States unto the said Swan Oleson as assignee as aforesaid and to his kin the trust of Land above described. To have and to hold the said tract of Land with appurtenance thereof unto the same Swan Oleson as assignee as aforesaid and to his kin and assignees forever. In testimony whereof I Abraham Lincoln President of the United States of America have caused these letters to be made patent and the seal of the general Land office to be hereunto affixed. Given under my hand at the City of Washington the first day of April in the year of the Lord one thousand eight hundred and Sixty one and of the independence of the United States the Eighty fifth. By the president Abraham Lincoln By W. V. Stoddard, sec'y. Recorded Vol. 110 page 430, Jan 9, 1863. 3 p.m. (Signature of the Recorder of the general Land office)

Swen Swenson's grandson, Walter Swanson, had the original deed to his family's government land. The pre-printed form is filled out by hand and has the seal of President Abraham Lincoln affixed to it. The secretary, Mr. Stoddard, apparently signed both his own and the president's name on June 1, 1861. Swenson's land was previously granted to a lieutenant in the War with Mexico. When the soldiers or their heirs no longer occupied the tract, it was returned to the government, which could then grant it to someone else.

Among the other Trolle Ljungby emigrants who can be identified in the Book of Records (1860) are Lars Johnson (Jönsson) who settled on 160 acres in Section 14. His great-grandson, Donald Johnson in Vasa, says that one parcel of 40 acres had to be sold before 1877 to pay for a team of horses. Peter Johnson (Per Jönsson, brother of Lars Jönsson), O. W. Peterson (Ola Persson), and Ola Larson settled in Section 12.

Thus the cluster formed by emigrants from Trolle Ljungby in the eastern part of Vasa was completed. Later that cluster extended into Featherstone Township (Plat book, 1877).

The Civil War and the Prosperity that Followed

The hard times, 1857-1860, and the Civil War that followed curtailed emigration from Sweden as well as from other countries until 1866. The same was true for Trolle Ljungby. Trued Pearson wrote that when President Lincoln asked for volunteers, Hans Mattson offered him (Pearson) the rank of lieutenant if he would volunteer. Out of consideration for his family, Pearson regretfully declined. However, he did all he could to recruit bachelors. No one was drafted in Vasa, "but it cost us a lot of money because we had to pay each volunteer between $50 and $100.00 until we had reached our quota," he said, adding that the Irish settlers, who were usually Democrats, sympathized with the rebels. The young men in the Irish colony did not volunteer. The Republicans called them "copperheads," Pearson wrote.

Mattson's Company D, Minnesota Third Regiment, consisted of young Swedes and Norwegians. The company was held captive by the rebels in Murfreesboro, Tennessee, between December 31, 1862 and January 2, 1863. Mattson was ill and on furlough in Minnesota when the capture took place. Many of the boys thought it would not have happened if he had been there. "It was a shame for the whole regiment as well as for Company D," Trued Pearson commented. Some of the soldiers from Vasa died in the South, but most returned in ill health. The records show that 22 of the men in Co. D died and ten were discharged with disabilities. In his *Vasa Illustrata*, Norelius listed 47 men from Vasa who served in the war. Of these, Nils Abrahamson, Ola Anderson, and Mathes Person belonged to the Trolle Ljungby group. Ola Larson, the son of Lasse Pehrson, also served, but he did not come to Vasa until after the war. All four survived.

The war was followed by a crime wave in Goodhue County in 1866, which included the shooting of cattle and burning of grain stacks. Letters from America often tell of how honest Americans were, saying that it was unnecessary to lock one's doors. In Goodhue County, however, before the turn of the century, there were thirteen murders and 125 cases of assault in the county. The offenses included grand

and petit larceny, burglaries, horse theft, illegitimacy, drunkenness, and unlawful fishing.

The Second Group of Settlers from Trolle Ljungby, 1865-69

The prosperity in the United States following the Civil War attracted a new influx of immigrants from Sweden. Meanwhile, some provinces in the old country experienced a famine in 1868-69. It did not come to that in Skåne, but the dissatisfaction there mounted when the peasant uprisings against the nobility in the 1860s resulted in firings and evictions. At the same time, the population 'explosion' made it more difficult for young people to find work or farmland to rent. Hans Mattson's emigration propaganda in Sweden added to the America fever. 1869 became a record year for emigration thus far from Sweden and also in northeastern Skåne. See more information about these settlers in my *Minnesota Swedes, Vol. II.*

The emigrants from Trolle Ljungby arriving in Goodhue County in 1869 signed up as members of the Lutheran churches, thus indicating they planned to stay. However, only some of them can be found in the Federal Census for Goodhue County of 1870. Apparently, they went somewhere else to find temporary work, returning before the next census was taken. Hans Mattson may have told them that railroad workers were in high demand. The railroad companies often provided family quarters.

A few of the families from Trolle Ljungby arriving in the late 1860s and early 1870s founded settlements in the southern part of Welch Township close to the Cannon River. Other farms owned by former Trolle Ljungby residents were scattered throughout the county. Welch Township, which was called Grant before 1872, was among the last to be secured by early settlers. One county history states:

Although claims were made in 1855-56, they were soon abandoned for the deserted homesteads in the south part of the county. These opportunities were eagerly watched by the temporary pioneers of this township, and not until 1857 and '58 was a permanent settlement made. These changes were so common that it is impossible to trace out the first claim that was secured. (*Goodhue County History*, 1878, p. 416)

The cluster of Trolle Ljungby emigrants in Welch Township consisted of farms owned by Olof Swenson-Wahlin,[v] Ola W. Swenson,[vi] Ola Swanson (D. O. Swanson),[vii] Anders Nilson (Andrew Nelson)[viii] and Mons Pehrson,[ix] all of whom had arrived in Goodhue County, 1865-69. Swen Magnus Bloom, not from Trolle Ljungby, also had a farm there.[x]

A Goodhue County history book notes that John Bloom and D. O. Swanson were among the first permanent settlers in Welch Township. One Red Wing newspaper reported on sales of real estate in January of 1869. According to the register of deeds, two sales had been made since December 1, 1868: Andrew Nelson and Ole W. Swanson had purchased from Pascal Smith one quarter in Section 31 and another quarter in Section 32. The purchase price was $800.00.

The price that Nelson and Swanson paid was actually less than they would have paid for railroad land. The availability of both homestead and railroad land was very limited in southeastern Minnesota in 1868-69. Railroad land was not available at all in the 1860s and 1870s in the western part of Welch Township where the Trolle Ljungby emigrants settled. (The price of railroad land varied between $5.00 and $15.00 per acre.)

Ola Peterson Daun, who arrived with his wife, Olu, in 1869 settled on 40 acres in Cannon Fall Township. See listings for Daun, Ola Peterson and Olsdotter, Olue Svenson Peterson in my *Minnesota Swedes, Volume II* and interview with Phyllis Pladsen.

Much progress had been made since the first emigrants arrived from Trolle Ljungby. There were stores and churches even in the countryside and travel was easier. From about 1858 until 1871, the Burbank Stage Coach was in use on a route between La Crosse and St. Paul. The trip took 49 hours which included a seven-hour rest at Winona and eight hours at Red Wing. It was also possible to travel by stagecoach from Red Wing to Cannon Falls and on to Faribault via Northfield. The first railroads were built in the 1860s and 1870s to connect the waterways and to access and settle the interior. The railroad between Winona and St. Paul, which stretched through Goodhue County, was laid in 1866. Red Wing got its first railroad service on September 29, 1870 (St. Paul and Chicago Company).

Those who settled north of Cannon River in Welch Township lacked communications, especially to the south. There were no bridges across the river and no roads through the hills. These settlers had to be self-sufficient for a long time. When we drove up the hills through the forest from Vasa to that neighborhood in the fall of 1992, the road was nearly washed out after a heavy rain. The telephones were out of order.

We met with Janice Olson, who was born on the farm that her great-grandparents Ola and Pernilla Swenson Wahlin (later Wahlen) settled on and which her brother took over. The farm had been in the family for over 100 years and is listed in *Century Farms of Minnesota*. About the land Janice said, "It has always been hilly and rocky. We wish the Swedes had settled some other place. We wish they had settled over at Northfield [where the land is] real nice and level." When she was young they still slaughtered all the animals on the farm, even the big cattle, because transporting them was too difficult, she said.

Helen Fredrickson, the great-granddaughter of Andrew Nelson, who arrived from Trolle Ljungby in 1865, remembered the family farm in Welch Township. "The river would get high sometimes, but they didn't have any farmland down by the river because it was a real high bluff. They were up on top of the bluff." Her grandparents did their own butchering and canned the meat.

Lawrence Nelson, grandson of Bengta Larson who emigrated from Trolle Ljungby in 1879, said that the Cannon River had flooded for one-hundred years. There was erosion which did not occur on flat land, but flat land was often sandy, he said. The river did not always freeze in the winter, but when it did, people walked across the ice to Vasa. "They were all Swedish around Welch. That was a Swedish town for quite a few miles," Nelson said. His grandparents always spoke Swedish.

Everal Nelson, Red Wing, said his grandfather Jöns Nelson and his family came over in 1873. They stayed with friends the first winter in Welch valley not too far from Cannon River. Their quarters were up in a little attic, so they had to climb up a ladder. "That's where they stayed with their two children the first year they were here." A number of years later they bought a farm in Welch, "a large farm right on top of the hills from Cannon River. Every day they had to drive the cattle down to the river for water. It was a long steep drive. In the winter they had to cut a hole in the ice, so that the cattle could drink. "They had very low barns usually, not very high, and just dirt floors in them," Everal said.

Norris Nelson recalled that his grandparents, the Andrew Nelsons, settled in sections 31 and 32. They lived in a dugout in the hillside. And that's where they spent the first winter, and then they built a house up on top of the hill... I remember we used to walk out on this bluff. It was way up high—and the railroad track came back around there...."

Wallace Weberg said it would have taken Norelius one whole day to walk from White Rock to Welch. Later, when two railroads came through Welch, that town outgrew Vasa in the 1880s. "They had passenger train service through here, so they could commute between Red Wing and Cannon Falls and any place they wanted to go." Welch had a hotel, a feed mill, sawmills, and a stockyard at one time. It also had saloons, Wallace said.

In a historical sketch, Katherine Hellquist wrote that D. O. Swanson and his wife Pernilla both of whom came from Trolle Ljungby in 1868, "bought a tract of wild land in Welch Township, Minnesota, and literally carved a home out of the wilderness."

From 1882 the town of Welch was served by two railroads, the Milwaukee Road, built across Goodhue County by Chicago, Milwaukee & St. Paul, but abandoned west of Cannon Falls in 1918, and the Chicago Great Western built by Minnesota Central, which was abandoned in 1982. The railroad companies sold some land, but we were told that it was usually swampy land and not for sale until the land grant was almost up.

The Third Group of Settlers from Trolle Ljungby, 1880-1881

In 1880-81, eight more families arrived from Trolle Ljungby. They were headed by Anders Lamberg,[xi] Per Nilsson Ljung (Young),[xii] Bengt Persson Rosenquist,[xiii] Per Svensson Vallin,[xiv] Jöns Trulsson Walberg,[xv] Sven Persson Trolin, Nils Nilsson Rooth,[xvi] and Carl Andersson Ståhl (Steele).[xvii] All except Rosenquist and Walberg stayed in Goodhue County. As far as is known, only one of the remaining six men purchased land in Goodhue County and it was a very small parcel. In some cases, their sons, who were also born in Sweden, became farm owners.

The Last Trickle of Settlers from Trolle Ljungby, 1907-1912

The large Brodd family from Trolle Ljungby and Nymö moved to Vasa in 1911 from Balaton, Minnesota. The family rented farms in Vasa.[xviii] The last large family from Trolle Ljungby to settle in Goodhue County was headed by Sven Bengtsson (Swan Benson).[xix] He probably arrived in 1907 and his family in 1912. The family lived in Red Wing, Welch, and Belle Creek before moving back to Red Wing in 1928. By that time, it had become increasingly difficult to establish oneself as a farmer in Goodhue County. See more information about these settlers in my *Minnesota Swedes Vol. II.*

Agriculture

After the Civil War prices rose. The prosperity benefited all classes, including workers and farmers:

To pay all debts was easy. Every bit of land in Vasa was tilled and brought the most luscious harvest of prime wheat, for which the farmer could get one hundred dollars for a couple of loads. Thus many of us became capitalists.... The land in Vasa rose in price as never before or since. (Trued Pearson)

Wheat became a dependable source of income. It generally produced between 15 and 30 bushels per acre according to Pearson. In a letter dated October 26, 1865, Swen Olson let his relatives know how much he had harvested on his land that year and what he could get for it. He was obviously proud of the results:

Wheat 1,185 bushels, barley 58 bushels, oats 686 bushels; how much corn I don't know, but it will probably be about 250 bushels. Together with what I have rented out or everything that is grown on my land it amounts to 2,639 bushels not counting corn, beans, and potatoes.

A diary written by John Malberg, who lived in Spring Garden, shows how the wheat prices fluctuated in the Vasa area. When he started his diary in 1869, he received 66 cents per bushel. He usually sold his wheat either in Cannon Falls or in Red Wing. The price of wheat increased in the 1870s and decreased in the 1880s. For the years 1870-74, he received an average of 91 cents per bushel; 1875-79, 94 cents; 1880-84, 88 cents; and 1885-89, 62 cents per bushel. The highest price Malberg received for wheat was $1.60 on May 14, 1877, and the lowest, 40 cents in the fall of 1878.

The wheat prices in Kristianstad län, Sweden, show a similar pattern, but with higher prices (Dollar value $3.25): 1870-74, $1.25 per bushel; 1885-89, $1.03 per bushel (284 bushels to a hectoliter).

Malberg also grew an unspecified amount of corn. During the 1880s he harvested less wheat and more barley and oats. In 1891 he added rye.

According to Pearson, the price of wheat increased for at least 15 years until the soil was depleted of nourishment. In Sweden, where the farmers kept much more livestock, the soil could be replenished with manure. The price decrease in Sweden was caused by import of cheap foreign wheat. Some of it came from the American Midwest.

Red Wing was the world's leading primary market for wheat. It was the only place for 30 miles where wheat could be sold. Pearson recalls that from the time the harvest began until the next spring, the streets in Red Wing were crowded with loads of wheat whenever the weather conditions were favorable. Red Wing had no railroad at the time and the wheat was transported on barges on the river, usually to La Crosse and via Milwaukee to Chicago. Many merchants in Red Wing became rich. When the Scandinavian wheat growers found that they were not always treated fairly by the merchants, they decided to form a cooperative. They bought a storage facility in Red Wing and hired Pearson to take care of it. The business was profitable for the first couple of years, but when three more cooperatives entered the business, the merchants convinced the shipping companies to raise the freight from Red Wing to Milwaukee by eight cents per bushel, which was returned to them as a discount. Pearson soon lost what he had earned the first two years for the cooperative, plus some of his own money. The wheat growers in Vasa sold to the highest bidder and not always to the cooperative. Pearson resigned, and that was the end of the cooperative.

In 1866, a Red Wing newspaper reported on the prosperity that the town enjoyed. In one year, Red Wing exported 550,000 bushels of wheat, 75,000 barrels of flour, and one hundred tons of hides. The total amount invested in new buildings in one year was $288,325. Red Wing constructed a new courthouse of red brick, a new school, a Methodist University, and several hotels (*Goodhue County Republican*, Sep. 21, 1866).

With all this progress some setbacks could be expected. The harvests in the area were hurt by the potato bug in 1865 and the chinch bug in 1880. That year there was not enough wheat left for seeds. The growers then started to raise more hay for cattle. A farmer in Featherstone Township recalled that the yield was only 12 bushels to the acre that year which was reflected in the 1880 Agricultural Census. "No one realized they [the bugs] had come to stay for several years until the farmers learned how to conquer them by means of more diversified farming with less wheat and barley sown," he said. Even the corn fields were destroyed when they were next to the wheat fields. As soon as the wheat was harvested, all the green grass and wheat was destroyed by the bugs, so there was nothing left for them to live on. They would not starve. Somehow they would rather crawl twenty or thirty rods, even if it took them a week or a month to reach the nearby corn field. A soon as they got there, the first corn hills became black with bugs. Those that came lagging behind had to crawl farther and farther into the corn field. Finally half the field of corn was dead, and the cornstalks began to turn white; all their sap and juice had been sucked out by the chinch bugs. The corn was dead. No real corn ripened (Related by Alexander P. Anderson).

Malberg did not mention the chinch bugs until in July of 1886. At that time, he said, they were very bad. Vasa seems to have escaped the great deluge of grasshoppers that swooped down on Nicollet and neighboring counties in 1874 and laid their eggs that hatched more locusts in 1875 and 1876 until the farmers finally gained the upper hand by dragging the fields.

Day-to-Day Work on the Farm

The Malberg diary provides us with a good account of the seasonal round and the usual farm chores in Spring Garden. His children were small and he had to hire help. When not busy with farm work, Malberg hired out as a carpenter or worked on his own buildings. His diary starts in January of 1869. From January through March, he worked mostly for others. Following a couple of weeks in April with nice weather, the spring planting season began. Malberg usually attended church on Sunday. Sometimes he had to interrupt his work and make coffins for neighbors and friends who had died. In 1869, he made three coffins. The entries copied here concern mainly farm work.

1869:

Apr. 20	Went to [Cannon] Falls to get the sowing machine and tools.
Apr. 21-26	Dragged new land.
Apr. 28	Started to seed oats. Branberg took the oxen to Vasa for a load of lumber. Seeded oats.
Apr. 29	Seeded oats.
Apr. 30	Started seeding wheat.
May 1	Seeded wheat.
May 4	Seeded. Had Carl Anderson's machine. Dry weather.
May 5- 7	Seeded.
May 8, 10	Did after-dragging.
May 12	Started plowing for corn.
May 13-14	Plowed.
May 15	Cultivated the corn land.
May 17	Planted potatoes.
May 18-19	Planted corn.
May 28	Started building fences.
June 1	Worked on the new land.
June 2-8, 11	Fence work.
June 14-15	Replanted corn.
June 16, 17	Cut weeds.
June 22	Grubbed at Blomberg's.
June 23	Grubbed in the wheat.
June 25	Dragged the corn land.
June 26	Dragged the corn and potatoes.
June 28	Cleared land with Edlund and Carl Beckman.

June 29	Cleared land with Edlund and Carl Beckman. Repaired a plow and bought a reaper from Lagerstrom.
June 30	Cleared land with Edlund and Carl Beckman.
July 2	Dragged rutabagas and plowed corn.
July 4-5	Did road work.
July 7	Plowed corn.
July 8	Finished plowing corn. Had Beckman to work.
July 9	Did road work. Had Beckman to help.
July 10	Worked alone on the new land.
July 12-13	Plowed corn.
July 14	Went to Jacob and borrowed a plow.
July 15	Started breaking new land at noon.
July 16-17	Breaking new land all day.
July 19	Hard rain. Broke new land, 4 hrs.
July 20	Broke new land all day.
July 21	Finished breaking new land.
July 22	Brought home Jacob's breaking plow.
July 23	Started cutting hay.
July 27-28	Cut hay.
July 29-30	Plowed corn.
July 31	Finished plowing corn. Nice weather.
Aug. 3	Repaired hayrack.
Aug. 4	Stacked hay.
Aug. 5	Helped breaking land at John Lagerstrom's.
Aug. 9	Was at John Lagerstrom's with horses and broke new land.
Aug. 10	Cut hay. Rain in the morning.

Aug. 11	Cut upland grass.
Aug. 12	Started cutting oats. Used cradle.
Aug. 13	Cut oats, got the reaper on the field. Cocked hay. Heavy rain.
Aug. 16	Cut some wheat. Hired Beckman.
Aug. 17	Started reaping oats.
Aug. 18	Beckman started working for me. Finished oats.
Aug. 19	Started reaping wheat.
Aug. 20	Reaped. Nice weather.
Aug. 21	Finished new land…. Nice weather.
Aug. 23	Reaped wheat.
Aug. 27	Reaped. Nice weather.
Aug. 28	Finished reaping.
Aug. 31	Started stacking oats.
Sep. 1	Stacked one stack of wheat.
Sep. 2	Stacked one stack of wheat.
Sep. 6	Cut hay.
Sep. 7-11	Stacked wheat.
Sep. 15	Started plowing with horses.
Sep. 16	Somewhat dry, stacked some.
Sep. 17	Finished wheat-stacking.
Sep. 18	Stacked oats. Hauled wheat for Anderson.
Sep. 20	Plowed.
Sep. 21	Plowed and hauled hay. Jonson died in the afternoon.
Sep 22	Plowed and made a coffin.
Sep. 23	Plowed. Some rain.
Sep. 25	Rain in morning, cold. Cut corn. Frost during night.

Sep. 27	Hard frost this morning. Cut corn.
Sep. 28	Cut corn. Warm and sunshine all day.
Sep. 29	Cut corn. Warm.
Sep. 30	Cut corn, hard wind.
Oct. 7	Dug the potatoes and sent some wheat to the mill for flour.
Oct. 9	Rained. Lay a floor in the granary.
Oct. 11-13	Plowed.
Oct. 14	Repaired wagon for threshing.
Oct. 15	Was at Lundell's and threshed ½ day.
Oct. 16	Threshed all day at Lundell's. Nice weather.
Oct. 18	Threshed ½ day at Lundell's and started at our place.
Oct. 19	Threshed ½ day and machine broke down.
Oct. 20	Plowed ½ day and was at Mrs. Johnson's.
Oct. 21	Threshed ½ and the twine wheel broke.
Oct. 22	Finished threshing.
Oct. 23	Repaired around cow barn.
Oct. 25	Repaired stable. Fanned some wheat.
Oct. 26	Fanned wheat for Lagerstrom.
Oct. 28	Had a cheese party (The women made cheese.)
Oct. 29	Took up the root crop. Fanned wheat.
Nov. 1	Fanned wheat.
Nov. 3	Plowed. Warm weather.
Nov. 4.	Rained half a day. Plowed in the afternoon.
Nov. 5	Plowed half a day.
Nov. 11	Fanned wheat to go to Red Wing.
Nov. 16	Hunted deer.

Nov. 19	Hauled corn and corn fodder.
Nov. 22	Traded wagons with R. Miller and got mortgage on oxen.
Nov. 23	Hunted deer.
Nov. 24	Hauled corn and corn fodder.
Nov. 25	Helped Lundell butcher.
Nov. 26	Built a pig house.
Nov. 29	Hauled corn.
Dec. 2-4	Worked on new land with Carl Johnson.
Dec. 6	Worked on new land with Carl Johnson and drove sled back.
Dec. 7	Finished working on new land.
Dec. 8	Warmer weather. Cut wood.
Dec. 10	Rain. Repaired fence and piled grubbed wood on new land.
Dec. 13	Cleaned out the water well.
Dec. 15	Hauled one load corn fodder with oxen.
Dec. 16	Butchered a pig.
Dec. 22	Sacked up the fanned wheat.
Dec. 28-29	Worked on the sled.
Dec. 31	Year at an end (Translated by Viola Young Knutson).

The same year that the above notations were made, a Red Wing newspaper advertised the Victor Drill, Estely's Broadcast Seeder, Kirby self-raking machine, a vibrator threshing machine, and the Galena Breaking Plow. The prices were not listed. Before threshing machines came into use, threshing was done by oxen threading out the grain or by using flails to pound the grain loose from the chaff by hand.

Emil Kullberg, who was born in Vasa in 1872, is quoted as saying that when he was old enough to do farm work, the grain was cut by a reaper. Men tied the grain by hand using straw to tie the bundles. (The same technique was used in Sweden.) The first binder in use tied the bundles with wire. Soon the twine binder was on the market. The first threshing machine he worked with was a horse-powered rig. The steam thresher came next. In later years the gasoline tractor was used for threshing. Wages in harvest and threshing in the early days was $1.25 a day. A day was from daylight to dark with five meals of good food each day.

The Swedes in Isanti County also embraced the new labor-saving implements that were introduced in the 1870s and 1880s. As Ostergren explained, "Reapers and threshing machines were wonders of the day, perfect answers to the vexing problem of high labor costs that plagued rural districts everywhere in the Middle West."

Occupations of the Swedes in Goodhue County, 1870

Of all the Swedish-born heads of households and single adults in Goodhue County in 1870, 468 were farmers, 190 farm laborers, 156 laborers, 54 day laborers, 49 housekeepers, and 34 domestics. Other occupations or 'none listed; totaled 200.

The percentage of farmers is high because they didn't have to own their farms to be listed as farmers. The largest number of farmers could be found in Vasa Township. Of the 167 farmers of Swedish birth in Vasa, 147 owned their farms in 1870 for a total real estate value of $299,820.00. The average value of their farms was $2,040.00. Twenty farmers rented their land.

For Goodhue County as a whole the average value of farms owned by 339 Swedish-born farmers was $1,860.00. This clearly indicates that the farms owned by Swedes in Vasa were larger than those owned by their countrymen in other townships. But the value of the farms owned by Swedes in Goodhue County was the third lowest of any nationality in the county. Only farmers from Holland and Austria owned less. In contrast, the Norwegian-born farmers operated twice as many farms as the Swedish-born and their farms were also worth more (Average value $2,368.00). The most valuable farms were owned by native Englishmen and Scotsmen. Thirteen percent of the farms in Goodhue County were owned by native Swedes in 1870.

By 1870 all the farmland in Vasa was occupied. If someone wanted to sell, the price was likely to be too high for newly arrived land-seekers from Trolle Ljungby. However, both single and married men could obtain work as farmhands. The "greenhorns" provided cheap labor, and sometimes landowners took advantage of their situation. Once the newcomers had saved some money and gained experience, they could start out on their own by renting a farm.

Successful Goodhue County Swedes

Vasa Illustrata, published in 1905, names many successful American men born in Vasa Township with college degrees and some who had earned Ph.D. degrees. Only one woman was mentioned, Miss May Anderson. She was a Fine Arts teacher at Gustavus Adolphus College in St. Peter, Minnesota, which was started in Red Wing in 1862. Hamline University was founded as an academy in Red Wing in 1854, and Hauge College or Red Wing Collegiate Institute, which closed in 1932, started as a military school in 1871. The city also had a fashion-school for girls between 1889 and 1920. Red Wing at one time was considered as the site for St. Olaf College which located in Northfield.

From interviews with descendants, we have learned that farm girls of the third generation received a relatively good education. In order to attend high school, the farm children had to be boarded out with relatives in the cities. Girls, in particular, often lived with their grandparents who had retired in the city. Farmers' sons seldom attended school beyond the eighth grade because they were needed on the farm. In later years, the boys also attended high school. Many of the girls who graduated from high school went on to a one-year teacher's college and became grade-school teachers, while others went to secretarial school. These were opportunities that farm girls in Sweden did not enjoy in the early 1900s. There, it was considered to be more useful to educate boys beyond elementary school, but even that was rare in the countryside.

Two men from Goodhue County achieved national fame in the fields of politics and agricultural science. One of them was born in Sweden and one was the son of immigrants.

John Lind, governor of Minnesota, 1899-1901, came to Goodhue County from Sweden with his parents in 1868 when he was 14 years old. He was born in 1854 in Kånna, Småland. Having lost his left arm in an accident, he studied to become a teacher and then a lawyer. In 1873 he moved to Sibley County. Before and after serving as governor, he represented Minnesota in the U. S. House of Representatives for a total of four terms. Having started his political career as a Republican, he switched to the Democratic Party before running for governor. He served on the board of the University of Minnesota, and was elected regent in 1893. For several terms he filled the office as president. In 1913, President Wilson appointed him to serve as his envoy in Mexico. During the First World War, he acted as chairman of the Advisory Council to the Secretary of Labor in Washington. Governor Lind visited Vasa in 1899. After the war, he returned to private law practice in Minneapolis. He died in 1930.

Alexander P. Anderson, an agricultural scientist, was born in Featherstone Township in 1862, the son of Swedish immigrants. He studied in the country schools (the first one-room schoolhouse in Featherstone Township). He taught school in his home district both before and after a year at the university. He earned Bachelor and Master of Science degrees. In 1895, he studied at the University in Munich, Germany, which awarded him a Doctor's degree. He served as state botanist of South Carolina, as bacteriologist at Clemson College of South Carolina, and as assistant professor of Botany at Columbia University in New York City, where he carried on independent research at the New York Botanical Garden. Meanwhile, he continued an early study of the starch granule and discovered a method of exploding it, which led to the commercial products known as Puffed Rice and Puffed Wheat. This invention made Anderson world famous. In 1917, he returned to Goodhue County and built a home in Burnside Township, where he continued his experiments until his death. For 30 years he was identified with the Quaker Oats Company of Chicago which manufactured the products he invented.

The Swedish-born brothers Magnus and Swan J. Turnblad, who grew up in Vasa, became well-known editors and publishers of *Svenska Amerikanska Posten* in Minneapolis, a Swedish-American weekly newspaper. They were born in Vislanda, Småland, and came to Vasa with their parents in 1868. Swan J. moved to Minneapolis at the age of 19 and worked as a typesetter for *Minnesota Stats Tidning* and *Svenska Folkets Tidning* for a few years. In 1887, he became the business manager of *Svenska Amerikanska Posten*. Under his leadership, the paper's subscriptions grew from 4,000 to 40,000. The success was deemed to be largely due to Magnus Turnblad's editing skills. Magnus, who had started out in the grocery business, was a scholarly man while Swan distinguished himself as a businessman. When visiting Sweden in 1897, Swan J. obtained a large library of books for free. Swan Turnblad assured himself of a place in the annals of Swedish Americans by donating his turreted mansion on Park Avenue to the American Institute of Swedish Arts, Literature, and Science in 1929. The mansion remains as the home of the American Swedish Institute. Swan Turnblad died in 1933 and is buried in the Vasa Lutheran Church Cemetery. (Magnus was born in 1858 and Swan in 1860. Their father was Olof Månson.)

The most successful of the earliest adult migrants from Trolle Ljungby was probably Swen Olson, known as Swan Olson. Having worked as a farmhand in Sweden, he made great progress in America. He owned 320 acres in Vasa Township, a house in Red Wing, and 800 acres in Idaho. Having moved to Red Wing, he served as supervisor of the town. John W. Swenson, who was born in 1854 in Trolle Ljungby and emigrated as a single man in 1873, also owned 320 acres in Vasa Township. Eventually, the farm ownership passed to his only son.

Ethnic Settlement Patterns

The Swedish population in Vasa expanded to include almost all of Cannon Falls and Welch townships (except for an Irish presence); the major portion of Leon Township, the northwestern part of the Belle Creek (which was for the most part Irish); the northeast corner of Warsaw and the northwest corner of Featherstone. In Featherstone there was a predominance of Yankee Swedes and Germans. The Scotch and Irish lived in Stanton Township and in the northern part of Warsaw. The Irish were never strong in Goodhue County with the possible exception of Belle Township.

The Norwegian settlements stretched far and wide in Goodhue Township. Wanamingo, Roscoe, and Kenyon townships were as Norwegian as Vasa became Swedish. In addition, the Norwegians had settled Cherry Grove except for the town of Fairpoint, which was mixed, and almost the entire township of Holden, as well as Minneola except for the northeastern part which was German. The Norwegians also lived in the south half of Warsaw Township and in an area in the center of Belvidere Township. Hay Creek, Frontenac, Wacouta, Central Point, Goodhue, Zumbrota, Pine Island townships were strongly German, as was most of Belvidere. Red Wing and Burnside were mixed. There was an Indian reservation in Burnside and a small colony of settlers from Luxembourg in the southern part of Belvidere Township. The Norwegians had the strongest ethnic presence in the county. The Swedes came second and the German third (Source: Plat Book).

Swedish geographer Helge Nelson separated the Norwegians and the Swedes in Goodhue County and found that in 1880, 15.4 percent of the foreign-born whites were native Swedes and 14.5 percent native Norwegians. Ten years earlier the Norwegians dominated.

Second Generation Swedes and Norwegians in Goodhue County

1910 Both parents born in Sweden	3,020	9.5%
1910 Both parents born in Norway	3,552	11.2%
1930 Mixed Parentage, Swedish	3,236	10.3%
1930 Mixed Parentage, Norwegian	4,071	13.0%

While there were more native Norwegians than native Swedes in Goodhue County in 1870, the Swedes took the lead in 1880 and kept it through 1930. However, there were more Norwegians of the second generation than Swedes through 1930, which indicates that the Norwegians had more children and/or more mixed marriages.

The Norwegians settled mostly on the flat land, as for instance, in Wanamingo and Kenyon townships to the south, while the Swedes preferred the hillier land to the north in the county, a rolling landscape with thick black soil.

Assimilation

Introduction

The first white settlers had to cope with Indians, prairie fires, grass-hoppers, and violent storms. As we have seen, the Native Americans were usually friendly toward the Swedish Americans, but nonetheless, they created a new kind of fear for them. When the Indians moved away that fear diminished. Having experienced much class struggle in Sweden, the Trolle Ljungby emigrants were probably discouraged to learn about the slaves in the United States. However, the letters to Sweden show that they believed the Civil War was fought to abolish slavery, and they considered that to be a just cause. Having been treated harshly by the landowners in Skåne, they supported the North and some volunteered for service. Few were active in politics, but they voted for Abraham Lincoln's Republican Party.

Diseases, such as tuberculosis, caused many deaths in their new environment. Among the causes of death reported between 1870 and 1877 were fever, croup, consumption, inflammation of lungs, dysentery, cholera, catarrh, childhood dropsy, scarlet fever, typhoid fever, accidents, nervous fever, summer complaint, hemorrhage of the lungs, accident, appendicitis, lightning, scrofula, and diarrhea.

Steven Hedeen told us about an early cemetery (*gravbacken*), in the Jemland settlement, where many small children were buried after a bad flu epidemic. In the 1860s and 1870s, most of the funerals held in Vasa Lutheran Church were for children and youth.

The Scandinavians soon learned that there were some things they could not control. The weather was more extreme in Minnesota than in Skåne. The summers were hotter and the winters colder. They did not complain. Being used to sleeping in unheated rooms in Skåne, they could endure the winters even in primitive cabins. However, the cyclones that ravaged Vasa, some say, seemed like a punishment from God. These devastating storms came without warning and were over in a matter of minutes. Yet, they resulted in the loss of life and destruction of property. The first cyclone that affected Vasa hit in 1865, killing one person and injuring nine. The second cyclone in 1879 was far more devastating. It killed nine people, injured 30, and destroyed the Vasa Children's Home. Four of the children at the home were killed and 18 injured. Houses and crops were destroyed. The damage to private property in Red Wing was estimated at $12,000. *The Red Wing Republican* named the individuals who were affected, almost all of them Swedes:

Commencing by tearing down trees in the school section, it crossed the Red Wing and Cannon Falls road at the house of Charles Roos, where it tipped over a granary. Gathering force and volume it next struck the house of M. Turnquist, cleaning the place entirely. This performance was duplicated at the house of Mr. Lindstedt. A young son of Mr. Lindstedt was killed and the rest of the family, four in number, injured severely. Then an unfinished building belonging to P. Jonson was strewn around and the house of N. Anderson was cast into a wheat field, Mr. and Mrs. Anderson being slightly injured. The Orphans' Home was scattered in all directions with frightful results. Three children was [sic] found dead, one died later, and fifteen were severely injured. Mr. and Mrs. Stran[d]berg and Mr. Wigman were injured. The residence of Mr. and Mrs. Holm was carried past the Orphans' Home, and Mr. and Mrs. Holm killed, a son of the family found nearby, dying later. The hurricane just passed the Lutheran church but lifted the roof off the parsonage. The next victims were E. Swanson and a four-year-old daughter, who were killed during the destruction of the house. Mr. Swenson died the next morning, Mrs. Swenson was badly injured, and the daughter escaped injury. Frank Hallberg lost a child eight months old and all his property. Thence, in due course Ola Anderson, August Peterson, Peter Larson, Mr. Gulbranson and Peter Johnson lost their houses, barns, and other property. Other buildings and property were destroyed. (History of Goodhue County, 1909)

Vasa happened to be in the center of the storm, but Red Wing, Burnside, Belle Creek, Featherstone, and Wanamingo were also affected. The news about the cyclone reached Sweden, and N. P. Granquist replied to an inquiry:

You want to know how far from us the cyclone hit last summer. It was 3 1/2 miles from here about one half Swedish mil, so we did not suffer from it. But we got a heavy rainstorm at the same time, so all that rain damaged the grain for us and many others. The cyclone swept away the houses and more or less damaged others in Vasa and several people were killed. (Nov. 22, 1879)

The Christian faith which the Trolle Ljungby emigrants brought with them from Sweden helped them endure the difficulties they faced. It was one part of their heritage they did not want to change. In the Vasa Lutheran Church and other Swedish-American churches, they could hear God's word preached in Swedish. By giving confirmation classes in the Swedish language the church ensured that the whole family could benefit from a Swedish sermon. In the 1930s, the Swedish language services were limited to once a month, and in the 1940s, when the need had diminished, they were discontinued. With the demise of the first generation, English became the language in the homes as well as the church, but the Lutheran faith remained strong.

The progress of assimilation can be measured in part by determining the emigrants' rate of naturalization, language skills, the children's education, and employment opportunities, division of labor, social life, and customs.

To declare one's intent to become a citizen was an important prerequisite for acquiring government land (and in Minnesota for voting). My study of the status of all Swedish-born men aged 21-85 residing in Vasa Township in 1900 revealed that the rate of naturalization in the Trolle Ljungby group was ten percent higher than in Vasa Township (79.6 percent).

While there were no resident aliens in the Trolle Ljungby group, nine of the other aliens who had resided in the township for five years or more were heads of households and two servants. Others in this category were listed as boarder, widower, single, and father (one each). Few scholars have attempted to research the rate of naturalization among the Swedes. When comparing the figures for Swedes in Chicago in 1870, it is evident that the prospect of becoming a landowner was an incentive for naturalization in Vasa and probably also in other rural areas. In his study about Swedes in Chicago, Ulf Beijbom found that only 16 percent of the Swedish-born in Chicago were naturalized by 1870 although among businessmen the percentage was 37 percent.

Language Skills

The 1900 Federal Census gives information about people's ability to speak English and whether they had reading and writing skills. Of the 455 Swedish-born adults residing in Vasa Township in 1900, 63 females (born 1871 or earlier) and 43 males (born 1884 or earlier) were listed as unable to speak English (together 23 percent). All adults and school children could read, but 37 females (born 1849 or earlier) and 23 males (born 1850 or earlier) were listed as unable to write (13 percent). In 1900, 68 percent of the Trolle Ljungby emigrants, who could still be found in the census, spoke English compared to 67 percent of all Swedish-born in Vasa Township. Interviews with descendants have revealed that many who were adults when they arrived, especially women, never learned to speak English. Nonetheless, the majority of all Swedish-born adults in Vasa (77 percent could speak English in 1900. Here are some of the comments made by their descendants:

 Steven Hedeen: My grandparents preferred to speak Swedish.

Helen Hyllengren: As long as my grandparents lived, we would talk Swedish to them, half English, of course.

Everal Nelson: My dad's parents never messed with English. I never ever heard them saying a word in English.

Lawrence Nelson: I think my grandmother could talk a little English, but my grandfather couldn't talk English at all.

Janice Olson: Grandpa and Grandma wouldn't speak English to us.

Stanley Swanson: About his parents, I hardly think they spoke any English at all. (Mother was born in Sweden.)

Arnold Risberg: Mother's mother preferred it [Swedish], but she could speak pretty good English too when she had to.

Ole Brodd: My mother never learned any English at all. My father finally did....

Hazel Weberg: He [Grandpa] would talk English quite a bit, but Grandma couldn't.

Bernard Anderson: It was a slow process. If they stayed around here, they didn't have to learn English either.

The Children's Education

The first school district in Goodhue County was organized in Red Wing in 1854 under the provisions of the territorial school law. Eight more school districts were quickly established, but did not have a schoolhouse. Classes were held in barns, attics, kitchens, lean-to-shacks, or wherever a room was available. Red Wing built the county's first schoolhouse. In the late 1850s, several townships built school-houses, including Vasa. The schools had to operate at least three months each year to be eligible for public funds.

Alexander Anderson, born in 1862, wrote about the school in his home community in Featherstone Township. The schoolhouse was built in 1858:

The new schoolhouse was the place where we all met during the four months of school each winter. Entertainment, spelling schools, prayer meetings, missionary meetings, revival meetings, debates, phrenology, lectures, singing classes, and Sunday school were all held in the schoolhouse.

He went on to say that the younger children started school in November. Older and bigger boys and girls came later, during the winter months. In 1872, when the Featherstone Township Board held the annual school meeting, it was decided that the school would be in session for 36 weeks and divided into three terms: a fall term of sixteen weeks, a winter, and spring term of ten weeks each, except for the school in the South Building which was opened on the 23rd of October for 29 weeks.

The Federal Censuses of 1880 and 1900 had a column which stated whether children were "at home" or "at school." Generally, children aged six through fourteen were listed as having attended school during the year. As a rule, children did not attend school after the age of 14, which was also the case in Sweden.

In the public school, children were not allowed to speak any other language than English. The rule extended to the school yard. Walter Swanson told us he had to 'stay after' one day because he was caught saying one Swedish word as he was leaving the school yard. "Then... it was a sin almost," [to speak Swedish], Walter said. This treatment made the children believe that the Swedish language was bad and best and best forgotten. Nearly all of our interviewees received their elementary education in a one-room schoolhouse. Newly-arrived immigrant teenagers often sat in the back row to listen and learn English.

The Vasa Lutheran Church started a parochial school on November 15, 1856. The first teacher was Jonas Engberg. Each church member between 21 and 55 years of age was asked to pay 50 cents a year toward his salary, but some substituted potatoes for the money, and the potatoes subsequently froze in the cold schoolhouse. Norelius wrote that the subjects were Christianity, Basic Swedish, Writing, Mathematics, Singing, and English Exercises. The school was not in session during the years 1857-61. From 1862 to 1864, Miss Lovisa Peterson was the teacher. She was succeeded by Jane Nelson and Lars Anderson, both teaching school in the church basement. From 1870 classes were also held in the various wards. S. F. Westerdahl taught in the Church Ward and the Skåne Ward. From that time, the congregation tried to realize a two-month session of elementary school in each ward. The parents paid 50 cents a month per child.

In 1875, when the congregation employed Mr. P. T. Lindholm as schoolteacher, the school was in session for eight months in five wards. In 1876, the school year was divided into three semesters. The smaller, and less advanced children attended the fall semester held in October, November, and half of December. During the least busy time on the farms, January, February, and March, teenagers and young adults could attend the so-called high school. The intermediate course was offered during the months of May, June, and July. In 1876-77, the largest number of students, 85, attended the fall semester, while 57 chose the winter term and 46 the spring term. The higher course was taught in English, but few students had the necessary basic education to follow the course plan, so requirements had to be lowered. Some of the students had to leave early because they were needed on the farms. The success of this course depended much on the weather. Students came from as far away as Spring Garden, and it was therefore necessary to find accommodations for them. The parochial school was never self-sustaining. The fee of six dollars per semester for the high school, and three dollars for the middle and beginners' school did not cover the cost, and parents who could not pay were excused.

Eric Norelius wrote in 1905 that if the congregation could have continued the way it started while it had the benefit of the good schoolteacher, P. T. Lindholm, it could have maintained a good high school in Vasa. He described Lindholm as an excellent teacher who knew how to inspire children and youth and awaken their interest in song, music, and book learning. During Lindholm's days, song and music were practiced more than ever before or since. Lindholm resigned in 1881 to become a teacher at Gustavus Adolphus College in St. Peter. Although the parochial school in Vasa had some good teachers after that, including N. L. T. Nilson, who later earned a Ph.D. from the University of Chicago, the special higher course was not mentioned after 1881. Instead, the children were divided into three classes according to their abilities. Examinations were held.

As a result of the higher course, some students could continue their education at Gustavus Adolphus Academy and College. In 1884-85, seven former Vasa parochial school students studied there. When the church celebrated its 100th anniversary in 1955, it could proudly point to eight sons of the congregation who had become ordained ministers. One prominent former student was Swan Turnblad. In his biography it said that he attended the "Lindholm High School" in Vasa. Since Vasa never had such a high school, it must refer to the parochial course taught by P. T. Lindholm.

From 1904 the congregation had no regular schoolteachers, but young women from the community served as temporary teachers in the various ward schools, among them Esther and Hanna Granville. After the public schools were extended to nine months, the children in the Swedish settlements attended Swedish church school only during the summer months. Our interviewees told us that at the "Swedish school" they could speak Swedish freely. The lessons in Christianity were in Swedish as well. Their formal religious education ended with confirmation classes after which they were confirmed in the church in the Swedish language. The first confirmation in Vasa Lutheran Church was held in 1857.

One can assume that there were long periods of time when many Swedish immigrant children did not attend school at all. They may have tried to make up for it later. In his letters to Sweden, 1855-1865, Swen Olson is strangely quiet about his children's schooling. The Federal Census for 1880 notes that his children, Andrew, 20, Olof 18, and Caroline 16, had attended school during the year, but not the younger children, who were 6 and 8 years old. Mr. Malberg notes in his diary that his 20-year old son had attended school in Vasa for a short period in 1878. No doubt, it refers to the parochial course for older students. The Malberg Diary has the following notations about school:

October 4 [1870]   Held annual school meeting.

October 9   Sent school reports.

September 30 [1872]   Enumerated the schoolchildren in the district.

September 30 [1873]   Took census of schoolchildren.

March 14 [1874]   School is out.

September 28 [1874]   Nailed up notice for school meeting.

November 9   Made out a contract with the teacher.

November 21   Left Bennet at school.

February 4 [1875]   School is out.

September 30   Took census of schoolchildren.

January 14 [1878]   Bennet went with C. Hagstrom to the Vasa School.

March 17   Bennet went to Vasa for his trunk. Started school January 15 and finished March 15, 2 months or 5 weeks.

July 19 [1879]   Bennet to Cavelin for Examination (testing).

The Work Places

While most of the Trolle Ljungby emigrants in this study lived in the countryside, there were those who settled in Red Wing. The many factories that employed workers of various nationalities provided the best melting pots in an immigrant society. Swen Tufveson, who had arrived from Trolle Ljungby in 1856, worked in a saw mill in Red Wing in 1870. He later became a machinist.

The 1870 Federal Census shows that many young girls who were born in Sweden worked as domestics in American households in Red Wing. They could be as young as eleven. Of the Trolle Ljungby emigrants listed in the membership book of First Lutheran Church in Red Wing most were women who had married Swedes from other communities in Sweden, but some of the Trolle Ljungby emigrants who joined in the 1880s were men. Many of the second generation worked in Red Wing as we will see from the interviews. The Swedes were instrumental in the founding of some of these work places.

The earliest manufacturing businesses operating in Red Wing were engaged in brick making, quarrying, and tanning. Brick making began as early as 1855. The first clay came from a pit in Vasa. The Red Wing Brick manufactured ten million bricks annually. Local lime manufacturers cut limestone from the bluffs near Red Wing. Four lime works operated in 1879. R. L. Berglund produced 250 barrels of slaked lime for the building trade each week, while Danielson & Betcher made 75 barrels a day. Charlie Oleson and G. A. Carlson produced 90 barrels daily each at their respective operations. The yellowish limestone buildings that can still be seen in Red Wing were constructed of limestone quarried in the city. The industry died out when concrete blocks came into use. John Johnson (married to Betsey Swenson from Trolle Ljungby) owned a stone quarry in 1900. Anders Danielson (married to Inga Swensdotter from Trolle Ljungby) was a stone contractor.

The tanning industry was started in 1855 by John Melander, a newly-arrived immigrant from Sweden. He was succeeded in 1857 by S. B. Foot from Pennsylvania, who together with G. K. Sterling established the G. K. Sterling & Co. in 1861. In the beginning, they made moccasins of buffalo hides that were tanned with the hair left on. These shoes were worn by the pioneers in the 1860s and were still the standard footwear for school children in the 1880s. Both the tannery and the shoe company were still in business in Red Wing in 1996. The two companies employed thousands of people through the years, including women.

Swedes also worked in the wood processing plants making wagons, sash, doors, and blinds, as well as furniture. The Erickson & Swanson Furniture factory was founded in 1874. Two furniture factories operated in the city from about 1880 until 1928. One specialized in bedroom furniture, ladies' desks, and bookcases, while the other made parlor and dining-room furniture. Claus Johnson (married to Kjersti

Olson from Trolle Ljungby) was a gluer in a furniture factory in Red Wing.

The Red Wing Iron Works was completed in 1866. The city's flour industry started in 1873 with the construction of the Bluff Mill. From 1878 it operated as a joint venture with the Diamond Mill. Together the two mills employed one hundred people and had a capacity of 850 barrels a day. Before that, water-powered mills dotted the countryside. These mills ground the wheat raised by settlers, and never attempted to build up markets outside their immediate vicinities.

A German immigrant by the name of J. Paul started the Red Wing pottery industry by setting up a shop in 1861. The Red Wing Stoneware Company was incorporated in 1877. In the 1890s, three local stoneware companies operated in Red Wing. The coarse clay which overlay the finer potter's clay in the pits was finally put to use in October of 1891 when the Red Wing Sewer Pipe Company was organized. Carl Joseph Pearson (married to Carolina Swenson from Trolle Ljungby) worked at the Sewer Pipe Company in 1910. In 1895, the workers were paid only 12 1/2 cents an hour and hoped to get 14 cents and a nine-hour day.

The state commissioner reported in 1878 that Red Wing's three flour mills had annual sales of $1,284,985 and employed 85 men. In addition, Red Wing had four lumber mills employing 148 persons, six wagon works with 47 workers, two cooperage establishments with 80 men on the payrolls, four stone-and marble quarries with 97 employees, four breweries with 15 men, two potteries with 14 men, and one foundry with another 14 employees.

Later, Red Wing also had companies that made hats and gloves. Occupations listed in the censuses include blacksmiths, gun makers, harness makers, and cigar makers. The town provided many work opportunities for both men and women. The railroad which came to Red Wing in 1870 catapulted its citizens and the surrounding area out of their isolation. It also provided employment. Ole Nelson from Trolle Ljungby worked as a laborer for the railroad in 1900. The village of Goodhue became a railroad town as did Cannon Falls, Welch, Kenyon, and Zumbrota. Vasa did not have a railroad, but at one time it had a post office, a creamery and two grocery stores.

Women's Work

The pioneer women carried a heavy work burden, especially during the first few years as can be seen from the following except from a historical sketch:

To begin with the people would work up just a small plot of ground and plant grain. Oftentimes the women would harvest it by hand and the men spent all harvest season out among the English farmers who had machinery and could work their whole farms. They had made money in the East before coming here. During the first winters the men would go to the Wisconsin woods and hire themselves to chop wood..... All the while the women had to manage by themselves as best they could at home.... Here my mother drove our cattle and Swan Nelson's oxen to water every day in the winter. (Judith Gull, original in English)

In the Malberg Diary there is no mention of Mrs. Malberg helping with field work, but neither is there any evidence of Mr. Malberg assisting with the milking. He usually hired men to bind the grain. Elsie Mae Lersch remembered the potato digging and the corn husking on her parents' farm in Wisconsin in the 1920s. Her mother was the daughter of a Trolle Ljungby emigrant. "We did most of that by hand," she said. "Mother always helped."

Mrs. Dorothy Holmes wrote in her memoirs, "My mother told me that they, the kids, would follow the reaper and gather the cut grain and tie it into bundles. I have an idea that *'gamla grandma'* was along too." When Dorothy married Chester Holmes in 1921, they drove directly home after the ceremony and milked the cows. Dorothy got her first washing machine in 1925. It was a manual type with a wooden pole to pull back and fourth. When her little daughter got her finger caught in the gears and had to have it amputated, Dorothy got rid of the washing machine and used the washboard instead. (Original in English with some Swedish words included.)

In the letters written by Trolle Ljungby emigrants, one has to read between the lines. If the women had not worked in the fields and barns, it would most likely have been mentioned in the letters to Sweden. As the dairy herds got bigger, and milking machines were not common until long after the rural electrification program was started in 1936, it was often necessary for the women to help with the milking. Some areas did not have electricity until in the late 40s or early 50s. From the interviews we have learned that some women did the milking. Myrtle Hilan said, "Dad never milked, never, never milked." Her mother took care of that chore. When Myrtle became a farmwife in 1929, she helped her husband with the milking. They took the children with them to the barn. Stella Ingeman, who married in 1939, milked eight cows together with her husband. "We both did," she said. Lola Nelson, born in 1925, recalled helping her father. "When my brothers left home, I graduated to hired man. I milked cows, up 5 o'clock in the morning. I helped him plant corn. I helped him hay, and that was with the fork and driving the horses."

The Lamberg girls, Sharon and her sister Janet, helped their mother milk 14 cows before going to school in the morning in the 1950s. Both girls became teachers. Nearly all public schoolteachers were women. Sharon quit teaching when marrying a farmer. At planting and harvest time, she told us she climbed up on one of the huge tractors or combines and helped out in the field.

Recalling his childhood, Ole Brodd emphasized that his mother's work did not change in America. "It was the same." His mother and grandmother both brought their weaving looms from Sweden and his grandmother also brought her spinning wheel. The family arrived in 1903.

In a historical sketch about the Ingeman family, it says: "Grandpa built Grandma's loom and Grandma made carpets for the house. She spun some yarn and made stockings. Grandma's loom was so big, it filled one room upstairs. It always stood in the first room above the stairs.... Grandma had carpets that were used in the winter and then different ones were put down for summer. Grandma made candles too." (Lucille Nelson)

Apparently, the women's work did not change much from the accustomed practices in Sweden. Women in general performed the same chores as in Sweden, but as far as we know they did not have to go out and do workdays for others. However, neighbors helped one another. Not all farm women had to work outside, but if there was a shortage of males in the family, the females had to do men's chores.

Modern conveniences for the home arrived earlier than in Sweden. They were not always welcome. Helen Hyllengren recalled that when her mother got her first washing machine, which had a gas engine, she said she didn't want it, because she could wash better than the machine. She had a big wash boiler and boiled and scrubbed the clothes. When women were widowed, it was sometime difficult for them to make ends meet. They had to manage with whatever was available. Mrs. Hyllengren's grandmother never had a pension. She lived alone on East 7th Street in Red Wing. "Times were hard. They didn't have much. They didn't get much rent from their farm when they rented it out. I don't know really how my grandmother lived." She did not take in any boarders or washing and ironing as many widows did, Helen said.

Mr. Malberg, who was a carpenter as well as a farmer, could probably afford to buy labor-saving appliances before many other farmers. Mrs. Malberg got a clothes wringer and a wash boiler in 1875, which was much earlier than women in Sweden benefited from such conveniences. Since it was more difficult for the farmwives to travel to distant store locations and to leave the children, their husbands usually took care of the grocery shopping. The items that had to be purchased were few. Mr. Malberg's shopping list, 1869-1879, included bluing fluid for the wash, but mainly it consisted of sugar, coffee, salt, herring, tobacco, cotton fabric, carpenter nails, and occasionally shoes or boots. The staples were purchased in large quantities, so they would last a long time. The farm produced other food items. There was no need to buy yeast in those days. The recipe was quite simple. "Boil one pound of good flour, a quarter of a pound of sugar and a little salt in two gallons of water for one hour. When warm, cork it close. It will be fit for use in 24 hours." (The Malberg diary)

Social Activities

The Swedes in Goodhue County created their own entertainment for the most part. They founded singing clubs, bands, debating societies, and sport clubs. They arranged picnics and church socials, and entertained guests at home.

One correspondence in Vasa reported the following to a Red Wing newspaper in 1871:

I will inform your readers that we have in this town a singing club which commenced its regular term last Monday. R. S. Summer, teacher, to keep on for a couple of months at least. We have also a debating society which meets once a week to discuss different questions for mutual benefit and instruction. (Goodhue County Republican)

Mildred Collins at the Vasa Museum with the Edison Home Phonograph

The Swedes celebrated the Fourth of July as enthusiastically as any native-born Americans. As early as 1874, the Lutheran Church in Vasa arranged a large picnic for the occasion. A Red Wing newspaper reported on the event July 7, 1874: "The Swedish Evangelical Lutheran Church of Vasa had a picnic last Saturday. About 1,000 persons were present. The Declaration of Independence was read by Hon. J. W. Peterson, Hon. T. G. [Granville] Pearson, orator." *(Goodhue County Republican)*

Walter Swanson told about "big doings up at the church on Midsummer. Near the Vasa Lutheran Church, there were large picnic grounds, which were used for the celebration of both Swedish and American holidays," he said. But none of our interviewees could recall that they decorated maypoles for Midsummer.

A group of Swedes and Norwegians founded "The Leon Literary Debating Society" in Leon Township on January 20, 1896. The first officers were: J. A. Young, president; J. A. Peterson, vice president; C. E. Pearson, secretary; S. M. Urevig, usher, and G. V. Young, treasurer.

From the Minutes of the Literary Society

Out of three suggestions for debate, the first meeting chose, "Resolved that the Indians have suffered more through the white man than the black man." (The n-word was used.) The debaters could debate in any language they chose. At their next meeting January 23, the debate on the first subject resulted in that the opening side won. The next subject for debate was, "Resolved that the immigration to the U.S. should be abolished." It came up for debate on January 30th. Again, the judges decided that the opposing side had won.

Other subjects suggested for debate were: "Resolved that city life is preferable to country life." (Opposed), "Resolved that education is better than wealth." (Agreed); "Resolved that the women should have the right to vote." (Not debated); "Resolved that intoxicating liquors have done more damage than war." (Agreed); "Resolved that the pen is mightier than the sword." (Opposed); "Resolved that a Republican form of government is preferable to a Monarchy." (Agreed); "Resolved that the minerals have created more wealth than the vegetable." (Agreed); "Resolved that the white man had the right to take land from the Indians." (Agreed); "Resolved that the arts are more pleasing to the human eye than nature." (Opposed); "Resolved that it would be more preferable to marry for money than love." (Not debated); "Resolved that married life is more preferable to single life" was debated instead (Agreed).

Later, the same subjects that had been debated earlier were chosen once again, but from a different angle. For instance, "Resolved that the black man has suffered more through the white man than the Indian," again resulted in the view that the Indian had suffered less. The subject of the women's vote finally came up in November. The judges voted that the side in favor had won. One new subject "Resolved that strikes are not beneficial" was voted in the affirmative. Many other subjects came up for debate. The literary entertainment included selective readings, declamation, singing, and speeches.

Vasa Illustrata portrays a Children's Trio, a children's choir, the mixed choir Lyran, and another mixed choir, the Spring Creek Choir, consisting of four men, four women, and their director, a large Jubilee

Choir, and the Vasa Band. Each of the twelve young men played a horn instrument. Bernard Anderson's father and grandfather both played in the Vasa Band. "They practiced once a week and traveled around and gave concerts," Bernard said.

Wallace Weberg told of the boxing club that he belonged to in White Rock. "It was an unusual sport down there, but my parents said when I came home with a bloody nose... 'You probably knew what you were asking for.' An Irish guy trained us and introduced us to boxing," Wallace said. Other sports the youth engaged in included baseball and basketball. Milton Swenson recalled a basketball team called "House of David" that came to the Woodman Hall and played. "They put on a good show," he said. The local team played against the teams in Red Wing and Cannon Falls. Swenson described the *"Olle i Skratthult"* shows:

He was down to White Rock in that hole, mind you. But it didn't go so good for him because he had worked for a farmer by the name of Manne Benson years ago, so he brought his company down, you know, to show off a little bit. But the company didn't like it in a small community. They felt they were degrading themselves a little... so they sat out in the car until they had to go in and play a little bit and then go back out again. But here in Cannon Falls.... he was here many times, and it went over big here. He even had a play at one time about a couple of farm families.... (See interview)

Milton also said he used to see Edvard Persson movies in Red Wing. He remembered the song, *Lite grann från ovan* (A little bit from the above).

Aurora Swanson recalled that they had a youth club at the church and a community club in the Town Hall. "It was fun to go to the youth club," she said. "They had ball games and then perhaps a boy came and asked if he could accompany you home." That was how she met her husband Hilding. Aurora never attended dances.

Stella Ingeman remembered the barn dances. "The young people would fight at the dances sometimes. The Irish wanted to take over and the Swedes weren't going to let hem. Swedish music was a must." They danced the schottische.

Mildred Peterson was a musician and played in her husband's orchestra at dances. She played the piano and the piano accordion. They performed all over Minnesota, she said, and seldom got home before 2:00 a.m. Her grandparents, Jöns and Elna Nelson, shared her parents' household in Red Wing, and they loved to have parties. "Grandpa didn't care if he had 50 guests. He'd pray and sing, do all kinds of things, to entertain them."

In a historical sketch from Spring Garden, I found the following about how young people entertained themselves:

They met in the basement of the church, but that was not enough, so they started to have dances in the new barns that were being built in the community. They had a great time learning to dance. Many also played games. (Glorian Anderson)

One Fourth-of-July dance "raised the roof" with the minister who was very much against dances. As a result some members of the Spring Garden Lutheran Church left that congregation and joined the Cannon Falls Lutheran Church.

The old letters I have studied indicate that Christmas parties depended on the weather conditions. The Malberg diary mentions only two parties during the entire year of 1869. One was a cheese-making party and the other a New-Year's party.

In Trolle Ljungby, Ola Lundborg wrote about New Year's parties in 1889. The letters from Vasa acknowledge New-Year's gifts received from Sweden.

Customs

We often hear that the immigrants wanted to become Americans, but most wanted to carry on at least the most significant Swedish customs and make them a tradition for their children. In the case of the Trolle Ljungby emigrants, it almost seems like they wanted to forget their past.

From what we have learned from the interviews, they did not pass on the story of the Ljungby Horn and Pipe. The descendants have no memories of Swedish fairy tales, but the grandchildren of Jöns Nelson recalled stories about ghosts and trolls. The descendants relate that their immigrant forefathers were very reluctant to speak about their lives in Sweden. Gladys Eckholm could not recall her grandmother ever mentioning anything about it. Janice Olson recalled, "I remember talking to Grandma and asking her about Sweden, and she would cry... she told about how they stood on the ship and waved until she couldn't see them [the relatives] anymore." Naturally, the immigrants longed for their loved ones in Sweden, but it did not mean they regretted their move. Mildred Peterson recalled that her grandfather Jöns Nelson appeared to be angry about the conditions in Sweden. He had married above his social class which was one of the reasons the family emigrated. On the other hand, Amanda Swanson, who was born in Welch and who had never seen Sweden, inspired her granddaughter Betty Jane Withers to learn more about the old country by showing her things that had been brought by the family from Sweden.

Swedish clothes were out of fashion in the Vasa area. One letter-writer feared that his emigrating nieces would bring too many Swedish dresses with them to America. He advised them to bring the fabric instead, and mentioned silk, so that it could be sewn in American fashion. One visitor to Vasa wrote about the party-like clothes worn by the worshipers who attended the Vasa Lutheran Church in 1872. Hans Mattson commented that in some cases the young women's dress was almost ridiculous. The immigrants must have become more conservative in their dress as they grew older, because many of our interviewees told us about their grandmothers' long dark dresses, large aprons, and bonnets.

It is surprising that the emigrants from Trolle Ljungby did not continue the genuine Skåne tradition of making *spettkaka* (a cone-shaped cake) for special occasions. The needed equipment could easily have been made in America. It is true that there were special female bakers, who made it in Sweden, but one would think that someone from Skåne would know enough about it to carry on the tradition.

We know of only three Trolle Ljungby families in Vasa that raised geese, something that was very common in Skåne. Geese required water for swimming. They provided the families with food, as well as goose down and feathers for pillows and mattresses. One letter-writer in Vasa asked his niece in Trolle Ljungby to bring pillows with her to Vasa stuffed with lots of new feathers.

The food traditions preserved from Sweden were the same as in any other Swedish-American community, *lutfisk, sill, sylta, korv, ostkaka* (cured fish, pickled herring, head cheese/jellied veal, sausage, cheese curd pudding), etc., especially for the Christmas holidays.

Viola Young Knutson wrote that they always had *dopp i grytan,* which meant that they dipped their bread in broth at noon on Christmas Eve. They ate *lutfisk* for breakfast on Christmas morning! (This may have been the tradition in Skåne at the time, but as far as I know, *lutfisk* was eaten for dinner in the rest of Sweden.) Viola says they did not have a Christmas tree until 1906. In the old house, there were hooks in the wooden ceiling on which they hung their Christmas stockings on Christmas Eve (an American tradition). The next morning, they would be filled with candy, nuts, apples, and oranges. "In the new house," she said, "Mother always had an oleander tree that we would decorate." Two weeks before Christmas they used to butcher a hog or a steer. Her father made a brew from hops for Christmas.

There were quite a few who used snuff, said Bernard Anderson. Even women sniffed snuff. Olu Jönsdotter, mother of Elna Skog, sniffed it because she claimed it improved her eyesight. Virginia Fanslow's great-grandmother, Anna Stina Anderson, also sniffed snuff. Tobacco was not grown in Goodhue County, but Steven Hedeen said, "Quite a lot of tobacco was raised down by Lanesboro."

The older people loved their coffee. Walter Swanson's grandmother Elna used to drink her coffee from the saucer. "And you had to have lump sugar and cream on the table," he said. Women made wine (from wild grapes, elderberries, or dandelions) and served it to company in small glasses with either a piece of candy or a cookie. Some of the men mixed whiskey in their coffee before they went out to work in the morning, especially if they had a cold.

Comparison with Isanti County Rättvik settlers

This chapter is divided into six parts:

1. Introduction and Hypothesis

2. Pre-existing Differences

3. Comparison of Agriculture

4. Comparison of Demographics

5. Adaptation to American Society

6. Conclusion

Introduction and Hypothesis

In 1960, Frank Thistlewaite recommended that scholars look at the Great Atlantic Migration as a "complete sequence of experiences whereby the individual moves from one social identity to another." The first (Swedish) non-academic research along these lines, *En Smålandsocken Emigrerar,* was published by Långasjö Emigrantcirkel in 1967. It registered the fate of individuals from the parish of Långasjö, many of whom had settled in Chisago County, Minnesota. Hans Norman became the first Swedish academician to research groups of emigrants in both the sending and receiving areas. His book, *Från Bergslagen till Nordamerika*, published in 1974, analyses the social and demographic changes that affected emigrant groups who settled in Worcester and Wisconsin. In the United States, Robert C. Ostergren studied the emigration from Upper Dalarna to the Upper Middle West, mainly the emigrants from Rättvik who settled in Isanti County, Minnesota. His book, *A Community Transplanted*, came out in 1888. Ostergren concludes, "At best it was a partial transplantation, brief emergence of something that resembled in certain ways the organism from which it came."

Dr. Ostergren and my advisor, Dr. Ulf Beijbom, then director of the Swedish Emigrant Institute in Växjö, suggested that if would be interesting to compare how the group from Trolle Ljungby in Goodhue County reacted to the new land and American society compared to the

Rättvik group in Isanti County. While the settlers from Rättvik came from a farm-owning background, the Trolle Ljungby group consisted mainly of former tenant farmers, crofters, and farm workers under the large castle estate that dominated Trolle Ljungby.

My hypothesis: One might reasonably expect that the background of the landless Trolle Ljungby emigrants (tenant farmers, crofters, and farm workers) influenced their encounter with land and American society in ways that might have differed from that of 'landed' emigrants like those from Rättvik. If there was no difference, it might suggest that the 'free land' and the democratic American frontier were great equalizing factors that made pre-migration experiences irrelevant.

Pre-existing Differences

We knew in advance that there were many differences in the background of these two groups. The Rättvik emigrants had owned fairly large forest farms in Sweden with an average of only three acres of arable land, while the Trolle Ljungby emigrants came from the sparsely wooded plains of Skåne, where most of the land was arable. They had no accustomed level of landed wealth. Nonetheless, many were born on tenant farms that had been rented by their ancestors for generations. However, they had no hope of ever owning their farms because the count was not selling. Neither did the tenant farmers and members of their families have any prospects of buying other farms. Basically, they had two alternatives: renting a farm from the count or working as servants on his estate. In the mid-1850s, a third alternative became a possibility—that of emigrating and becoming landowners in the American Middle West.

Rättvik was a much larger parish than Trolle Ljungby both in size and population. In 1880, Vestra Ljungby (later Trolle Ljungby) had a population of 1,929 in an area that was only about half a square *mil*, while Rättvik had a population of 8,022 in an area more than ten square *mil*. One Swedish *mil* equals about seven English.

The number of emigrants from each of the two parishes was fairly equal, 1,086 for Trolle Ljungby and 1,003 for Rättvik (according to excerpts), but the transatlantic emigration from Trolle Ljungby began earlier and continued for more than 60 years, 1850-1914, while it lasted less than 30 years in Rättvik, or from about 1864 to 1893.

The Rättvik emigrants did not begin to arrive until 1864 when the best and most conveniently located government land in southeastern Minnesota was already taken. However, they could still take advantage of the Homestead Act of 1862 further to the north in Isanti County. Here, they became more isolated than the Trolle Ljungby group in Goodhue County. While for instance the pioneers in Vasa walked about ten miles to Red Wing for supplies, the early settlers in Isanti County had to walk all the way to Taylors Falls or Anoka. In either case it was a three-day walk.

The topography of Isanti County was vastly different than in Goodhue County. The first emigrants from Rättvik settled on clayey soil in the oak forest in Cambridge Township. Later arrivals had to be satisfied with the sandy soil on the aspen and oak brush prairie of west central Springvale Township or the brush prairie in Athens Township. In contrast, the rich prairie soil in Vasa consisted of two-foot black loam. The lumber trade was important in Isanti. Ostergren remarked that the main "crops" were wheat and logs. While wheat production was very important in Goodhue County there was a shortage of timber.

Ostergren does not say how many of the Rättvik transatlantic emigrants settled in Isanti County, only that at the end of the settlement period (about 1885) there were 109 Rättvik households in the county. The Trolle Ljungby group in Goodhue County consisted of at least 128 households with more than 300 individuals who were emigrants. In 85 of the households the husbands and most of the wives were from Trolle Ljungby. In 29 households, the wife was from Trolle Ljungby, but not the husband. In 14 households at least one of the spouses was a child upon arrival. The group included 11 single people with children and 30 single adults without children. Many of the single people subsequently married and formed additional households, while others moved away from the area. The Trolle Ljungby group had much in common with groups from other parishes in the Villand district, such as Nymö, Kiaby, Oppmanna, Ivetofta, and Viby.

Comparison of Agriculture

My study of the Trolle Ljungby group's agricultural achievements has been limited to Vasa Township, which had a total population of 1,157 in 1880—the highest ever recorded in the township. All were Swedes except for one Norwegian family and one mixed Norwegian-Swedish family. I have included a brief comparison between farming in Trolle Ljungby, Sweden, and in Vasa Township.

The farmland in Vasa Township covered 20,602 acres. In 1880, 24 farmers in the Trolle Ljungby group owned 2,893 acres (14 percent), of which 2,164 acres were tilled. Their average farms size was 120.54 acres, just a little smaller than the average 130-acre farm in Goodhue County as a whole. According to Ostergren, the average size of farms owned by Rättvik emigrants in Isanti County was 147.9. The difference, however, is obvious when comparing the areas of tilled land. In 1880, the Trolle Ljungby group averaged 74.8 acres of tilled land. In Isanti County, the average size of tilled land held by 382 native Swedes was only 20.1 acres. For the Rättvik group, the corresponding figure was even smaller or 17.9 acres. (The Rättvik farmers in Clay County, South Dakota, whose land was probably comparable to land in Goodhue County, had converted about one-third of their land to cropland by 1880.) The Isanti Swedes improved more land after 1890. Originally, the Swedes in Isanti County acquired 80 acres of homestead land and 40 acres of railroad land for a total of 120 acres, while the first Swedes in Vasa Township acquired 160 acres of government land.

In 1880, the percentage of tilled land devoted to wheat was larger in the Trolle Ljungby group than in the Rättvik group, or 52 percent compared to 47 percent. However, the Rättvik group used a larger percentage of their tilled land for oats and corn.

Bushels per Acre 1880 and 1890

Goodhue County harvested more bushels per acre of all small grains, wheat, corn, oats, and barley than Isanti County. This fact confirms that the soil was more fertile in Goodhue County. As we have seen, Vasa Township experienced a devastating attack of the chinch bug in 1880, resulting in a reduced crop of wheat. In Vasa, farmers received less than 12 bushels of wheat per acre compared to the normal 15 to 18 bushels. The Trolle Ljungby farmers in Vasa harvested 12.51 bushels of wheat per acre. Apparently, other small grains were not affected by the chinch bug.

As reported in 1880 and 1890, the harvest remained fairly constant except for the corn yield which decreased in both Goodhue and Isanti counties. The acreage devoted to each crop in Isanti was much smaller than in Goodhue. For barley, it was 17 acres versus 30. In 1890, the Villand District in Sweden produced a larger yield of wheat and rye per acre than farmers in the two Minnesota counties, but a lower yield of oats.

No bushels per-acre figures are available for 1870, but at that time the Trolle Ljungby group in Vasa harvested an average of 1,032 bushels of spring wheat, 102 bushels of corn, 222 bushels of oats, 39 bushels of barley, and 18 bushels of potatoes per farm. Only two of the farmers in the group grew rye at that time (*Statistics of Agriculture*).

Livestock

In 1880 the Trolle Ljungby group averaged more horses and swine than the Rättvik group, while the latter kept more cattle, oxen, and sheep. According to the figures from the 1870 Agricultural Census, the Trolle Ljungby group at that time averaged 2.94 horses, 2.36 dairy cattle, 2.89 other cattle, and 2.31 swine per farmer. Among them, they owned only seven work oxen and no asses or mules. The large number of horses in Vasa already in 1870 indicates that the settlement had passed the frontier stage. The figures are basically the same in 1880 except for "other cattle" which showed an increase of nearly two per farm. Sheep had also been added by 1880.

With the introduction of creameries around the turn of the century, the dairy production increased. In Vasa, F. L. Engberg bought the former Baptist church building, moved it, and started up a creamery. In 1898, he sold it to the Vasa Co-op Creamery. The creamery then proved to be the best "gold-mine" they had in Vasa, according to Emil Albert Kullberg, who was born in Vasa in 1872. In the beginning, the cream was hauled three days a week.

In comparison with farms in Skåne, the average number of livestock, except for horses, is small especially if one considers the size of the farms. In Trolle Ljungby an operator who farmed as little as 25 acres generally owned two horses and four to five cows in addition to sheep, hogs, and chickens. Someone farming 50 acres usually kept eight to ten cows. In Vasa, a farm twice as large kept only two to three cows. The farmers in Minnesota relied more on the production of grain crops than on animal husbandry and did not keep more dairy cows than needed for their own consumption of milk, butter and cheese. It was more profitable to sell the grain than using it as feed. The swine production was held down by the low price of pork. It went as low as three cents per pound in 1879 according to Mr. Malberg.

In Sweden, the swine production was relatively large already in the 1850s. The combined area of Villand, Gärd, Albo, and Trolle Ljungby reported the percentage of livestock on larger farms in 1851 as follows: Horses 17%, Oxen 6%, Dairy Cattle 16%, Other Cattle 18%, Sheep 19%, and Swine 24%.

The Farm Retention Rate

In researching the farm-retention rate of the former proletarians from Trolle Ljungby in Goodhue County, I found that they developed a family-farm tradition. An astounding 89 percent of the farmers belonging to the Trolle Ljungby group listed in the Vasa Agricultural Census in 1870 were still farming in Vasa in 1900, or had either rented out their farms or transferred them to heirs. For the farmers in the same category listed in the 1880 Agricultural Census in Vasa the corresponding rate was 75 percent. These numbers indicate that those who arrived earlier had the highest rate of farm retention. Many developed a tradition of landed wealth.

In the Isanti community, 47.5 percent of the farms were liquidated between 1885 and 1915, while 3.13 percent were transferred to heirs either before death or after, which would allow for a retention rate of 50.63 percent. Ostergren found that the Isanti community, which included former *torpare* (crofters), had a higher liquidation and transfer rate (after death) than the Athens community, which was settled mostly by former small land-holders. In the Athens community, 31.8 percent of the farms were liquidated between 1885 and 1915, and 1.03 percent transferred. Both communities had a strong presence of Rättvik emigrants. Ostergren concluded:

Land ownership was always important to the crofter as a stepping stone to economic independence, but the relationship was often not as permanent as it was for the freeholder. Land could be converted to capital that would allow one to take advantage of local, non-agricultural opportunity or to leave the district altogether in search of opportunity elsewhere.

One might caution that the better quality of the prairie land in Athens Township may have contributed to the lower liquidation rate. Although

I have no actual liquidation figures for Vasa to compare with, it seems that the high farm retention rate in 1900 (an average of 82 percent) among the members of the Trolle Ljungby group would leave room for a liquidation rate of a maximum of 18 percent by 1900 compared to an average of 40 percent in the Isanti and Athens communities by 1915. While these figures are not directly comparable, the resulting differ-ence is significant enough to allow for deviations in calculations. As Isanti County was settled later, one cannot use the same year for com-parison. It is clear that the liquidation rate was higher among the farmers in the two communities in Isanti County that included farmers from Rättvik than among the farmers belonging to the Trolle Ljungby group in Goodhue County.

'Bad years' could affect the harvest. Bengta and Nels P. Granquist rented an 80-acre farm in Vasa. In 1879, he wrote:

We have had two bad years in a row. Last year we did not get more than 343 bushels of wheat and then we had to leave one third of that [in lieu of rent]. Then to make matters worse, the wheat was so poor that we got only 25 cents a bushel in the fall, but now in the spring it went up to 50 cents. This year we got 400 bushels and have gotten between 95 cents and one dollar for it, so it has not been so bad this year.

Of oats and corn we have no more than we can use for the cattle. Those grains are priced at about 25 cents a bushel. But we are blessed by God and have enough to eat and drink and then no one ought to be dissatisfied. We have to hope for better times....

Granquist is listed in the 1880 Agricultural Census, at which time he kept two horses and two milk cows. He reported that the farm had pro-duced 150 pounds of butter, 443 bushels of wheat (on 28 acres sown), 125 bushels of Indian corn (on three acres), and 104 bushels of oats (on two acres).

Of the total 3,306 farms in Goodhue County in 1880, 2,865 were cultivated by owners, while 43 were rented for fixed money rental, and 308 for share of products for a total of 10.6 percent rented. It should be noted that Goodhue County had a much larger population than Isanti County, 29,651 compared to 5,063 in 1880. In Isanti County, almost all the farms were cultivated by owners in 1880, but in 1900 about one farm out of every ten was worked by either a cash or share tenant. The latter percentage was the same for men from Trolle Ljungby who had arrived before 1870.

In Vasa Township in 1900, 42 percent of the farms were owned mortgage free and 28 percent mortgaged, while 30 percent of the farms were rented.

In the Trolle Ljungby group, 60 percent of the farms were owned mortgage-free and 13 percent mortgages, while 27 percent were rented.

When comparing the agricultural achievements of the Trolle Ljungby group with all the farmers in Vasa Township, I found that not only had the farmers in the Trolle Ljungby group cultivated more land per farms by 1880, they had also harvested more bushels per acre of wheat and owned more cattle. In 1900, 60 percent of their farms were mortgage-free compared to 42 percent of all farms in Vasa. The percentage of owned farms versus rented farms also favored the Trolle Ljungby group. Thus, they did very well compared to all farmers in the township.

Summary

The Vasa Township farmers tilled much more of their land during the first years than the Swedes in Isanti County, but it should be noted that their land was easier to clear. Many of the settlers from Trolle Ljungby had the advantage of arriving early when good farmland was still available. They acquired it for $1.25 an acre, and as we have seen, farm ownership was very important to them. Being used to the open landscape in Skåne, they chose a good place to settle. The Trolle Ljungby emigrants who arrived in Goodhue County in the late 1860s and settled north of Cannon River had to work harder to clear the land.

It was not unusual that the Trolle Ljungby emigrants had to find other means of support before establishing themselves as farm owners. Some worked temporarily for cash after they had taken their claims, while others hired out as farmhands or rented farms. It seems that the Trolle Ljungby emigrants were more critical about the quality of the land than the Rättvik emigrants. Many who came too late for claims preferred the more expensive land in Goodhue County to cheaper and less fertile land elsewhere. No doubt, their farm experience in Trolle Ljungby, which was on a larger scale than in Rättvik, was a plus. Members of the Trolle Ljungby group settled in clusters as far as possible. My research has also documented that many family farms were established. At least eight of those farms were still owned by family members in 1993.

The farmers in both groups wished to acquire land, and they went directly to Minnesota to achieve that goal. According to one early pioneer, it was more important to "go west" (from the eastern seaboard) as soon as possible and acquire land than having cash in one's pockets. If the emigrants brought money from Sweden, they were likely to spend it before they knew how much it was worth, but if they had to work for it in America, they would know its value, he reasoned. The main prerequisite for success appears to have been farm-work experience and a will to work very hard.

Goodhue County entered the post-settlement period in the late 1860s when the settlement of Isanti had just begun. Isanti remained a frontier area into the 1890s. The arrival of the railroad in Red Wing some twenty years earlier than in Cambridge and the subsequent industrial growth also contributed to a faster pace of acculturation in Goodhue County. The Trolle Ljungby emigrants had an exceptional desire to make it in America because they appreciated the freedom to be their own masters. The way they emphasized the advantage of living in "the land of freedom" reminds one of the letters written by members of the Swedish religious commune in Bishop Hill, Illinois, except for the religious overtones in the latter.

Comparison of Demographics

Sweden versus Vasa Township

When studying the Trolle Ljungby household registers, one is surprised by the many boarders listed in each household. Some worked for room and board, while the parish paid a nominal fee for paupers and orphans. Even elderly parents living with children or perhaps in a separate cottage on the property were classified as boarders. In Vasa, parents were listed as either "father, mother," or "in-laws" depending on their relation to the head of household. Unrelated members of the household, who were neither employed as domestic servants nor farm laborers, were listed as boarders. Presumably, they paid for room and board.

In my study of population censuses for Vasa Township the most surprising finding was the large number of grown children living on their parents' farms. In Sweden, children above the age of 14 seldom lived at home. Those who did worked for their parents. Other grown children had to hire out. In Vasa, it was not unusual that two adult children in their 20s lived at home even though they had teenaged siblings. Many waited for an opportunity to take over the farm. When their parents stayed on the farm, and their grown sons and daughters delayed marriage, an obvious maturation of the community occurred.

Fertility and Marriage Patterns

Ostergren looked at what happened to the family during the post-settlement period:

The rise of a new generation is a major feature in the maturation of rural communities, although the rate of new family formation is much tempered by inheritance strategies. The proportion of eligible young women who are married is generally less than was the case during the frontier period, since declining economic opportunities has the effect of delaying marriage in addition to discouraging couples from having large numbers of children. There are also more unmarried young adults living at home despite the high rate of out-migration among unmarried men and women in their twenties.

Comparison with other areas

While the total number of children living at home in Vasa was large, the number of young children declined as the population began to pass into the post-settlement period. In other words, Vasa followed the long-term American trend toward lower fertility levels in aging settlement districts. Having compared the fertility and marriage patterns of Vasa Township with two townships in Isanti County and two other studies of Swedish settlements in Pepin and Burnett counties in Wisconsin, as well as a few Norwegian settlements in Wisconsin and Minnesota, I found that the fertility rate was relatively low in Vasa compared to other Swedish settlements, but higher than in two Norwegian settlements.

The decline in fertility in Vasa corresponded with the general theory that it begins roughly three decades after settlement or once land availability begins to fall off sharply. Although the decline in fertility in Vasa was significant (-26.85), it was less so than in the German settlement of Bradford in Isanti County (-37.4) and the Old American community in the same county (-42.3) as documented by Ostergren. Using figures from the state censuses in 1885, 1895, 1905, and 1915, he found striking deviations from the norm in Cambridge West (+0.9) and Athens (+8.8), Isanti County, where the fertility actually increased from 1885 until 1915.

The later period of study in Isanti makes sense, as that area was settled later than Vasa. However, it is difficult to explain the significant difference. Out-migration occurred in both groups. The Rättvik people moved mainly to South Dakota and members of the Trolle Ljungby group acquired land in Kittson County in northern Minnesota or further to the west in Idaho and Montana.

The Trolle Ljungby emigrants produced many children during the settlement period. They saw the opportunities in America, and their children were needed to help cultivate the land. However, after the Civil War, there was little land to cultivate in Vasa, and the population aged. When the older generation continued to be in charge of the farms, as was often the case, many young people moved away from the community. Work opportunities in nearby Red Wing attracted both males and females.

The young people in the Isanti study area had more room to expand in the agricultural sector. Ostergren writes that after 1890, the percentage of improved farm acreage climbed dramatically. "Farmers were grubbing and breaking land with renewed enthusiasm." The lumber industry provided additional income. Thus, the Rättvik group lived in an area that remained a frontier area for a longer period of time than was the case in Vasa.

By dividing the married women of childbearing age in Vasa Township into three different age groups, 1860, 1870, 1880, and 1900, and calculating the percentage of each group, one can get an indication of the gradual change toward older women that occurred.

In 1860, the overwhelming majority of married women of childbearing age, 20-49, were in their 30s. However, already in 1870, there were more women in their 40s than in each of the other two groups. Although women above the age of 50 with children were not included in the child/woman ratio study, it is interesting to note that in 1900 they made up 78 percent of the total number of married women with children. This shows that a maturation process had occurred, which indirectly may have affected the prospects for young people in the agricultural sector.

Hans Norman, in his study of Pepin and Burnett counties in Wisconsin calculated his child/woman ratio on children 0-14 years of age with mothers aged 15-44 and came up with an average of 3.79 children per woman in 1880 in Pepin County, which includes the Stockholm settlement. The figure for Pepin County was in line with the fertility in Sweden, while the figure for Burnett County was lower. By using the same method of calculation as Norman for Vasa in 1880, the result is an average of 2.95 children per mother, and 3.1 for the Trolle Ljungby group. Thus the fertility was higher in Pepin County, which was settled by Swedes at about the same time as Vasa; however, it should be noted that Norman's figures are based on the entire county and not specifically a Swedish settlement.

The following statistics includes Sweden:

Average Number of Children, Aged 0-14 per Married or Previously Married Woman Aged 15-44, 1880

Sweden	3.42
Pepin County, Wisc.	3.79 (Norman)
Burnett County, Wisc.	3.13 (Norman)
Vasa Township, Minn.	2.95
Trolle Ljungby Group, Goodhue County	3.10
Trolle Ljungby Group, married in the U.S.	2.82

These numbers show that the woman/child ratio was higher for the Trolle Ljungby group than for Vasa Township. The figures also show that that the average number of children in the Trolle Ljungby group was lower when the women were limited to those married in the United States.

Jon Gjerde in his study about emigrants from Balestrand, Norway, who settled in Wisconsin and Minnesota, calculated his figures on children aged 0-14 born to women aged 15-49 in three different townships. For 1880, he found that the child/woman ratio was 1.46 in Vienna Township, Dane County, Wisconsin; 2.4 in Arendahl Township, Fillmore County, Minnesota; and 1.68 in Camp Township, Renville County, Minnesota. In comparison, the fertility in Vasa was high in 1880. In Arendahl Township, Minnesota, there was a 51 percent decrease in fertility rate between 1860 and 1880. While a direct comparison cannot be made due to the different base used by Gjerde, his figures from 1880 show that the fertility was lower in his study areas than in all the other areas documented here. Yet his over-all figures, which included data from 1860, were higher than in the sending area of his study. He attributes this to women's earlier age at marriage. One of the consequences of earlier marriage and larger segments ever married was increased fertility. When including the Gjerde study, my study shows an average rate of fertility.

In Vasa, women's average age at birth of first child was 27.26 in 1880 and 25.35 in 1900. Even though women began their childbearing at an earlier age in 1900, the woman/child ratio decreased, so other factors must have affected the outcome. As Ostergren pointed out, declining economic opportunity may delay marriage and discourage couples from having large numbers of children. In the countryside in Sweden, the largest number of births occurred in the female age group 26-30.

As we have seen, the average age at marriage of all women with children in Vasa Township in 1900 was between 25 and 25.5 years of age. As a comparison, the average age of marriage for women in Isanti County, 1865-1885, was 24.5. In the countryside in Kristianstad län it was 26. If one is going to read anything out of these figures, it would be that the slightly lower age of marriage in Isanti may have contributed to the higher fertility in that county.

The number of married women in Vasa decreased with every census. In 1870, 170 married women, aged 20-49, lived in Vasa Township. In 1880, they numbered 140, and in 1900, only 100. The reason for the decline does not seem to have been a shortage of men to marry. In 1870 the males made up 54 percent of the total population and in 1880, 55 percent.

Hans Norman documented the man/woman ratio in three Swedish-American study areas. In Pepin County, Wisconsin, the males made up 57 percent of the population in 1880 compared to 55 percent in Vasa Township. In Trolle Ljungby, Sweden, in 1880, 51 percent of the total population consisted of females. However, the number of unmarried men was greater than the number of unmarried women.

The declining fertility of the Trolle Ljungby group was in line with other documented Scandinavian and non-Scandinavian post-settlements enclaves except the Rättvik group. However, if one looks closer at Ostergren's figures, they show that the increase occurred before 1905 in Cambridge West and before 1895 in Athens Township. After that, the fertility decreased also among the Rättvik emigrants.

Summary

My research shows that Trolle Ljungby group's fertility was low compared to that of the emigrants in Ostergren's and Norman's Swedish-American studies, and to the national Swedish rate, but high compared to Gjerde's findings among Norwegian Americans. The number of children per married woman was higher in the Trolle Ljungby group in 1880 than in Vasa Township except among couples married in the United States. Thus, old-world fertility patterns were more likely to prevail among couples who had been married in Sweden.

Adaptation to American Society

There is no doubt that the emigrants from Trolle Ljungby appreciated the free and open American society and the opportunity to acquire land of their own. They enjoyed living in a tightly knit enclave. They adhered steadfastly to the protestant faith of their homeland and socialized mostly at events arranged by the church. The Swedish language churches provided an institutional completeness that safeguarded ethnic boundaries and values, including the native language. It organized youth activities and parochial schools, while other recreational programs, such as music and singing groups, literary societies, and sports clubs were founded with or without the assistance of the church as a first line of defense against intermarriages. Although the Swedish ethnic group was the dominant one in Vasa for a long time, the Germans made inroads. The Swedes had to learn to interact but they knew their geographical boundaries. Their social encounters with the Irish could be hostile while their business relations were cordial.

Ostergren documented how the Rättvik emigrants settled in clusters and transplanted their neighborhoods in Sweden to Isanti. Many of the Trolle Ljungby emigrants also settled in clusters. Kinship was an important factor in the Skåne Ward, where most of the early settlers were from the village of Vanneberga. The cluster extended into the Småland and Spring Creek wards. In the late 1860s, a cluster developed in Welch Township, just north of Vasa Township. Later there was a concentration of first and second generation members of the Trolle Ljungby group in Leon Township, south of Spring Garden Lutheran Church. Most were descendants of Nils M. Swenson.

Members of the Trolle Ljungby group who purchased farms in Cannon Falls Township did so close to the Vasa boarder. When it was no longer possible to obtain farms in the same neighborhood as relatives and friends, new arrivals spread out in Vasa and other townships. While the Swedes slowly integrated into American society, they retained a close relationship with one other. Still, Americanization was unavoidable for the simple reason that their children born in America became Americans.

According to Ostergren, Swedish-American communities in the early twentieth century Isanti County could be viewed as more traditionally Swedish, in some respects, than the places in Sweden from which their inhabitants came. When the migration from the sending community ceased and contacts with Sweden were broken, the culture was allowed to fossilize. Isanti did not experience any significant influx of industry until well after the turn of the century. The Swedes in Vasa, on the other hand, lived relatively close to industrial centers such as Red Wing and Cannon Falls. Their old-world culture was not allowed to fossilize.

New immigrants from especially Halland, Sweden, to Vasa in the first part of the twentieth century brought fresh influences that were mixed with the old. It is difficult to determine which of the customs were passed down from Trolle Ljungby and which were added by later immigrants. The descendants mixed the customs of America, Sweden, and Norway.

What the Trolle Ljungby group had in common with the Rättvik group was: A large Swedish presence; cluster formations and out-migration; early adaptation to American agriculture; Fourth of July celebrations as early as the 1870s; a strong church affiliation; a social life mainly limited to their own Swedish peer group; little or no involvement in politics.

Other Swedes in Vasa Township were exceptional in that they participated in politics before the Civil War. One eyewitness wrote that many Swedes were elected to town offices in Vasa Township already in 1858 when the township was founded (Trued Pearson). The local elections were non-political. (See Politics in the Chapter "Swedes in Goodhue County") The Isanti County Swedes did not participate much in government until in the 1890s.

After the demise of the first generation, the Swedish language began to die out except in homes where new immigrants kept it alive. It was a gradual process, but in the 1940s the Skåne dialect had largely died out in Vasa, while the Dalarna dialect in Isanti lingered as documented by Folke Hedblom. This can probably also be attributed to the later settlement of Isanti County. (Folke Hedblom researched Swedish dialects in America in the 1960s.)

The Rättvik group lived in a decidedly Swedish area as late as 1900. A whopping 89.5 percent of the foreign-born in Isanti County were still Swedish-born at the turn of the century. In 1880, the foreigners born in Sweden and Norway made up 46 percent of the total population. The corresponding figure for Goodhue County in 1880 was 29 percent. However, Vasa Township was almost 100 percent Swedish in 1880.

In 1900 the rate of naturalization among adults in the Trolle Ljungby group was 80 percent compared to 70 percent for the Vasa Township. The rest of the adults (20%) had obtained their first papers. When looking at their ability to speak English in 1900, the difference is small, but the Trolle Ljungby group had an edge.

The best evidence of the Trolle Ljungby emigrants' satisfaction and acclimation is their low return rate to Sweden. Only three percent of all emigrants from Trolle Ljungby returned to their home parish compared to an average of 15.2 percent for all Swedish emigrants to North America during the entire emigration period.

Conclusion

As long as 'free land' was available, the Trolle Ljungby emigrants' background as landless peasants did not influence their encounter with the land and American society in Goodhue County in ways that differed much from that of land-owning emigrants like those from Rättvik. Most deviations in the behavior and progress of settlers from

Rättvik and Trolle Ljungby can be explained by the earlier peopling of Vasa and the prevailing local conditions.

The 'free land' and the democratic American frontier were indeed great equalizing factors. When government land was no longer available and the frontier had moved further to the west, the pre-migration experience mattered. For the land-hungry emigrants from Trolle Ljungby who arrived in the 1870s or later when farmland had become costlier, there was a marked difference from what the earlier settlers had experienced. If they had no start-up capital and wished to farm and live among their peers in Goodhue County, they had to become sharecroppers or at best farm renters. To be merely a sharecropper was not much better than being a tenant farmer in Skåne, although in America, they had a chance of becoming farm owners.

The low farm liquidation rate among farmers in the Trolle Ljungby group indicates that the former proletarians did not have the liberal attitude toward the land that could be expected from a former landless class. Once the former proletarians had acquired land, they were determined to keep it as long as possible. Ownership was not a stepping stone to economic independence, but more permanent. For most it was a life-time commitment.

The letters written by the Trolle Ljungby emigrants show their appreciation of the freedom in their adopted land. They were glad to have escaped what they called the slavery they had experienced before emigrating. These Swedes wanted to be as much like Americans as possible and were eager to assimilate. To forget one's past seems to have been a condition for patriotism. The descendants we interviewed recalled the immigrants saying, "We are in America now, so we will act like Americans." In everything visible to the outside world, they sought to replicate American ideas from farming techniques to building style. In the 1890s, many Swedes in Goodhue County lived in two-story white Victorian houses with open porches on two sides. The American building style was very different from the sprawling low stone houses in Skåne.

Another result of my research suggests that the Trolle Ljungby emigrants were not as tradition-minded as the people from Dalarna in Ostergren's study. While the latter sought to replicate the social and cultural relationships of their Swedish past, there is circumstantial evidence that the Trolle Ljungby emigrants tried to forget their past.

The background of the Trolle Ljungby emigrants may actually have hastened their assimilation into the American society. As they became successful independent landowners in Goodhue County, they were ready to cut their strings to Sweden. As Hans Mattson observed, the new surroundings created a new man out of the former farmhand. Swen Olson is a good example. America gave him and his many children good lives. To learn the American way of farming was part of the assimilation process, but it was also imperative to the livelihood of the farmers. Assimilation into the social fabric, especially the English language, was naturally slower. The farmers from Sweden did not have many opportunities to mingle with Americans. Their wives had even less contacts with the outside world. Nevertheless, they too clearly enjoyed their new life in America.

Letters dated 1855 – 1881

Introduction

Of the 15 letters published here, one was sent from Trolle Ljungby. An appeal for old letters in the Trolle Ljungby area gave better results. When Lennart Olsson, sexton at the Gualöv Church, learned of my project, he began a search that resulted in a collection of 16 letters written by Trolle Ljungby emigrants either from America or during the journey. Two letters of personal nature are not included here.

The letter collection:

The letter originating in Trolle Ljungby is a handwritten copy in somewhat modernized spelling and therefore easy to read. It was in the possession of Bernard Anderson, Vasa. The letters from Swen Olson are in the original handwriting and some of the words are difficult to decipher. Punctuation was used sparingly, and the spelling is often phonetic. Lennart Olsson assisted with the deciphering of nicknames and words written in the local dialect. Regretfully, many words are illegible. The original letters, Nos. 2-15, were in the possession of Lennart Olsson (since deceased). I have deposited copies and verbatim transcriptions at the Swedish Emigrant Institute in Växjö, Sweden.

These America letters are especially interesting because the writers are related. Ola Anderson was the brother of Swen Olson's wife, Karna Andersdotter. Another sister, Signe, and a brother, Swen, also immigrated to Vasa. In the next generation, Ola's niece, Bengta Nilsson, and nephew, Ola Nilsson, immigrated to the same place. Their cousin, Anders Andersson, also emigrated, but we have no letters from him.

The letters presented here in English have been freely translated for easier reading. I have omitted many words and sentences of no importance as well as repetitious phrases. The spelling of personal names varies a great deal and has been made uniform to match the spelling used in the preceding chapters.

Swen Olson's first letter to Sweden has not been found. That would be the letter in which he would tell about the journey and the travel route. However, we have what is probably Olson's second letter to his family in Trolle Ljungby and four subsequent letters written by him that describe the conditions in the new settlement.

Through the letters written by Ola Anderson, 1857-1875, we can follow him from a teenager to a mature man. Meanwhile, his writing skills improved. The letters from Swen Anderson, Bengta Nilsson, and her husband, N. P. Granquist, and Ola Nilsson are relatively well written, probably thanks to the better education they had received. The letters in this collection have one thing in common. Both men and women refer to life in Trolle Ljungby as slavery while they praise the freedom in America.

The letters also show how a pattern of chain migration among relatives could develop. In 1855, Swen asked his brother-in-law, Ola Anderson (Karna and Signe's brother) to come to America. Ola emigrated in 1856. Karna died about 1862 and Signe before 1871. Their brother Swen arrived in 1866. In 1875, Ola Anderson wrote to his sister in Sweden, saying that he would be happy to welcome her daughters Karna and Bengta [Nilsson] to Vasa. Bengta emigrated in 1876, and in 1878, she wrote to her sister Karna, who then wished to come to Vasa, saying that she and her husband would welcome her. Karna did not come. She died in Sweden in 1880. Bengta's brother, Ola Nilsson, emigrated in 1881 and returned to Sweden in 1883 for health reasons.

No. 1: Letter from Anders Larson to Bengt Anderson in Vasa

Trolle Ljungby October 14, 1856

Dearly beloved children and siblings:

We thank you heartily for your dear letter of August 10. We can't tell you how happy we are to hear that you are in good health. Praise the Lord we haven't lacked that blessing either. During the summer we moved, not very far, but still it is a bit of news to relate. We have finally gotten a new croft building. Compared to the other crofts, it is both beautiful and comfortable, so we now have it nicer and more comfortable than before.

It was considerate of Bengt not to write earlier about the measles he suffered from during the last days at sea. You did the right thing when you gave Ingrid emergency baptism since the minister was so far away. We are happy to know those things. The children's physical and especially their spiritual well-being are always close to the heart of all faithful parents. [Quotes from the Bible, etc]

You write that your new house is finished and that you moved in on June 7 and now have enough room to house two families who have arrived from Hisby [?] Castle. [Norelius mentioned that some of the early arrivals were from Bosjö Kloster.] We also find that you have made a real-estate deal. We wish you well in all your endeavors. God will do anything that is good for us.

Mr. and Mrs. Bengt Anderson, *Vasa Illustrata*

Our neighbor lady is dead. She became ill Saturday before midsummer and died the following Friday. The farmhand has signed up for next year and will work for the same salary, 45 *riksdaler*. I, Nilla, haven't had to work so much at Hovgården because we have had Sissa here... and she has often gone there instead of me. [News about friends and neighbors]

We thank you so much for the American gold coin, a dollar. Mother was worried that especially Elna would fare badly during your settling days out there. [More news about friends and neighbors]

We want to greet you Bengt from a dear friend, the farmhand Sven Johnsson in Christianstad. [Old spelling] Uncle was heartened by the news your letter brought. Other America letters have made him sad and upset, but yours made him feel better. He is in good health....

We love to have word from you in your own handwriting. Finally, we send you, our dearly beloved friends and relatives, greetings from ourselves as well as from your friends and acquaintances, among them Lundberg. May the Lord always be your guidance and you will do well. Old Lina greets you. She appreciated Elna's greeting.

Your father, Anders Larsson

No. 2: Letter from Swen Olson

Mr. and Mrs. Sven Olson, *Vasa Illustrata*

November 14 or December 14, 1855

Dearly beloved parents, siblings, brothers-in-law and all friends:

We received your welcome letter in good health and with much joy on November 12. It was with great satisfaction we learned that all of you have your health, which is the most important. Now I will tell you what I can to the best of my ability. Here are very good plains which have neither stones nor trees, but here is a shortage of woodland because it is taken and it is difficult to get water out on the prairie. But I have a good spring on my land. I don't have as much woodland as my friends, but much better farmland and a water spring by the east end. It is a good place for the cattle.

I can't know when the land has to be paid for, whether it will be next fall or not, because now in the fall this prairie is cleared. If it will happen next fall, you ought to come soon if you plan to come. There is still room for a few next to us, but I do not know more than I can see. There is a shortage of water except on my land. Members of my family can build on my land. The cost of construction is minimal. Here we build with large logs and hew them on two sides. Then we lay them... and smear clay and lime between the cracks. These houses can be built faster than any other and they are warm. We don't have any pine, but we can buy oak, aspen, elm boards seven English miles from here, but they are much too expensive because they have to be shipped far from the large timber forests. We have a brickwork here in Red Wing, but stoves are used which have tin pipes with room for cookware and a baking oven. We have them inside the house so when we cook it gets warm in the house. The price varies between 10 and 30 dollars, all necessary cookware included.

We do not have any outbuildings. The grain is left outside.... Oxen and cows are expensive. One pair [of oxen] 400 *riksdaler* [about $100.00], a cow about ten dollars, bacon 16-17 cents per pound, butter 25 cents a pound, wheat flour about 10 dollars per barrel, potatoes about 50 cents per bushel. [Olson gives the prices in *riksdaler*.]

You might think it is expensive here, but note this: I have worked for a man, whom Ola Pehrsson knows, building on his house for 20 days at one dollar a day, plus food. It is the usual daily wage here. I consider it a loss that you keep Ola at home, and the loss for him and all of you is even bigger, because he could have taken for free as much land as I, 160 acres. It would have been enough for you, too.

Now, Father and Mother, you have to decide for yourself whether you wish to come or not. The move would probably be difficult for someone who is fairly comfortable and up in years. However, for my siblings it would be useful. You, brother-in-law Ola Anderson, come and take my brother Ola with you. You should be able to find a suitable place. Then we will help one another as best as we can with oxen so that we can break land ourselves. Breaking land costs between 16 and 20 *riksdaler* per acre. I have had four acres plowed this fall.... I beg your pardon for making a mistake in my last letter about the size of the land. [Olson goes on to explain how much 160 acres is in the Swedish measurements of the time.] One does not have to take that much, but for the price I believe there is a reason to take it while it is available. One cannot take more than 160 acres and not less than 40. With such soil, it is a smart thing to do. If you want to and have the desire, it's certainly better here than in Sweden, because this is the land of freedom. One has to work, but our work benefits no one else. If you come here, there is enough food and work on the land that I have and the rent is free.

A pastor has been here twice. He distributed communion to those who wished to partake. He wants to return and we took a vote about it, so perhaps he will come at Pentecost if he is well enough. He was rather weak when he was here the last time. He had the service in a home because the schoolhouse is not finished yet. If he comes to stay, he will get an annual salary.

You cried bitterly when we left, but it was not as much for us as for yourselves. One needs to be patient for one year. We can have the grain for food without buying it. See Hymn 482, v. 6.

Karna and Signe wish their parents would come here. If you want to come, we will take care of you in your old age if you stay with us. But anyone taking on the journey should not believe that everything is that well arranged at once. Before leaving, one should be prepared to face bad as well as good times. Not everyone has the right attitude or luck. It is up to anyone who plans to come here to ask God for guidance. Think about what is practical. It is not advisable to bring someone unless he is dependable.

For the journey, it is best to bring as much bedding as possible. We have no shortage of every day clothes here in Red Wing. The prices are good in relation to wages.

Provisions: The butter you should put in clay pots. Bacon, meat, 15 lbs of each; 4 lbs hardtack, the kind my mother baked for me, but some thin, one of each kind; peas, prunes, raisins, oatmeal, one pound of rye flour, one bushel potatoes, *lingon* berries, *sylta*; what we had was enough. You also have to look at what the captain recommends you should bring.

When the seasickness starts, stay up as long as you can; then when you go to bed the stomach settles down and you will get well that much faster. Bring laxative oil in case you should get constipated. Juniper drops are very good; *Hofvmans* [Hoffman's] heart drops and cramp-suppressing drops to take when you feel sick.

Brother-in-law Nils and Ingar, forest ranger Hans Pehrsson, you have to ponder it hard. All of you who have it good in Sweden should know that when you come here, you have to buy everything. But if one considers the future the prospects are good since one can become a landowner. Here one is free from all fees and taxes except on what one owns. It is figured according to what one has of grain... implements, what one reports. Every one-hundredth percent has to be paid in tax.

Now I will send these few lines in the name of God, so that He will give you the best guidance. Dear greetings to all of you, parents, and siblings, from the four of us. We are content and Märta is as chubby as sister Anna ever was. We are in good health.

Kindly signed, Swen Olson, the 14th, 1855 (The month was omitted).

No. 3: Letter from Swen Olson

Vasa January 12, 1857

Your welcome letter dated Oct. 31 was received on Dec. 23, 1856. It was a pleasure to hear that you are all well, and we feel better than what some say when they write to Sweden. Are you to believe one unwise or rather careless young man, who lies, while I can document everything I write?

My dear brother-in-law Nils Pehrsson, you cannot be serious about delaying your journey to this place. I see that you cannot come in the near future and you write you will come next year if I can decide on a place [for you]. That I can, but you don't have enough capital to purchase, because now the land is very expensive. If I wanted to sell my land, I could get $1,600 any day, and here are several who have sold this winter.

However, I will tell you about a new place near Geneva, located inland about 60 English miles from here, southwest of Red Wing, where a new town is planned, and there is much land to take for $1.25 per acre with plenty of timberland and water available. There are several in our settlement who plan to go to that frontier area next year. Many buildings were constructed last fall in that new town. If you, parents-in-law, brothers-in-law, siblings, and anyone of you should come here, then I will sell and accompany you to the new tract, where land can be had at the government price.

You, Ingar Andersdotter, my sister-in-law, are worried about what it is like to travel on he trains. One can sit inside the car. It is built of planks with a somewhat rounded ceiling with windows on the sides. There are chairs like in a church with a narrow isle in the middle. It does not travel faster than I could stand outside and look at the country and the American instruments which we cannot understand. One can bring as much luggage as one wants. We could take 5 pounds free of charge for each adult ticket. The luggage is locked securely in the luggage cars so one cannot get to it except when changing trains. The luggage cars are in the front. The people sit in the last cars. The steam engine pulls about 20 to 30 or up to 38 cars.

I hear that Ros-Ola's Nils writes that we are impoverished. It is probably true [or it might seem that way] because one cannot obtain large houses, or estates like the ones the noble family owns, but what we have is ours, both house and land. Here, one is not judged according to the old standard of implements and stone statues to decorate the walls with as they do in Sweden.

Please tell my father's sister, Bengta Nilsdoter, that Nils would rather take advice of Ros-Ola than of me. Ola Pehrsson was rejected by his fiancée and then he could not stay here, so he enticed my cousin Nels to go with him to Moline, Illinois, and from there to Monmouth. I told him what I thought would be best for him. Now, I have to say that he thought only about this winter, because he did not keep his land. If he had kept it until next spring he could have gotten 1,000 dollars without doing any work on it, but he sold it for $50.00.

I also hear that *åboen* Nils Jönsson [Jöns Nilsson?] who is married to my cousin Margaretha Eriksdotter from Vanneberga, desires to come here, and that would be possible, because those who cannot buy can rent land here. A couple of days ago, Pehr Månsson rented a place. He shall pay half of what he gets [sharecropping]. If you believe what I write, I could write a lot, but I hear that you believe someone who is not telling the truth. Finally, little Märta says thank you for the New Year's gift she received, which was a joy to her. Her eyes lit up so beautifully when she saw it, and even we received a New Year's gift....

Nothing more at this time, new or old, but a dear greeting to all of you at home, parents, parents-in-law, brothers and sisters as well as all brothers-in-law, and all other relatives and acquaintances in Sweden saying that we are in good health and enjoy this land of freedom. Kindly signed by Swen Olson

Be kind and send this letter to my father and let him know about the contents. Do not forget it. Thank him for all he has given me, for I have a good place here and live well.

No. 4: Letter from Swen Olson

Vasa July 12, 1861

Your letter dated January 22nd was received May 3rd.... We are happy to hear that you are in good health all of you....

I have to ask my dear Father-in-law to excuse me for not writing sooner, but I have been waiting for news about the fighting between the slave states and the Free states that are now in a terrible war. At this time, the Free states have 300,000 men on the warpath to defend freedom. Facing them are more than 200,000 men of the slave party who are against freedom and wish to defend the slave business, which is carried out the same way as we do business with cattle. Is that something [to defend]? No!

I will let you know how the soldiers are recruited here. The ones who want to go can go, the others are free [to stay] unless the war is in their state. Then they have to go if required. Every person who volunteers gets 300 dollars and 160 acres of land, food and clothes and free transportation if the war lasts between one and three years. They are enlisted for three years. If it ends in two or three months, the payment is the same as for three years. If someone is shot, I believe the same amount is paid.

You, who live in Sweden, have less reason to be frightened than we. After all, what bad effects did you have of the war between the French and the Austrians who fought in Italy? We are not affected by this war except that our products are worth only half because nothing is shipped out. The North is guarding the ocean around the South, so they will not get access to our business.

It was bad that you got the news that we now have a son without finding out his name. His name is Andrew S. Olson, because that name is both after his father and my father-in-law. No matter which of the two names he had been called, it would have been changed here. Anders becomes Andrew and Ola becomes Olof. He was born February 23 last year, and he is now so delightful. He runs in and out, prances, and tries to tell Mother what he has seen outside even though we cannot understand him. You would enjoy seeing him perhaps. You can see him because he looks so much like brother-in-law Swen that it could be him when Måns Swen was little. He has curly hair and is just as lively and ... as Swen Andersson.

You my brother-in-law Andersson writes that you plan to get married, and all of us here wish you luck in that endeavor. You say that you could have gotten someone with more money, but seek a spouse according to your liking.... I, Swen Olson, am not against the marriage, but I am sorry you will stay in Sweden and take on the bondage which will be a burden forever, because you could have been free from it. When one has the burden tied to a spouse, it is not easy to be free from it.

I and my dear wife ask you, Father and Mother, who will truly soon have reached the end, perhaps also we, that you do not get attached to what belongs to the earth, but to the treasure that is above that is ours by the grace of God if we do not reject it, because Christ the son of God has earned for us all eternal peace and happiness.

Nothing more this time but a dear and kind greeting to all of you, parents-in-law, brothers-in-law, sister-in-law, and all acquaintances from of us. We are in good health at the present time and live free of bondage.

Signed kindly by Swen Olson and Karna Andersdotter

I also send a dear greeting to your letter-writer, J. Wallengren. I and my wife Karna send a dear message to Nils Swenson and his wife and children that we live better than they can imagine and some letters relate. I have been waiting for you to come here, but it has been so long delayed that there is no hope. Tell my mother that Ola Swenson lives on my land not far from here—slow but steadfast.

Karna wants to know how Jöns Olsson's Kjersti is and whether she is getting married. Write back as soon as you have received our letter. Don't be discouraged. Next time you write, let me know if Uncle Nils has received the letter from Lasse Pehrson.

No. 5: Letter from Swen Olson

Vasa October 26, 1865

Keep well is my wish and my wife's. I will briefly answer the questions in your letter the best I can. For several years I have not thought of advising anyone to come, but I will answer your questions. The land prices vary a great deal according to location and condition. For untilled land the price per acre is ten dollars, but for a farm or homestead which is improved on one-hundred acres the cost is between two and three thousand dollars. When renting land, the renter pays one-third provided he has his own draft animals. If the owner supplies the draft animals and buys the seeds, the renter has to pay half of what he harvests.

200 *mil* west of here, there is virgin land as it was here when I arrived. There, every man who has reached the age of 21 can take 160 acres for nothing, and only pay for the papers, but the provisions are that one has to live on it and improve it as soon as possible. When they have lived on it for five years, they get their deeds; whether they have tilled ten or 100 acres does not matter.

The current prices are: Wheat $1.05, oats 40 cents, barley 60 cents per bushel, meat 10 cents [per pound], bacon 8-12 cents, a dozen eggs 15 cents, a pound of butter 20 cents, honey 25 cents a pound.

I will also let you know how much grain I harvested this year. Wheat 1,185 bushels, barley 58 bushels, oats 686 bushels. How much corn I don't know, but it will probably be about 250 bushels.

Together with what I have rented out or everything that is grown on my land it amounts to 2,639 bushels not counting corn, beans, and potatoes. This is on my own land. I hear that you believe that I have used Ola's land, but far from it.

Regarding your trip here, I don't want to give any advice because many things will be different than at home. Some think that large buildings and complete farmsteads are available the same as at home, ready to move into, but it is not like that. Here one builds one's house according to one's assets. It has to be like that for the time being.

Now, I and my family send a dear greeting to all of you. We all live well and are in good health, which we also wish for you and your children.

Kindly signed, Swen Olson

Brother Pehr and his wife are here and they are in good health.

No. 6: Letter from Ola Anderson

Vasa January 12, 1857

Mr. & Mrs. Ola Anderson, *Vasa Illustrata*

Now for the first time I want to write a few lines to you, parents, siblings, and brother-in-law, and all relatives and friends from all of us. We are living in the sight of God, feel good, are in good health, and like it well in America.

I thank you kindly for helping me get to this land of freedom. I like it so well here that you could not have given me a better gift in Sweden than permitting me to leave. While I was traveling, I knew that my dear mother worried a lot and also my sister Ingar, but I trusted in God and was blessed both on water and on land. I also thank you my sister for advising me to leave. I am thriving and growing in America, so that my clothes are now too small for me. I was not old enough to take a claim when I came here, but I have not forfeited that American right. I can still do it, but I think you my parents and siblings should come here. If you were to come, we would go to the interior and there we could make a good land deal, but I hear that you are still as hesitant about the journey as you were when I was home.

I have worked for both Swedes and Americans. I worked in a mill for six weeks at one dollar a day, plus food. We celebrated Christmas at the place of my brother-in-law, both Swen and I, and we had Christmas the same as in Sweden.... I am staying with my brother-in-law and plan to remain with him, so that we can harvest together. We have seeded winter wheat on three acres and we have six acres corn and potatoes. It is tilled, and we plan to plow more next spring. I we stay healthy we will fence in 75 acres in the spring. We plan to build houses of lime-stone next spring. We can burn lime on our land because here is plenty of limestone.

I would like to know whether you Brother Anders plan to become a soldier in Sweden or come to the land of freedom. It is not as difficult to travel to America as you think. There were no questions about the passports in Göteborg. They were meaningless. They didn't ask us, or the soldiers, for the passports. We bought the small slip of paper; then we were Americans and free men in Göteborg.

When we came to New York, there was much to see, you know. There were ships in the thousands. We met three Swedish ministers. We stayed there two days. They held four services for us. Several thousand people disembarked, all kinds of people from all over the world, and we were all together in one house, and in three days during the previous week 6,000 had disembarked. Thus you shouldn't believe that only Swedes come to America.

It is not as dangerous as you think to travel on the trains. Now I will end my own letter. Karna and her family greet you. They are healthy and feel well.

[The following is from Ola's sister, Swen Olson's wife.]

I, Karna, am in better health now than when I lived in Sweden and I run around as easily. I hear that you sister Inga are expecting and we wish you luck. Signe has moved to a city called Cannon Falls, and she was there two months and earned two dollars a week. It is as far from here as to Red Wing. She will begin to work on the 14th of this month at the same place in Cannon Falls. She likes to work for Americans. It is a tavern which is the same as an inn. She wishes she could have all of you here. You, dear Mother, should not worry about us because we are no further away from each other than we can send a message.

Little Märta wants to send a greeting to all of you, but especially to her aunt's children. She talks about them often. When we read your letter, Märta heard it, and said, "Aren't they coming here so I can have a grandpa and grandma and friends here? If *Morfar* (Grandpa) comes here, I will dance with him." Finally, she said she has no *mormor* (grandma) here, so she has to take Per's Sissa as a *mormor*. Her talk is a lot of fun and we enjoy her very much.

Don't believe what the old saloon lovers say or what anyone says who don't care to work more than a day now and then, because they only write gossip letters.

I am sending a greeting to Nils Jönsson in the village. I want to know how he is and how he likes the stillness and if there is going to be an *åbo* (farm renter) there or if you feel like coming to America and be free of the slavery that prevails at home [meaning at the castle farm].

Now, farewell our foster land, our valleys, hills, and shores. We commit them in the hands that bless land and sea. May God bless our friends; Help them in all distress and danger. Include them in your care. May God be with you.

Amen.

Ola Anderson

> Ola Anderson was born Aug. 25, 1838 in the village of Östra Ljungby, Trolle Ljungby, and emigrated from that parish to Vasa in 1856. He married Nilla Nilsdotter, born Oct. 25, 1841 at Tosteberga 18, Trolle Ljungby. She emigrated from Trolle Ljungby in 1866. They both died in 1912. Children: Nils Judin (Eugene) born Jan. 24, 1868, Etta Clarinda born July 6, 1870, Arthur Edward b. May 8, 1872, Selma Evelina b. Oct. 6, 1874, Anna Mathilda b. Sep. 30, 1876, and Alfred Stanley b. Oct. 7, 1879 (d. in 1899). The Andersons owned a farm in Featherstone Township.

No. 7: Letter from Ola Anderson

Vasa July 12, 1861

God's grace and peace be with you all.

Since I have the opportunity, I too will send a few dear greetings to you and thank you for your letter that I received through brother-in-law A. Jansson [Signe's husband] a couple of days ago, from which I learn you have your health and feel well. I can say the same until this moment.

I left Baileytown with my relatives and friends the last week of April to return home. The trip went well. It was a pleasure to travel. I stayed in Chicago five days to see the big city, which was rather fun. Entire blocks are built of expensive marble in four to five stories. I couldn't count the city's churches, but they are close to 200. I visited the largest of them and they had windows in the ceiling. The Jewish Temples were not open on Sundays, so I could not observe their service. The Swedes have four denominations, Lutheran, Methodist, Baptist, and Episcopal. I also visited our Swedish educational institution [Augustana Seminary] because I was acquainted with some of the students. There are 16 students at present. The city is ten-square *mil*, but New York is 36-square *mil* with two and one half million inhabitants. Sweden has only 3 ½ million in population or inhabitants. I traveled through Wisconsin 500 miles on the railroad and then home toward Minnesota.

The people who were baptized (in the creek) were not from Skåne. Our party is steadfast [Lutheran] and many have been awakened. The baptism was performed by a minister in the open air in a so-called Jordan's River, or as we call it Belle Creek. All who were there could join in the singing.

Now I ask you if you want to travel with me if I come home to get you. Answer me the next time you write.

I want to tell you a true story. President Abraham Lincoln is the son of a farmer. His father was killed by a wild Indian while the son was little. He worked in the forest, chopped some wood for pay, and hired out to big landowners. He tilled and fenced 160 acres of land, himself.

He received God in his childhood and became a living Christian. Since then he has lived his whole life as a true Christian, and now he has advanced to the highest post in the land and sits in the president's chair.

Nothing further this time but a dear greeting to all of you, also a dear greeting to your letter-writer J. Wallengren. I thank you heartily for the advice sent by both him and you.

Signed kindly, Ola Anderson

No. 8: Letter from Ola Anderson

January 5, 1871

My devoted brother-in-law Nils Pehrsson, sister, and your children:

We wish you a happy New Year, good health, and wellbeing.

In brief, I want to pen a few lines to answer your letter that arrived in good order, and from which I learned that you were well at the time. My family and I enjoy the same blessing....

I'm glad to hear my old mother is well enough to be up and around. I join you in wishing she will be treated with love up to the end and that she can remain at the same place where she was raised and worked so hard taking good care of us.

You say in your letter that you have heard a rumor that our sister Signe is dead, and this is true. It happened soon after Father's death ... and she left her mourning children and husband. I assume you have received more detailed information from her husband about it. In case you haven't, I will tell you what I know. She was ill on and off from after Christmas. I assume it was the ague chill, which often bothered her. She became severely ill 16 days before her passing. Her husband related that she departed in good spirit. The last time she became ill she knew she would not get up again, but looked forward to the hour of redemption. She was convinced she would meet her savior.

I don't know her two eldest children whom she had with her first husband. Signe was the guardian for them, and now the guardianship goes to the stepfather. He mentioned in his letter that the two eldest children say they want to come to me, and this would be my wish also.

I have not heard anything from Brother Swen since I wrote to you last time. Thus I don't have anything to tell you about him. Swen Olson and his family send their greetings No change there. Everyone had an enjoyable and happy Christmas season.

I have heard that Per Nilsson shall become double *åbo* [probably means that he is going to rent two farms.] I suppose he has breathed enough freedom here so that he does not sell himself at home.

O. Anderson

No. 9: Letter from Ola Anderson

Vasa, Minnesota, March 15, 1875

My faithful sister and your beloved children:

Your letter dated February 7 arrived a few days ago. I see that you my sister still feel poorly although you don't say what disease you have. My wish, as well as that of my family, is that this letter will find you in better health. I can tell you that my family and I are well.

From what I understand from your letter, Bengta and Karna want to come here. I hope it is like your letter says that you have your dear mother's permission, so that it does not hurt her and leads her to an early grave. I look forward to seeing you, but I don't want you to leave unless she agrees.

Regarding what you should bring, I can mention a few things. Clothes you should not take or have made to take along. Bring only what you have just sewn. Every-day clothes for women like the ones worn in Sweden are not used much here. But if you have any fabric which is not cut or sewn you should take it with you. Aprons you can bring as many as you want if they are hand-woven. Kerchiefs only what you need for the trip; shawls you can take but not too many. Sheets, only very nice and big ones, and if they are pure linen; Otherwise few are needed. Swedish style pillowcases are not used much here. But you can bring pillows stuffed with lots of new feathers because it would pay. If you would like to buy some fabric such as silk for dresses you should not sew or cut it at home but make sure you buy enough. Here you need 11 yards in sufficient widths. Place all un-cut material of value inside pillows in the bottom of the trunk in case there will be an inspection when you disembark. Put the oldest stuff on top.

As far as the food is concerned, you will get it aboard, but it is good to have a little extra consisting of dry bread, meat, and such, according to one's taste. I hope that Ola Månson who has traveled the distance recently can give you better information than I. I can greet you from Swen Olson and his family. They are living and have their health all of them as far as I know, and also from brother Swen. He is here with me....

Respectfully, Olof Anderson

No. 10: Letter from Swen Andersson

"Götheborg" June 1, 1866

My dear sister:

Thousand thanks for your welcome letter, which I had the pleasure receiving from you. It hurts me to think I was so tardy in writing that you had to remind me, but I hope you will overlook it and forgive me. I can no longer unburden myself on you or anyone else. Instead, I have to realize that we are so far apart that you, my kind sister, cannot care for me in all respects as you have done before. I thank you dear sister so very much for all the cautious advice in your letter. With God's help, I will try to live up to them as far as possible.

With this letter, I'm enclosing a small remembrance of myself which Ola should have as a memory of Uncle Nils Swensson. He asks me to greet you so much, and I send his and my greetings to all of you relatives and friends, saying that we have our health and feel well. As soon as we get to America, we will write and let you know how the voyage went. Greet your husband and all your children from me and say that I am satisfied, so if God grants me health and everything goes well, I cannot expect anything better on such a long and difficult journey.

[Comments about his travel companion Nils Swensson]. We get along so well in all respects, and we are as concerned about one another as we are about our own person. It is nice to have someone to depend on.

I will now end my little chat with you for this time with many hearty greetings and a friendly farewell to all of you.

Signed by your dearly faithful brother and friend, Swen Andersson

> Swen Anderson was born Mar. 13, 1840 (?) and emigrated in 1866 from Trolle Ljungby. He was the brother of Ola Anderson and Karna Andersdotter, who was Swan Olson's first wife. The letter was written to his sister Ingar Andersdotter in Östra Ljungby. Her descendants still lived on the farm in 1996.

No. 11: Letter from Bengta (Betsey) Nilsson

Minneapolis July 20, 1876

My dearly beloved mother and siblings on the other side of the ocean:

First of all, I have to thank you sister Karna for the welcome letter. It was nice to hear something from Mama and siblings. Please excuse my delay in writing. I could have written sooner, but it is soon enough, because you must have received a letter from Uncle Ola. He said when I was down there that he was going to write to Sweden. I was there in June and moved my trunk from there to Otto [Ola?] Larson's because Swen has his home with him. He has his clothes there too. There, he has a different home than with Uncle Ola. I have taken my money away from Uncle because when I was there he promised me ten percent interest, and I got only eight. I don't think I will stay there any more because I am better off with people who are not my relatives. He wrote to you that he would take care of me, that you did not have to worry at all, but I can take care of myself. I didn't want to continue to work for him like a slave for nothing as Swen did. He worked for him for such a long time, but when he left he didn't get anything for the time he had been there. It would have been the same for me, but I insisted, so I got most of my money. Swen has still not been re-imbursed for the curtain material. I plan to go down to the coast next summer.

Greet Måns and Anna and their little girl from me. If they feel like coming to America, he would not make a bad choice, but he has to decide for himself, because I don't want to entice anyone and get the blame for it if he doesn't like it. I will write more to him in my next letter when I know more.

Now I will close with a dear greeting from myself and Swen to Mama and my brothers and sisters, Per, Måns, Ola, Anna, Karna, and Uncle and Aunt and their children as well as Nicklas' Jöns, that you can do, Karna. Greet all other relatives so much from me. Many greetings to the Simon girls.

Signed humbly and hastily by me, Betsi Nils Son

P. S. I'm sending my portrait to you, my Mother in life and death. Write to me as soon as you get this letter. You should write the address the same as when you write to my uncle, but you should write my name instead and the box number 91. Dear *mamma*, be so kind and send your portrait to me. I talked to Nils when he came from Sweden. I thank you for the dear greeting he brought to me.

No. 12: Letter from Betsey Nilsson Granquist

God's grace and peace be with you all, now and always. First I have to thank you my dear sister for your welcome letter which I received as a New Year's gift. It was so welcome because we had waited for a letter from you. Thank you also for the beautiful New Year's gift that you and Mother sent to us. Then I want to answer your question about coming to America sometime in the future. Both Nels and I want you to come. It would be a much better future for you than going at home as a slave. I want to tell you truthfully my dear sister that I would never go to [or live in Sweden] more than I already have, because I live here in much happiness and freedom. If the Lord will guide you as surely as he did me, you can begin your journey in a good mood, because it is not at all dangerous. One has to put one's trust in God whether on land or water and everything will go well. If you want to come here, we will be happy to have you. Nils wants you to take his sister Anna with you. She would be dumb to go there at home and work hard. You can tell her that. If you are coming, write and tell me how everything is at home, whom Per shall have as a wife. I suppose he will marry someone else instead of you. If you have as much desire to go as I, then you will be happy to leave. Come, so we can clasp each other's hands once again. I don't want you to live in a shack at home. I hope Per Sven's Hans has visited you over Christmas. You can go with him, but do not get attached to someone from home during the journey. Tell Anna Swensson that she should be happy to leave because she has someone to come to. Betsy is married to our landlord, and she has it good. No woman in Ljungby parish has it better. Nils and I were at her wedding before Christmas. She now has three stepchildren and her husband is 50 years old.

Then I want you to write and tell me truthfully how it is with Mother so I'll know, because I am so worried about her, but I feel that when brother Per shall have everything at home, then he should also want to arrange for caring for our old mother It is his duty. I have so much I would like to tell her, but I can't do it since we are so far from each other, but I am sending thousands of warm greetings to my dear mother and siblings, Pehr, Måns, Ola, Karna, and Anna [sister-in-law]. How about a nice letter from Måns? Many greetings to Uncle and his family,

Signed by me, Bengta Granquist

Dear sister, write me back as soon as you get this letter, and you will soon have an answer.

> Bengta Nilsdotter was born Apr. 2, 1851 in Trolle Ljungby and emigrated from that parish in 1876. She married Nels P. (Persson) Granquist in 1876. She died 18 Mar. 1936 at a hospital in Rochester, Minn. Nels was born Aug. 13, 1849 in Trolle Ljungby and emigrated in 1869. He died Feb. 11, 1932 in St. Paul, Minn. The couple had three children: Nils Alfred b. July 25, 1881, Ida Carolina b. Nov. 27, 1883, and Manda Josephine b. July 21, 1886. Manda (Maud) married Clarence Alfred Julius Plaas and they had one child, Paul Anthony Plaas. Manda died in 1939 in Yakima, Wash. Paul Plaas died Aug. 8, 2003 in Troy, Lincoln County, Montana. He had three sons. (Some of this research was performed by Allen Olson).

No. 13: Letter from N. P. Granquist

Vasa January 7, 1878

Our dearly beloved Mother, Mother-in-law, brothers-in-law, and sisters-in-law:

[The usual religious and health remarks]

First we have to thank you for your welcome letter which we received in good health on December 30th. It was dated December 3rd. It was a dear New-Year's gift for us to receive. [The usual about health]

You think it would be nice to talk with us in person and this is true, and it would not be impossible if you desire to come here. We are not worse off than we could receive you, and I believe you would get better care in your old age than what you can get at home under the present circumstances. But I don't want to entice anyone to come to America, especially not someone who is old and comfortable, because they cannot improve on their situation wherever they go. But for young people like brother-in-law Måns and many with him who have no other possibilities than working their way, it would be a big advantage to come to America, because it is much easier to get ahead here than in Sweden. At least we would not want to trade Sweden for America.

You want to know what the house is like that we live in. The outside is painted white and it's pretty big. Bengta says that the two rooms are the same size as your house, and then we have two smaller rooms. You can get more information from Per Sven's Hans from Kjuge after he has returned home if his trip goes well. He was here before he left for Sweden. He is likely to come and visit you, because I sent a songbook with him for you, Mother-in-law, and Bengta sent a little oil cloth for Karna.

The Christmas parties are few this Christmas because the roads are bad. Here is no snow and no frost in the ground. We did have sledding snow for a couple of days three weeks ago, but that snow has melted.

I can greet you from Swen Anderson. He has visited us on several occasions since I wrote to you last time. He has stayed with Sven-Måns's boys from Östra Ljungby this fall. Nothing further this time, but a dear greeting from us.

Signed by N. P. Granquist and Bengta Nilsdotter

One more time we are asking you for your portraits. Greet Per, Måns, Ola, Karna, and Anna. Write as soon as you get this letter and you will have an answer sooner, for the waiting is just as long for us as for you.

The end

No 14: Letter from N. P. Granquist

Vasa November 22, 1879

Dearly beloved Mother-in-Law, Sister-in-Law, and brothers-in-law:

[The rather lengthy introduction has been omitted here.]

Now, we want to thank you, Mother, for the large Bible which you gave us. It was a memorable gift to receive for we cannot forget you as long as we live and neither do we want to. It is nice to hear that you have gotten such a good harvest at home. Then you can manage without any big worries for your bodily needs especially if the prices are high on what you have to sell.

Our harvest was much below average, so that now we can say that we have had two bad years a row. Last year we did not get more than 343 bushels of wheat and then we had to leave one third of that [in payment of rent]. Then to make matters worse, the wheat was so poor that we got only 25 cents a bushel in the fall, but now in the spring it went up to 50 cents. This year we got 400 bushels and have gotten between 95 cents and one dollar for it, so it has not been as bad this year.

Of oats and corn we have no more than we can use for the cattle. Those grains are priced at about 25 cents a bushel. But we are blessed by God and have enough to eat and drink and then no one ought to be dissatisfied. We have to hope for better times.

You want to know how far from us the cyclone hit last summer, It was 2 ½ miles from here about one half Swedish *mil*, so we did not suffer from it. But we got a heavy rainstorm at the same time, so all that rain damaged the grain for us and for many others. The cyclone swept away the houses and more or less damaged others here in Vasa and several people were killed.

Signed by your son-in-law

No. 15: Letter from Ola Nilsson

Liverpool, May 16, 1881

Dearly beloved Mother and brothers:

Since we are now so far apart, I will pen a few lines to you and let you know that we have arrived safely in England. We left Malmö last Thursday at 3 p.m. and came to Newcastle Sunday the 15th at 7 a.m. Then we played and danced until 2 o'clock in the afternoon and arrived in Liverpool at 9 o'clock in the evening. There an agent came at once and asked in a loud voice if there were any emigrants for the National Line. Then we went with him to a place where we spent the night and we got coffee, butter, and coffee bread. We got the same for breakfast. Later we had meat and potatoes for dinner and it tasted very good. The food on the ship was also good, but I didn't eat any except fish and potatoes. I want to tell you that I was not seasick for one minute, but there were so many who were very ill. Now we will go out on the Atlantic on Wednesday the 18th, and then they believe we will arrive in New York on the 27th if God will grant us health and the journey goes well.

I have to tell you that we have traveled through six tunnels and two of them were as wide [long] as from our place to the Bäckaskog station and the others somewhat shorter. It was so dark that we couldn't see a thing.

We have bought a revolver each today. It cost 7 crowns and one can load 6 bullets at one time and shoot them off all in the blink of an eye. We received 50 bullets at the same price. Lars and I have exchanged our money for both English and American currency. The English we are going to use on the ship. Also, I want you to know that we are sleeping on the 6th floor. We are ten men to the room. Now I have related a little bit about the travel for you. Finally, I ask you my dear Mother not to be sad for my sake because if God is with me and I stay well, I will make it in the new world. Eriksson asks me to greet all of you from him. Now I have to end my writing for this time.

Signed by me Ola Nilsson

Greet Måns and Anna and the children so much from me. Also, you must greet Uncle and his family and tell him that I have my health and feel good.

> Ola Nilsson was born in 1862. He returned to Sweden in 1883. He was married twice, the first time to Elna P. and the second time to Olu P., who had lived in Paxton, Illinois, 1891-98. Ola had 13 children, and one of them is Anna Magnusson in Bromölla.

Interviews with descendants

Introduction

As we travel the roads in 1992 to meet with Swedish descendants in the area, we notice exposures of rock where the highways cut through the hills, but that is the only rock we see in Vasa. We are told that black loam covers the red subsoil to a depth of two to three feet. The farmers grow corn and soybeans. Their homes are usually surrounded by hardwood trees and evergreens. Every farm has at least one silo, oftentimes four or five. Dairying and cattle-feeding are on the decline, but some dairy herds are seen close to the barns. Beef cattle and some riding horses graze in the meadows.

The Vasa Lutheran Church sits mightily on top of a hill amid the rolling landscape. There is also an older edifice from 1862 that houses a museum, in which artifacts, old clothes, books, and documents are displayed. The exterior of another building, which used to be an orphanage, has been beautifully restored by the family who bought it and lives there. The former elementary school has been taken over by the church, and is used for Sunday school, church offices, and social gatherings. The schoolchildren are being bused to Cannon Falls. The village stores are gone.

Having made our way to the 20-foot porous sandstone cliff called the White Rock we find that it looks naked in all its whiteness. On closer inspection, we notice many different shades of pastel colors in the rock. The steep-sided cliff has lost its protective cap of limestone and disintegrates as frost and rains dissolve the surface. When the first settlers arrived it was about 50 feet high. The surrounding trees tower the cliff, and it can no longer be seen from a distance. The Indians used to give the white rock special reverence. Later, the gypsies gathered there. Wild gooseberry bushes and other thorny underbrush make it rather difficult to come close. Many of the interviewees recalled climbing to the top of the rock as children and having family picnics on the grounds. Young couples went there on dates and carved their names in the rock. The White Rock cliff in Goodhue County seems to have had the same prominence as the *trollasten* in Trolle Ljungby.

Only a few of the residents we spoke with had heard of or seen the latter.

For the purpose of obtaining more information about the Trolle Ljungby emigrants settling in Goodhue County than the statistical and other written sources can give, about 40 interviews were made with descendants living in the area, of which 19 were men and 22 women. One man had emigrated with his parents, 38 were direct descendants born in the United States, and two were spouses of descendants. They were ordinary people who had worked hard to achieve relative security. Some of them were still working at the time we met with them. The interviewees were born between 1898 and 1947. All except five were senior citizens.

The majority had a farming background. Some of the men devoted their entire career to farming, while three combined farming with other occupations (tannery work, trucking, and insurance). One was handicapped. Six of the men were not involved with farming at all. Their occupations were: mechanic/inventor, clerk/mechanic, county maintenance employee, salesman/real-estate agent, variety storeowner, and grocery store manager. Another descendant, Professor Stephen Rosenquist of Bloomfield Hills, Michigan, was interviewed in Sweden. Quotes and data from his family history can be found in the chapter, "Background History."

The 20 recordings made with 22 women (published in 1996) include interviews with two sets of sisters. Five of the women had been teachers before they became farmwives, one a former music teacher, and another was still a public school teacher at the time of the interview. Other occupations included one pottery decorator/farmer's wife, one musician/homemaker, and one office clerk/homemaker with teachers' training. Four of the women had a college education. One of the men had a college degree. At least five of the men never attended high school, while nearly all the women were high school graduates. All the women, most of them daughters of farmers who were second-generation Swedes received a much better education than was the norm in Sweden at the time. Thirty-five of the interviewees were of 100 percent Swedish stock. Four were of mixed Scandinavian heritage while two were Swedish on one side of the family and non-Scandinavian on the other. Twelve had married spouses of Swedish stock; eleven had married German-Americans; six were married to spouses with Swedish and Norwegian or Danish background; four who were re-married had chosen one Swedish spouse; five had spouses of mixed heritage; one had married an Italian American. Two had not married. Nearly all the interviewees were Lutherans. One had converted to Methodism and one to Catholicism. Another was a Baptist for several years, but had returned to the Lutheran faith. The Lutheran faith is no doubt the best preserved part of their heritage. Most of the descendants did not know where their ancestors came from in Sweden or anything about the immigrant ancestors' background. Only four had visited Trolle Ljungby, but several had traveled to other parts of the world. The two women who were interviewed later are not included in the above findings.

The interviews give us insight into the lives of three generations, sometimes four. Comments about the Great Depression were common. The men were usually more talkative than the women. The oldest man served in World War I, and six others in World War II. What follows are summaries of the interviews with quotes. The tapes and transcriptions contain more information.

The most dramatic finding is that many of the young people married within the Trolle Ljungby group. While this was more likely to occur among the earlier migrants, it happened also in the early 1900s. Working with this material one gets the feeling that almost all the descendants are related. There is a tangled web of relationships that is difficult for an outsider to unravel, but some kinship can be mentioned. Walter and Stanley Swanson were related to Donald Johnson, Bernard Anderson, Virginia Fanslow, Stella Ingeman, the Webergs, the Risbergs, the Hokenstroms, and possibly also to the Young family. Betty Bender was a descendant of Swan (Swen) Olson and had many relatives, including Marian Terborch, and members of the Weberg and Risberg families. Norris Nelson and Helen Fredrickson were related to the Prink, Knutson, and Youngberg families. Everal Nelson, Mildred Peterson, Betty Jane Withers, and Hazel Hokenstrom-Weberg were blood relatives. Arlan Banks was related to the Mons Swenson descendants, including Milton Swenson's wife and also to Mrs. Bender. Ole Brodd was related to Aurora Swanson through marriage. There are other relationships that I am aware of and probably many more of which I am unaware. The personal history contains much information which could be researched further. The information obtained from descendants has been augmented with data from the Swedish-American church records, federal censuses, and plat books. The narratives are presented in alphabetical order according to the interviewee's last names. The spelling of the surnames has changed through the years. The following list shows the relationship between the migrants and the interviewees:

Immigrants and interviewed descendants

Early arrivals

Anderson, Bengt, Vasa: Bernard Anderson, great-grandson

Lars Johnson, Vasa: Donald Johnson, great-grandson

Nelson, Anders, Vasa: Stella Ingeman, granddaughter

Olson, Swen, Vasa: Marian Terborch and Lorain Deden, Betty Mae Bender, all great-granddaughters

Pehrson, Lasse: Walter Swanson, Stanley Swanson grandsons; Virginia Fanslow, granddaughter, and Donald Johnson, great-grandson

Swenson, Swen, Vasa: Walter Swanson, Stanley Swanson, Wallace Weberg, grandsons; Virginia Fanslow and Stella Ingeman, granddaughters

Later arrivals

Anderson, Ola and Margaret: Doris Landon, great-granddaughter

Anderson, Kjersti Truedson: Gladys Eckholm, daughter, and Elsie Mae Lerch, granddaughter

Brodd, Sven Olson: Ole Brodd, son and immigrant

Daun, Ole: Phyllis Pladsen, great-granddaughter

Hokenstrom, John Nilson: Hazel Weberg, granddaughter

Johnson, Olof: Stella Ingeman, granddaughter

Bengt Knutson (Persson): Mildred Schultz, granddaughter

Lamberg, Nels: Donley Lamberg, Sharon Nelson, Janet Larson, grandchildren

Martinson, Anna Jonson: Helen Hyllengren, granddaughter

Martinson, Pehr: Myrtle Hylan, granddaughter

Nelson, Andrew: Norris Nelson, grandson, and Helen Fredrickson, great-granddaughter

Nelson, Bengta Larson: Lawrence Nelson, grandson

Nelson, Jöns: Mildred Peterson, granddaughter, Everal Nelson, great-grandson

Person, Per: Sterling Nelson, great-grandson

Risberg, Ola: Arnold Risberg, grandson

Risberg, Nils: Betty Jane Bender, granddaughter

Skog, Elna Weberg: Earl Skog, grandson

Steele Anders Karlsson: Steven Hedeen, grandson

Swanson, John W.: Aurora Swanson, daughter-in-law

Swenson, Mons: Arlan Banks, Eldon Anderson, Luella Swanson, grand-children

Swanson. D. O.: Betty Jane Withers, great-granddaughter

Troline, Sven Persson: Donald Trulen, grandson, Marlene Thompson, great-granddaughter

Truedson, Nels: Harriet Nelson, granddaughter

Wahlen, Olof Swanson: Janice Olson, granddaughter

Weberg, Nels: Wallace Weberg, Betty Mae Bender, Virginia Fanslow, grand-children

Weberg, Peter Jönsson: Lola Nelson, granddaughter

Two interviews that were made later were not included in the first edition, but are now incorporated in alphabetical order with the others. Those interviews were recorded with:

Mildred Schultz, Charles City, Iowa, the granddaughter of Bengt Knutson (Persson) b. 1861 in Trolle Ljungby, who emigrated in 1882. Mildred was the eldest of 14 children born to Bengt's daughter, Hattie Knutson Swinton.

Phyllis Pladsen, White Bear lake, Minnesota, the great-granddaughter of Ole Daun, b. 1832 and his wife Ola b. 1840, both born in Trolle Ljungby. The couple emigrated in 1858. Their daughter, Emma b. 1877 in Cannon Falls, became Phyllis's grandmother.

Anderson, Bernard

It was only Hans Mattson who could afford to go back

September 17, 1992

Bernard Anderson

Bernard was very interested in his background and credited that to his grandparents on his mother's side, who lived with his parents for several years. They spoke only Swedish. "It was a slow process. If they just stayed around here, they didn't have to learn English either. There used to be a grocery store in Red Wing, Hanson & Gustafson, and that's where all the Swedes went. They could talk Swedish there up to the late '40s. And there was a store in Vasa too at the time," Bernard said.

Rudolph Ackerson, a grocery store owner in Vasa, was a first cousin of Bernard's dad. He was also the grandson of Bengt Anderson from Trolle Ljungby. Ackerson owned many farms and rented them out. His daughter, Margaret Johnson in Woodbury, a suburb of St. Paul, still owned the former Norelius farm in Vasa.

Bernard continued, "My mother's parents never learned English very well. There was a lot of Swedish spoken that I heard." He had retained quite a bit of it. *Svenska Amerikanaren Tribunen* was always read in his home and still was. The Vasa Lutheran Church had Swedish services once a month through the 1930s. About his paternal ancestors, Bernard knew that his great-grandfather Bengt Anderson arrived together with Walter Swanson's grandfather, Swen Swenson, from Trolle Ljungby in 1855. "On the neighboring farm where they first settled there is a hole in the ground where they built their first cabin. It's still there, that hole in the ground," Bernard said. While many of the descendants stayed in the area, there were those who went out west to farm. "Grandmother Anderson had two brothers who went to Plenty Wood, Montana. About 1906 or 1908 it kind of opened up out there. When they homesteaded they got 320 acres. Around here it was 160. When the Swedes left, other nationalities came in. All these ethnic areas have gotten more mixed up. There is no difference in how they farm," Bernard said. He thought it would be fun to know a little more how his great-grandparents farmed. "I suppose it was a learning process for them," he said.

About politics, Bernard said that the Swedes followed President Lincoln example and became Republicans. He could not remember any Swedish politicians. The local elections are non-political, he said. The Vasa post office was just for the ones who lived in the village. They went there and picked up their mail. His dad started a rural delivery. When Bernard's father (Almer) was young, he and his brother played in the Vasa Band. Almer played the tuba. Walter and Stanley Swanson also played in the band.

Bernard went to a one-room schoolhouse for eight years. He remembered when they got electricity in 1938 after which they could have hot lunches in school. They had a hot plate they could plug in. In the winter they brought their skis and during recess they skied on the hill by the school. When Bernard attended high school in Red Wing there were school buses. At the age of 15, Bernard got a driver's license without taking a test. His brother, who was three years younger, had to take the test. In the winter the car was up on blocks. They didn't have snow removal like they do now, Bernard said.

Recalling his boyhood years on the farm, Bernard mentioned the first corn-shelling machine. "That was quite a thing. We didn't have to shell corn by hand. It was a tough job picking corn by hand. There wasn't that much corn raised then compared to now. They raised more small grain, wheat and barley and oats and some flax. It was after the war that the corn pickers came." The first tractor his father had was a

Nielsen. It was sold by a local dealer and there weren't too many of them around." The second tractor they had was a John Deere. It had iron wheels and was the first one they used for plowing.

Bernard and his brother Richard farmed their ancestral homestead in Vasa. Richard was married and had a family, while Bernard was single and lived on the farm. They were diary farmers. Most of the corn they grew was used for feed. The milk was shipped to Hastings. "The trend nowadays is toward bigger dairy farms. There are even some around here that have 100 cows." Bernard said.

Bernard had visited Trolle Ljungby and seen the *trollasten*. As far as he knew, he had no relatives in the area. "It looks pretty nice down there. Trolle Ljungby was flatter than here. It probably wasn't really level, but not as hilly as here," he said. Neither his grandparents nor his great-grandparents ever visited Sweden. "It was only Hans Mattson, who could afford to go back," Bernard said. His mother, who was born in Sweden, went back three times. The interviewer was Lennart Setterdahl.

> Bernard Anderson was born Sep. 4, 1930 in Vasa. His great-grandfather was Bengt Anderson, b. 1829 in Trolle Ljungby, who emigrated from there in 1855 with his wife Elna Larsdotter, b. 1825 in Fjelkestad. Six children were born in Vasa: Ingrid in 1855 (m. Pehr W. Peterson), Bengta in 1859 (m. P. G. Anderson from Dalhem, Älvsborg's län), Alfred in 1861 (m. Anna Britta Back), Anna in 1862 (m. Swen Ackerson from Färlöv), Nellie in 1864, and Esther in 1868 (m. John B. Back from Väröbacka, Halland). Alfred's son Almer Bernard married Judith Johnson from Väröbacka in Halland and they became the parents of Bernard and Richard.

Anderson, Eldon and Glorian

He could have asked his mother

February 10, 1994 and June 12, 1994

Eldon Anderson

Eldon said he asked his mother many questions, but wished he had asked more. In the 1870 Federal Census both Eldon's grandfather and great-grandfather were listed as farmers, but in 1880 the great-grandparents lived with their son Peter while their son Mons was married and lived on the next farm. The two farms were in Section 23, Leon Township. Eldon showed us the places in the plat books where his relatives on his mother's side used to live.

"Mons and Peter were brothers. They owned it together. When Mons got married they divided it," Eldon said. Mons owned 200 acres and Peter 120 acres of land (Plat book for 1894). Mons's four sons each got a farm of his own in the vicinity of their parents. The youngest, Reuben, did not have any children, so Mons let Eldon and his wife buy the farm that the Swenson family had settled on when they came from Sweden. The barn built in 1857 was still standing at the time of the interview.

Speaking of his mother's father, Eldon said: "Mons had money that they were going to inherit, and the farms were going to go to the kids. He bought them for them, and they didn't pay much for their farms. Oh, there was a lot of money there. He [Mons] made money. He was so tight that his wife had to go through his pockets to get money for groceries and clothes. If she asked for it, he would say no. That's how tight he was."

The Eldon Anderson ancestral family

"Everyone had a good laugh when Mons was kicked down in the manure pile by an old buck sheep. He had just gone out on the plank to tip the wheelbarrow over when the buck came up from behind. Mons did not get hurt, but when he got up he grabbed a 2x4, mumbled something in broken English, and went after the buck," Eldon said.

Mons died in 1914 and his wife who was 13 years younger lived until 1940. Their daughter Ida, Eldon's mother, lived until she was 101 years old. The family had a nice birthday party for her when she was 100. Eldon related how she did fancy work all her life even close to the end at the nursing home in Cannon Falls. "The week before [she died] she had made Santa Clauses out of yarn for all the grandchildren, and she finished that night, and I was there and talked to her. She said, 'I finished the last one. Now I got for all of them for Christmas,' and she had that much yarn left, and she said, 'I don't think I'm going to buy any more. I am going to rest for a while.' And she put all her needles away and stopped that night. I don't know how many nights later she got into the hospital. She just slept herself away and she was gone. It's like God had said, 'Now you have finished.'"

When Eldon was young there was a general store in Wastedo. "They came and delivered groceries once a week. So they did not have to go to town to buy groceries. And you were lucky if you got to town once a month. They had the nose to the grindstone. They worked and they worked. What they laid down to get to own this place, we would have never tried it now. We would have just plain given up and let welfare take care of us. With all that work they could eat anything and they didn't have any trouble with their blood because they worked it off. I can remember when I was a kid, breakfast was fried potatoes, fried bacon, fried eggs, and toast made over the flame in the stove. When they butchered they didn't think about cutting off the fat," Eldon said.

Eldon remembered that the general store in Wastedo carried an assortment of fabrics for the women's sewing. "They had bolts of fabric piled all the way to the ceiling. You had to have a ladder to get to the top one. When my mother was a kid they more or less stayed in the plain colored clothes. On the bottom, the skirt was usually plain on every picture. Mother always said that. You never saw them put flowers on the skirt. Flowers, if they had any, would be a pattern on the blouse." Eldon said. His wife, Glorian, said that her mother, Alice Bodelson, sewed everything herself.

With the accuracy of the former teacher she was, Glorian wrote down the stories that her mother Alice told her. When Alice's father decided to send his four sons to a school in Northfield, Alice had to go along and be their housekeeper. To keep her busy while the boys were in school her father brought her a sewing machine. "He bought bolts of cloth that she made into sheets, pillow cases, towels, skirts, and pants for the boys, also underwear, and dresses for the women. So often the machine was kept running far into the night," Glorian said.

Alice Bodelson had told her daughter, Glorian, about the food that was prepared and mentioned that cheese used to be made in the home. "Every housekeeper took great pride in the making of cheese." Glorian recalled that when she was a child they were still butchering and making sausage and *pölsa*. At Christmas they ate *lutfisk* and *doppade i grytan*. [Pölsa is boiled meat, mostly from calf lungs, etc. In Norway, *pölsa* is a sausage. *Lutfisk* is cured ling. *Doppa i grytan* means dipping bread in broth directly in the kettle.]

Alice Bodelson was the daughter of another Swedish immigrant family, the Vanbergs, and she could remember living in a clapboard cabin that was very cold in the winter. She slept next to a single-board wall. One night she woke up when her father came in to get the heaviest quilts to put on the horses. He was afraid they would freeze to death. The barn was only a lean-to made of boards. Her father was up all night working with the horses, rubbing their legs and leading them around, while her mother had to stay up and keep the fires going.

One of the stories Eldon told us was about the wild pigeons in the area. "It was a great sport at first, then a hopeless task for the children to help drive the pigeons away from newly planted fields. They came by the hundreds and settled down on a field so it looked black, and how they could eat the newly planted wheat! The children tried to chase them away, the men shot them, and the women dressed them and they were roasted for food. At last they moved on as more settlers moved in and helped destroy their nests." Eldon said, adding that the pigeon breasts were thick and good to eat.

Speaking of Halloween, Eldon said that years ago good deeds were performed that night instead of pranks. If a man had a pile of wood that had not been split, the young guys would get together and split the wood during the night. At the time Eldon's dad was a youngster, they started the pranks. When a neighbor, Emanuel Young, came out the morning after Halloween, he found his buggy on top of the barn roof! They had taken it apart, the guys, and dragged it up there and put it together. And there it stood," Eldon chuckled.

In more recent years, it was common that the young people messed with the car of bridal couples while they were at church to get married. Eldon used to hide their cars in the woods, but at one time when he had promised to keep a car for some friends, his own sons who knew where the car was decided to have some fun. They drove steel poles in the ground around the car, one each by the front doors and one in front of the car and one in the back so that it was impossible to move it. Eldon could hear them laughing when their prank was discovered.

At the 100th anniversary of the founding of the Spring Garden Lutheran Church in 1958, the congregation put on a play in the church parking lot. Reverend Arthur Chell was the minister at the time, and he and his wife, Evelyn (Signe Evangeline?)], had written the play. Someone had hired oxen which were put up in the barn at the parsonage. The next morning the oxen were gone. "I tell you, people just about went crazy. They traveled all over looking for them oxen and couldn't find them." They were found in a pig house just north of Eldon's farm. "A boy came and said, 'There's two big animals in the pig house with big horns.'" It was the day before the play. Local people acted out the roles of Pastor Norelius and other ministers. The play included a baptism and a wedding.

"It has never been a dull life. It has been lots of pleasures and fun," Eldon said. The interviewer was Lennart Setterdahl. Lilly Setterdahl interviewed Glorian Anderson, June 12, 1994.

> Eldon Anderson was born in 1922 in Spring Garden, the son of Ida Clarinda Swanson, b. 1890 in spring Garden, and John Leonard Anderson. Ida was the daughter of Mons N. Swenson (later Swanson), b. 1844 in Trolle Ljungby. Mons emigrated in 1866 with his father, Nils M. Swenson, b. 1815 in Trolle Ljungby, and mother Kjersti Person, b. 1820 in the same parish, brother Per, b. 1849, and sister Nilla, b. 1859. Mons married Eva Enberg (Engberg) and they had ten children. She was also of Swedish descent and lived on the farm next to Spring Garden Lutheran Church. Eldon married Glorian Bodelson, b. 1926 in Belle Creek Township, and they lived on the original Swenson farm, while two of their sons operated the farm. Glorian's father, Anton Bodelson, emigrated about 1886 as a 16-year old with his parents. The Bodelsons were also from Skåne. For a list of Mons Swenson's children, see the interview with Arlan Banks. Eldon Anderson passed away Mar. 20, 1997 in Goodhue County, and Glorian died Aug. 9, 2012.

Banks, Arlan

The big bull hides weighed one hundred pounds

October 7, 1992

Arlan talked about working in the tannery in Red Wing for many years and also about the lives of the Swedish farmers in Spring Garden. About his own family history, he knew that his father's father changed his name from Anderson to Banks when he went into military service because there were too many Andersons. The Federal Census for Leon Township in 1870 shows a Swedish-born farmer by the name of "Bank" Anderson, 65 years old. Due to the name change, one of Alan's brothers thought they were of English descent on that side of the family. Arlan had heard of Småland and Skåne, but not of Trolle Ljungby.

The old home on the original Anderson-Banks homestead burned down the night before this interview took place. Arlan's old grandparents used to live there in a walk-out basement. The basement had windows and a door, one bedroom and another room. Arlan was born in that house, which also had a first and a second floor, where the older folks lived. On his mother's side, Arlan was the grandson of Mons Swanson, the same as Eldon Anderson.

Arlan Banks

Arlan did not go to high school. His father farmed with six horses. When Arlan began to farm with his youngest brother, Don, they had tractors. "The first tractor we had was a little Fordson. We cultivated corn by horses, a single row cultivator," Arlan said. The soil was a productive black loam. Don served in the U.S. Navy during World War II. When Arlan married, he left the farm and went to work at the tannery in Red Wing.

"I worked for S. B. Foot Tanning, making shoe leather. I was there 37 ½ years. It was a hard place to work, heavy work with a lot of lifting. The big bull hides weighed over one hundred pounds, and you threw them around for three hours, and you knew you had been working. We bought the hides from the slaughter houses and salted them. We had wheelbarrows at that time. We had to haul it way out in the swamp. All the hair, we used to bail that up. They used it to make padding for rugs; it used to be all hair," Arlan said.

There were more than 300 employees at the tannery in the '40s. It was the biggest employer in town. The workers were unionized and made good wages and had fairly good benefits. Arlan worked there until he retired. At the time of the interview, he estimated the number of workers to 200. The hides were then prepared in Texas, where they burned the hair off, so there was nothing left of the hair, he said. The hides were shipped to Red Wing, where they made them into all kinds of leather for jackets, suede, shoe soles. They made so much leather that there was no way the Red Wing Shoe Company could use it all. It was shipped out, Arlan said. The tannery was owned by the Red Wing Shoe Company. The managers were still named Foot, but not the owners.

When his brother Don milked 100 dairy cows on the farm, Arlan was envious, but that changed. "He [Don] was losing $1,800 a month when the milk prices went down. He tried to keep the boys on the farm.... He lost the shirt. I made out better, but I sure didn't think so. The profit is not there anymore unless you got 1,000 acres," Arlan said.

He mentioned the pottery in Red Wing, where his wife worked in the office for a while. It went out of business because of the union's demands, he said. The Casino became the biggest employer. No one in his family had visited Sweden. There was no correspondence with Sweden that he could remember. His mother went to "Swede School" in Spring Garden. "Almost 100 percent was Lutheran," Arlan said. He added that half were Republicans and half Democrats. The interviewer was Lennart Setterdahl.

> Arlan Banks of Red Wing was born May 7, 1920. He was the grandson of Måns N. (Nilson) Swenson, b. 1844 in Trolle Ljungby, who emigrated in 1866 with his parents Nils M. Swenson, b. 1815, and Christina (Kjersti), b. 1819. They settled in Spring Garden, Leon Township. Måns married Elna Josephina Enberg, b. 1857 in Red Wing, and they had the following children: Mary Adelia, b. 1876, Carl Albert Julius, b. 1878 (m. Emma Marie Chelberg), Esther b. 1880 (m. Emanuel Young), Selma Adelia, b. 1884, Victor Manfred, b. 1886 (m. Frances Charlotte Edstrom), Alice Victoria, b. 1888 (m. George Banks), Elmer Alexius, b. 1893 (m. Myrtle F. Nelson), Florence Estella, b. 1896 (m. Carl Olson), and Rueben Sigfrid b. 1898 (m. Alma Swanson). Arlan's father, George Banks, was the son of "Bank" (Bengt Anderson), a Swedish-born farmer in Spring Garden. Arlan had two brothers. He married Margaret Norton b. 1930 in Lake City and they had one son and one daughter. Arlan Banks passed away 9 April 2012.

Bender, Betty

The snow piled up as high as the houses

September 29, 1992

Betty remembered the hard winters they used to have in Goodhue County and reminisced about her ancestors. As the great-granddaughter of Swen Olson, she could name a few of his many children. Hilma and Tillie went out west, she said. Agnes stayed in Red Wing, and Lena moved to Hallock, Minnesota.

Betty's grandmother Johanna Olson Edstrom lived well into her 80s on a farm in Leon Township before moving to Red Wing. "She was a milliner by trade, a wonderful seamstress, and beautiful homemaker. She could just do everything," Betty said.

Betty Bender

She remembered reunions on the Edstrom side, but said they were not like the Weberg reunions that were still being held at the time of the interview. "My mother's mother passed away when my mother was only three years old. She died of cholera. That was Betsey [nee Risberg, who died in 1900]. She was a very young woman." Betty's grandfather, Nels Weberg, died when she was a child.

All the Weberg girls became good homemakers. "They didn't have a mother to love them or show them what to do, but they all became wonderful homemakers. They knew how to set a beautiful table without much of an education. Mother went through the 8th grade, but she could have gone on to high school at the time, but of course, she had to stay home. She was very bright. I think they all married well. They had good husbands that took good care of them. They didn't have a lot of money, but they had enough to be comfortable. The eldest daughter, Esther, was the first to be married, and then my mother told me that when Esther started having her children, Mother was the one to go and help her with her babies. Esther married Frank Larson and he worked for the railroad," Betty said.

After that, Betty's mother, Mollie, worked as a maid for wealthier people in Red Wing and later as a seamstress for Munsingwear Industries that made underwear in Minneapolis until she married Reuben Edstrom. He died in 1990, but Betty's mother was still living at the time of the interview. Betty's parents, both born in America, spoke Swedish. "I didn't want to learn it. Now, I wish I had. But they spoke Swedish when they were talking about something they didn't want me to understand. I usually understood, but I couldn't reply. My mother was very good in Swedish. In fact she taught a little Swedish to some people here in Red Wing," Betty said.

"Our family life was pretty much centered around the church activities [St. Ansgar Lutheran Church in Cannon Falls]. My mother was Sunday school superintendent. She directed one of the choirs, she sang in the choir. She would sing at almost every funeral in Cannon Falls. She sang in Swedish and kept it up. She was very bright, very sharp. That was when they lived in Cannon Falls. Then in Red Wing, I think she taught Sunday school and sang in the choir [First Lutheran] and also sang in the Swedish choir. In the Bicentennial Year, she was one of the first to join the Swedish Singers in Wing, which was founded that year. They had other soloists, but she was one of the main one," Betty recalled.

"It was recognized that she had a good voice. She was asked to sing. The mortician would call her. She hardly got a penny for doing it. In her later years, maybe she'd get a dollar or five dollars. It was a lot of money," Betty said. She thought that her parents sacrificed so she could go to St. Olaf College and pay for all her private music lessons. "My dad did not have much money. To be music major is a lot more expensive.... It runs into a lot of money," Betty said.

Betty's father came from Spring Garden. The area where the Edge-wood Restaurant was located used to be her grandfather's farm. "My dad completed [school] really through the third grade because being the eldest son, he always had to stay home and help his father work in the fields. Later in life, he worked for the Minnesota Highway Department, and started out with a team of horses. They kept a cow across the street that my mother milked. Later he got a Model T. He loved to drive even in the worst snowstorm. He used to take the family out in the Model T which had big high tires. We'd be out running around the country, going to Red Wing when everybody else was bedded down at home, because he just loved winter going through the snow," Betty said. "They used to have blizzards so the snow piled up as high as the houses. The phone would ring at 4 or 5 o'clock in the morning and he had to direct the people who were going out to plow the snow. During the Depression he was out of work," Betty said.

He was a very sociable person, Betty added. He became a mason in the Masonic Lodge and at one time he was the Mayor of Cannon Falls. It was a non-political office. He served for about four years in the '40s. When the Farmers Labor Party came into Minnesota, "there were some very crazy circumstances. I just recall him saying one time that they took him to this room in some hotel and put a chair against the door and wouldn't let him out. I don't know what it was all about, so he was very upset," Betty remembered.

Equipped with a degree in music, Betty went to Wisconsin Rapids to teach. There, she met her future husband, Fred Bender. Her mother's first thought was, "Why throw away your education when you've just started to earn some money?" Betty and her husband lived in Minneapolis, where Fred was an investment and securities banker. When he retired he built a new house in Red Wing, and they moved there to get away from the big city and so Betty could look after her mother. The lumber came from a forest that Fred had planted 50 years earlier at his birthplace in Wisconsin Rapids. Their children married spouses of various nationalities.

Betty belonged to the Red Wing Piano Keyboard Association and the Minnesota Music Association. She talked about Red Wing as being a progressive town. It restored the Sheldon Theater for musicals, concerts, brass band performances, and private recitals, as well as old movies. A group from England performed there. At the time of the interview Red Wing had a choir, but no permanent orchestra. The interviewer was Lennart Setterdahl.

Betty Bender, Red Wing, was born Aug. 10, 1924 in Wastedo, Minnesota. She was the great-granddaughter of Vasa pioneer Swan Olson (formerly Swen), who emigrated from Trolle Ljungby in 1855. Her grandmother, Johanna Jubiliana, was born 1876 in Swan's second marriage. Johanna married Frank Edstrom, b. 1866, and their son, Reuben, b. 1898, married Molly Weberg, b. 1896, and they became the parents of Betty Mae. She had no brothers or sisters. Betty married Fredrick Bender, b. 1923 in Wisconsin Rapids, and they had two sons and one daughter. On her mother's side, Betty was the granddaughter of Nils Weberg and Betsey Risberg, both of Trolle Ljungby. Nils Jönsson Weberg, b. 1860 in Trolle Ljungby, emigrated from that parish in 1869 with his parents, Jöns Persson and Olu Jönsdotter. Jöns died shortly after arrival. Betsey, b. 1862 in Rinkaby, emigrated in 1879.

Additional information about the Swan Olson children born in his second marriage: Hilma married Axel Ramstedt and they moved to Wallace, Idaho, where Axel was in the mining and banking business. Tillie (Alma Mathilda) married another Ramstedt brother, Victor, and they moved to Moscow, Idaho, where they owned a dry goods store. Agnes did not marry. Lena (Carolina) married Charles Youngren and they farmed near Hallock. Betty Bender died Mar. 22, 2009 in Red Wing.

Brodd, Ole

He said he was Brodd's boy

April 15, 1993

At the time of this interview in 1993, Ole Brodd had lived five years in Sweden and 90 years in America. He was the only Swedish-born member of the Trolle Ljungby group we met in person. The family emigrated in 1903 and settled at first in Balaton, Minnesota. His two older brothers had emigrated in 1901. "They went to Balaton because my mother had three brothers that lived in Balaton," Ole said. That was the Monson family. The Brodd family later moved to Vasa.

Ole Brodd had many memories from Sweden. He recalled the date of departure as April 15, 1903. Since his father had been a dragoon for 17 years, a platoon of horse-mounted men came to say goodbye two or three days before the family left. The house they lived in had a thatched roof. The barn was attached. They had a tobacco shed and a built-in oven. The cooking was done on the hearth. Other memories include the rye bread his mother baked, the goose lard used as sandwich spread, and the feather beds and pillows, all stuffed with goose down. Some of the mattresses were brought to the United States.

The journey to America started at Malmö and went via Copenhagen and Grimsby, England, where they buried a little brother who had died at sea. In Liverpool, the family boarded a rebuilt cattle boat, a freighter that took them to Halifax, because the Cunard Liner had "busted its propeller." Ole said. In Halifax they almost missed the train. They arrived in Balaton on May 5th. "The three uncles of mine all owned their farms, but my dad, when he landed in Balaton with eight kids, had two hundred dollars left to his name, so he had to rent a farm," Ole said.

The family belonged to Sillerud Lutheran Church, where Ole's father was a janitor. Ole pumped the organ. At one time, when he went into town with his father, a lady asked him, "Are you God's child?" He answered in Swedish, "No, I'm Brodd's boy."

Ole Brodd showing an artifact from Sweden, a newspaper holder

"I didn't know a single English word when I started school," Ole said, and added that he stood by the teacher's desk a lot. "She was teaching me English words. She understood Swedish so it made it easier to translate the English into Swedish," Ole said. When the school inspector remarked that the boy Ole Brodd seemed exceptionally bright, Ole became embarrassed because he thought it was a derogatory word. He didn't know what it meant. "Everybody talked Swedish. It was all Swedish in the whole community, and the church was right in the center," Ole said.

While Ole's father was a delegate to a church convention in Red Wing in 1911, he met many friends and former neighbors from Sweden and decided to move to that area. The family filled two box cars with cattle, machinery, and other belongings, and went by train to Red Wing and from there to a rented farm in the Norrbotten Ward, Vasa Township.

"I didn't like farming, but after I was confirmed in Vasa, I hired out to a neighbor farmer for seven months for 26 dollars a month. I worked ten hours a day, seven days a week, and took one day off to go with my mother up to St. Paul, and when settling up, he [the farmer] deducted a dollar for the day I was gone," Ole said.

For fun, the young people used to go to dances in White Rock. "Town Hall was quite famous, popular for dancing. South of White Rock was all Irish. So there was a lot of fighting going on there between the Swedes and the Irish. Every dance, there was a fight of some kind," Ole said.

When World War I began, Ole enlisted in the Marines. After three months, he was transferred to the Marine headquarters as an armed guard for secret Navy mail. Ole Brodd was over 20 years of age when he finally got to attend high school. He finished in 2 ½ years and graduated from Minnesota College in 1921. Having attended the Hamline University for one year, he got a temporary job with the Standard Oil Company that lasted 17 years.

For five years with the company he handled buying street-corner lots for their stations. He then decided to go into business for himself doing the same kind of work and did that for 50 years. He sold out in 1990. The business was still active in Minneapolis at the time of the interview.

Brodd had visited Sweden two times, in 1956 and 1979. In '56 he visited his childhood home, which he said was completely remodeled. Following this interview recorded by Lennart Setterdahl, Ole visited Sweden once more. He was extremely hard of hearing and the questions had to be repeated by a hearing specialist.

Ole Brodd was born July 28, 1898 in Nymö. He was the son of Sven Olson Brodd b. in 1862 in Trolle Ljungby and Nellie Monson, b. 1862 in Nymö. Ole's brothers and sisters were: Nils b. 1884, Swen b. 1886, Kersti b. 1888, Alfred G. A. b. 1892, Anna Maria b. 1894, and

Esther M. b. 1901. Nils married Helga Swanson, a Trolle Ljungby descendant. Anna Martha married John Wiberg, who was also a Trolle Ljungby descendant. Following the death of Ole's mother in 1917, his father remarried and had another daughter. Ole Brodd has a daughter from a previous marriage, and three sons with his present wife, Ruth, nee Story. Ole Brodd died Feb. 11, 1996 at age 97.

Eckholm, Gladys

The pioneers lived in a cave at first

September 19, 1992

Gladys was one of the few descendants who remembered the original cabin where her ancestors lived. The Pehr Truedson family lived on 40 acres in Section 18 in Featherstone Township, the Spring Creek Ward according to the divisions of Vasa Lutheran Church.

"My grandfather dug out a part in the hill, so they lived in a cave while he built a log cabin, and the log cabin stood until maybe ten years ago. He built a four-room cabin. There was a large living room and a real long kitchen, and two small bedrooms. They raised eight children in the four-room house. He had only 40 acres, and they had a couple of cows and a horse. They built their home near the creek," Gladys said.

Gladys Eckholm

She remembered her grandmother Margareta Truedson, but not her grandfather who died in 1906. "She was rolypoly. Up until I was six years old we always conversed in Swedish, and she lived alone out there and the mailman would bring her groceries out for her," Gladys said. She recalled that her grandmother always wore long dresses and never pants, but several petticoats. "The creamer and sugar bowl and the spoon holder were always on the table. She had copper kettles," Gladys said.

Grandma Margareta used to serve grape wine with peppermint candy. The children got bananas which she had saved a long time. She had some personal habits that seemed peculiar to a little girl.

The Truedson boys saw their opportunities far away from Goodhue County. The eldest son, Nels, became a rancher in Spokane, Washington. William moved to Hallock in northern Minnesota. Theodore and Wendel acquired large farms in Cathy, North Dakota, and Sigfrid had a farm in Big Sandy, Montana. All the daughters except Gladys's mother moved to the cities. Kjersti married Nels Anderson who was born in Östra Wemmenhög, Malmöhus län. He was a carpenter and a farmer. Later, he built a livery stable in Red Wing and re-located there with his family. He worked as long as he could, but when he became crippled, it was up to his wife to support them.

"They had bought a house with—it must have been five bedrooms upstairs and two bedrooms downstairs, so she took in roomers. My father had built garages in the back yard. There must have been six or seven garages in the back that they rented out. She rented out rooms and then she took in washing and ironing for people. At night she went out and cleaned offices downtown. We always had enough to eat and clothes to wear," Gladys said.

Having studied at a business college in Red Wing, Gladys found work in the office of the Red Wing Shoe Company. Her salary was 30 dollars a month. She continued working even after she was married. Her husband, Roy Eckholm, was a butter-maker at the creamery. Both kept on working through the Great Depression. They had one son who lived in Rochester, Minnesota.

The family had been in contact with relatives in Sweden on the Anderson side. The relatives named Åkesson had visited Vasa and Red Wing a couple of years before the interview. They even sent a *spettkaka* once for a birthday. But Gladys has not been to Sweden, nor had her brothers and sisters. The interviewer was Lilly Setterdahl.

Gladys Eckholm was born Sep. 16, 1906 in Vasa. She was the daughter of Kjersti Truedson, b. 1866 in Trolle Ljungby, who came to Vasa with her parents Pehr Truedson, b. 1842 in Trolle Ljungby and his wife Margareta Persdotter, b. 1846 in Nymö, and a brother,

Nils. b. 1868. The following children were born in Featherstone: Lina in 1872, Knut Wilhelm in 1874, Arthur Sigfrid in 1880, Eric Wendel in 1881, Hilma in 1885, and Theodor in 1877. The family was related to Swen Olson. Gladys Eckholm passed away 30 Aug. 2005 in Red Wing. In the 1996 book, the picture posted with her story was an incorrect one.

Fanslow, Virginia

The menu consisted of potatoes for breakfast, dinner, and supper

September 28, 1992

Virginia Fanslow

Virginia used to stay with her grandparents on her mother's side during the summers (Walter Swanson' parents). That way there was one child less to feed at home in White Rock during the Depression. Her grandmother born in Sweden always spoke Swedish, and it was difficult for Virginia to understand her. She remembers running errands for her, getting the wrong things, and peeling potatoes. "They had potatoes for breakfast, potatoes for dinner—potatoes for supper, and there had to be enough to get the next breakfast in the morning, so it was a lot of potatoes." Virginia also had to polish the white shoes that her uncles, Walter and Stanley, wore when they played in the band. "They wore those white bucks. They were the hardest things to polish. White shoes in those days, no paved roads! They had gravel on the roads," Virginia said.

"Christmas was always at Grandma's house for many years, and then we always used to stay over night," she said. There was a big upstairs and they slept on the second floor without heat and covered themselves with lots of blankets and quilts and ran downstairs to the stove to get dressed. You could have several quilts on the bed. The women saved nice pieces of material, had quilting bees, and made quilts. Church was at 5 o'clock in the morning. Santa Claus came on Christmas Eve. He came in through the door. Was all dressed up and looked nice." Her uncles, Walter and Stanley Swanson, always sang in the church choir on Christmas morning. "Sometimes we made it, and sometimes we didn't because we had been playing with our toys we got," Virginia said.

About her great-grandmother, Anna Stina Anderson, Virginia said, "She had this old chest that had the two little drawers on the side. I can remember her little tiny glasses and then she always had a little box of snuff in that one little drawer. We could never figure out what she was doing in that room. Then as the years went by, Mother told me that she had her little snuff."

Virginia remembered the Julian and Ackerson stores in Vasa. Besides the groceries, they had overalls, shirts, socks, rubber boots, and gloves "It was really like a department store. And the merchandise looked the same for years," Virginia said.

The picnics at Vasa during the Depression years also came to mind. "The picnic grounds are not there anymore. The highway is kind of going through there now, and you don't see much of it. I can remember my grandpa giving us kids a nickel, so we went to the stand and got our ice cream cone for the day. I mean the times were hard and we just had a picnic and everybody brought something and then they had entertainment like the band."

Being a Weberg, Virginia remembered her uncle Philip showing her the graves of Pehr Weberg's four children who died the same year in 1892. She said the graves are under an old oak tree in the Vasa Lutheran Cemetery. Her dad had said that they died of black diphtheria, but the death records give tuberculosis as the cause of death. Growing up in White Rock, Virginia recalled the big white cliff by the same name. "When we went to grade school out there, we walked by the white rock all the time. We used to crawl up on that white rock. It wasn't all that high. We used to carve names in there. It was soft. We used to scrape on it and pick up different colors like shades of brown and pink. For every time it rained you could just see that sand. It kept getting shorter all the time," Virginia said.

Having retired from farming, Virginia's parents moved to Red Wing, where her father worked at the Sewer Pipe Company. Virginia married Le Verne Fanslow of German descent. She recalled what happened when she introduced him to Grandma Swanson. "She kind of pulled me in a corner and said to me. " Is he a Catholic?" I said 'no.' She liked him all the better, and Le Verne liked her. I started a new trend. We'd known each other in high school."

Virginia and her husband farmed in Hay Creek, where there weren't many Swedes. "I was the only Swede out there for many years. I didn't have any trouble." [Later there were three.] "I joined the Methodist Church. I should be an outcast, shouldn't I? But you see my husband was a Methodist. I thought there is no way we are going to drive to Vasa all the time."

She also talked about the Weberg reunions every other year. They started in 1969 and the second was held in 1970. Then it was decided to have them every other year and reunions were still being held in 1992. "More young people are coming now than before," Virginia said.

Her cousin Viola Larson found an old cookbook. "She is a great one to preserve the heritage. She will work very hard to find old things to bring to the reunion," Virginia said.

Having retired from farming, Virginia and her husband moved to Red Wing, where they operated an implement store. They sold chain saws that were made in Jonsered, Sweden. The couple had two sons and two daughters. The sons were both farmers in Hay Creek. "I have such a concoction of nationalities of whom my kids all married. It doesn't bother me at all," Virginia said.

Virginia and her husband belonged to the American Swedish Institute in Minneapolis. At one time they went on a two-week tour of Sweden that the Institute arranged. "We had one week on our own. So then we went to see Dorothy's (Walter Swanson's wife's) relatives." But they did not know about any relatives in Trolle Ljungby. Now we know that they indeed have relatives in Trolle Ljungby although they are very distant. The interviewer was Lennart Setterdahl.

> Virginia Fanslow was born Mar. 6, 1924 in Red Wing, the daughter of Titus Weberg, b. 1890 in Spring Garden and Rose Swanson, b. 1900 in Vasa, granddaughter of Swen Swenson. Titus was the son of

Nels Jönson Weberg, b. 1860 in Trolle Ljungby, and Betsey Risberg b. 1862 in Rinkaby. Virginia's uncle, Walter Swanson, was included in the interview. Nels emigrated with his parents. Åbo Jöns Persson, b. 1822, and his wife Olu Jönsdotter, b. 1821, and two sisters, Elna (Skog) b. 1855, and Else b. 1855 (died young). Jöns died and Olu lived with her daughter Elna Skog. Besides Titus, Nels and Betsey Weberg had the following children, all born in Spring Garden: Esther Antonia (Larson) b. 1885, Alice Angela (Heglund), b. 1887, Ruth Hildegard (Fredrickson), b. 1888, Thekla Paulina b. 1893, Dora Alvida b. 1894, Amelia Vilhelmina b. 1896, and John Philip b. 1899. Virginia Fanslow died Nov. 13, 2000 in Red Wing.

Fredrickson, Helen

Their needs were supplied, but not all their wants

April 12, 1993

Helen and Carl Fredrickson

Helen talked about her grandparents and the Great Depression. She was only three or four years old at the passing of her great-grandmother, Sara Nelson, who was born in Trolle Ljungby. Her great-grandfather Andrew Nelson, also born in Trolle Ljungby, had died before that. Together with Ola W. Swanson, Andrew Nelson bought one quarter in Section 31 and another in Section 32 of Welch Township in January of 1869. Helen gave the names of the Nelson children's spouses, and later we discovered that two of them were Trolle Ljungby descendants. Alma married Alvin Knutson. Henry married Amelia Youngberg, and became the parents of Norris Nelson (also interviewed). The eldest child, Emma (Helen's grandmother) married J. F. Hagberg, who was born in Dalsland, Sweden, and they took over the family farm near Cannon River. They farmed as long as they lived.

About her grandmother, Emma Hagberg, Helen said, "She was a very hardworking person. She brought up nine children. Two little boys died when they were just infants. You had to work hard in those days, no modern conveniences." Helen described the house. "It was a small house. There was a kitchen and a dining room and the two small bedrooms and the living room downstairs and an entry. And then there were two small bedrooms upstairs." Helen remembered Grandma Hagberg's divinity candy. "Grandma always had that for Christmas, and then she'd make some molasses cookies and frost them and we loved that," Helen said.

"Grandma always had long hair. She had a very heavy head of hair, and when she was going to wash it, it was a job because it was thick and long. When her daughters bobbed their hair she did not approve of it. She did a lot of sewing for the kids, and knitted stockings and sweaters. They did their own butchering and preserved the meat by canning it," Helen said.

Grandpa Hagberg was the janitor of the church for many, many years, and also the Sunday school teacher. He was an active churchman. They had the Swedish services in those days. "In the wintertime he would get up very early in the morning and walk to church. He could walk kind of cross country. It wasn't far. So he would get up and walk to church very, very early to get the stoves going in church, so it would be warm when the people came," Helen recalled.

"They always had to drive horses and sleighs in the wintertime and the church had barns put up with a lot of different stalls so that all the people could unhitch their horses and put them in the barn during the services. I remember when they went by horses and sleigh. They both [her grandparents] had dog-skin fur coats. I think it was dog skin. And then they had fur robes they would put in the sleds." Her grandparents had very little hired help. "Usually if they needed extra help, the neighbors would exchange help, they called it 'You help me and I help you.'" Helen's parents also farmed all their lives.

Recalling her school days during the Great Depression, Helen said, "We walked and we had about one pair of shoes and when that wore out we got another pair. We didn't have a lot of clothes. Our needs were supplied but not all our wants. A pastor at one time was talking about it and explained. 'It's a lot of things we want, some of them we don't need, but the Lord usually supplies our needs.'"

Helen graduated from a four-year high school and continued with one year of teacher's training, all in Cannon Falls. She says that attending teacher's college was something the girls could do that didn't cost much. "It was right in the same building as our high school." Soon there were more teachers than schools, and some of the new teachers were unable to find teaching positions. When Helen started to teach in 1934, her salary was $45.00 a month. She continued to teach for ten years, boarding out in the districts.

Having married a farmer, Helen's ultimate occupation became that of a farmwife. She did not have to work outside, because there were always enough men around, she said. The Fredrickson family has raised beef cattle for 35 years. At the time of the interview, they also had 26 dairy cows.

Helen had not visited Sweden and she had not heard of Trolle Ljungby. "All I ever heard was Skåne," she said. Grandfather Hagberg was in touch with a sister in Sweden, and Helen's husband Carl's relatives have visited Sweden. The interviewer was Lilly Setterdahl.

> Helen Fredrickson was born Apr. 14, 1916 in Cannon Falls Township. Her father was John Emil Sederblad, b. 1876 in Goodhue County, and her mother Alice Hagberg, b. 1889 in Welch. Alice was the daughter of Emma Hagberg, who in turn was the daughter of the Trolle Ljungby emigrant Anders Nilson and his wife Sissa or Sara Håkansdotter, who arrived in 1865. Besides Emma, they had the following children: Nils Edward b. 1870, Carl Richard b. 1872, Henry William b. 1874, and Alma Victoria b. 1883. Helen married Carl Fredrickson b. 1918 in Vasa. They owned a farm in Vasa and had two sons. Helen was related to Norris Nelson. John and Emma Hagberg's children were: Alice Elenora b. 1889, Agnes Victoria b. 1893, Esther O. b. 1895, Edward William b. 1899, Vendel Ferdinand b. 1901, Sidney Everett b. 1906, Earl Gilberg b. 1908, and Alton

Russell b. 1912. Carl Fredrickson died 12 March 2006, and Helen Fredrickson on 7 May 2006 in Goodhue County.

Hedeen, Steven

When the Indians came they'd hide the kids

April 12, 1993

Steven told stories going all the way back to the Indians. His grandparents Andrew and Anna Steele lived on a 40-acre farm in the Jemtland Ward in Section 16 of Vasa Township. In the 1910 Federal Census, Andrew Steel is listed as a carpenter and small farmer. He owned the farm mortgage free.

Steven Hedeen

Steven recalled: "They raised that large family on 40 acres of land. They had a chicken house and they sold eggs and would go up to Vasa and trade their eggs for groceries, and they had some cows. At the house, to go to bed they had to go outside and go up an outside stairway to get up to the loft. Grandpa Steele was a handyman, who could do anything. He used to do well work and fix pumps. And he'd done cement work. They were good gardeners. They always had fruit trees, and apple trees and berries and strawberries. A lot of it was woods. And they had to go down every day on Highway 19 to get the mail. At one time, he [grandpa] shot a bobcat along that road. They didn't raise a lot of crops. I suppose they had hay and maybe a little oats. In later years, I think he had a threshing machine."

In the old farmhouse owned by Steven's son, there was a trap door that was used to shelter the children for the Indians during the pioneer years. "When the Indians would come, they put the kids down in that trap door." Steven said. About the Indians, he added that there was a half-breed tract [in Wabasha], occupied by Sioux Indians, who had married, for instance, Scandinavians. Steven's older brothers and sisters learned to speak Swedish, but he could only understand it. He recalls hiding under his grandmother's apron because he was bashful. His grandmother Anna had a son, Alfred, before she was married, and there were speculations that his father was of the nobility or royalty, Steven said. Alfred went out west. The eldest Steele daughter, Maria Amalia, married Eddie Hedeen, whose parents were from Jemtland, Sweden. The Hedeens walked from McGregor, Iowa, to Vasa. When grandfather Hedeen arrived, he peeked into the little church during service, blocking out all the light inside and everybody got scared, Steven said. The Hedeen farm was in Section 33 near White Rock. Amalia came down to that area to work as a maid and that's how she met her future husband.

"Where we lived down there in old Jemtland, there was one of the best trout streams in Minnesota when we were kids," Steven said. They lived closed to Belle Creek. They also did a lot of hunting. When Steven was 13 years old, he went to work for a farmer for a dollar and a half a day. "I drove horses, plowed with horses. They'd have five horses on gang plows." He did a man's job, and the wage was the same as a man would get. "That was what the high wages was in those days."

Steven joined the Army at age 17. "I lied about my age and got in the Army. My mother had to sign for me. We were in the Aleutian Islands. We were in South Pacific and in Iwo Jima, and Okinawa. I was in five years, 11 months, and 13 days, two and a half years overseas," he said.

Having returned to civilian life, Steven took his high school equivalency test, worked for a road-builder, and drove bulldozers. He married an Army buddy's sister, and they bought a farm in Jemtland in 1948. "We lived there and we milked cows. We farmed quite a bit of land for a while [about 300 to 400 acres] and then we got out of it. Our youngest boy, David, farms now. He lives on the old home place. He bought that and he farms these 160 acres also." (Where Steven used to live.)

Steven Hedeen's main career was devoted to the insurance business. He operated his business from his home and also had an office in St. Paul. The headquarters for the Farmers Union Insurance Company was in Denver, Colorado. "I had a 17-county area here in southeastern Minnesota," he said. Steven was the only one who told us about tobacco growing in Minnesota. He insured all kinds of crops, among them tobacco, he said. "There was quite a lot of tobacco raised down by Lanesboro in that area in Minnesota. There was tobacco raised not so many years ago. I retired in '87, but I would say back in the early '80s, there was a little tobacco raised down in the hills. In fact we insured tobacco. The growers dried it in special barns, baled it, and shipped it out," he said.

Steven also told us about the hemp used for twine that the farmers used to grow. 'They raised wild hemp which is marijuana. They raised it like a crop. Now you can go down these valleys to Vasa, and you'll find wild marijuana growing all over," he said.

Steven thought it was getting harder and harder to make it as a farmer. "Land rents from between $100 and $115 an acre. There is no way that I can see that they can break even on it, but they have this big machinery and they got to keep it busy, using it," he said. The farmers grow mostly corn and soybeans, but Steven told us that a new crop, ginseng, was being grown for export to China. The interviewer was Lilly Setterdahl.

Steven Hedeen, Vasa, was born June 9, 1922 in Red Wing. His mother, Maria Amalia Steele b. 1896 in Vasa, was the daughter of Anders Ståhl, b. Apr. 27, 1863 in Trolle Ljungby and his wife, Anna Simonson, b. 1871. He emigrated in 1881 from Trolle Ljungby with his family. At the time of his emigration, he was listed as farmhand Anders Karlsson, together with his father, farmhand Karl Andersson Ståhl, b. 1830. His wife, Anna Månsdotter, b. 1830 in Fjälkinge, arrived from Trolle Ljungby in 1882 with daughter Maria Carlsdotter, b. 1869. The couple had a third child, Per, b. 1865. The mother and three children belonged to the Vasa Lutheran Church. In addition to Maria Amalia, Andrew Steele's children were: Anna Lovisa (Fredrickson), b. 1897, Lillie Rosalia b. 1899, Hilda Erika b. 1901, Elmer Fridolph b. 1906, Carl Wilhelm b. 1903, Esther Hellen b. 1909, and Lilly Frances b. 1912. He was in the Army from 1938 to 1946, Coast Artillery Corps, or Army Mine Planter Service. He was married to Joyce Marie Banitt (Bennet?). The son, David, was born in 1955. Steven Hedeen passed away Dec. 11, 2004 in Goodhue County.

Hilan, Myrtle

Her dad never milked

June 18, 1994

Myrtle Hylan and Janice Hinch

If we are to believe most of the America letters, the men milked the cows, but Myrtle emphasized, "My Dad never milked, never milked." She can't understand how her mother could endure all the work, "and then go out and milk at night." Of course, she milked by hand. Asked whether it was the same with all the men, she answered, "The men took care of the horses, and that was it. They did the field work and it was up to the women to do the milking." Her father used to take a nap at noon, but her mother never did. She had to do the dishes and think of something for the next meal. They always had forenoon and afternoon lunches. When it was Myrtle's turn to be a farmwife, she and her husband both milked. They took the children with them to the barn.

Myrtle never met her grandfather Pehr Martenson because he died in 1897. The only child of his who remained in Goodhue County was Nels. He had 12 children, nine of whom grew to adulthood. Myrtle is the youngest and the only survivor. All the children in the Nels Martenson family were born at home. There was no special midwife. Anybody who could come helped. Mrs. P. A. Peterson was one of them. No doctor was needed. The family had an 80-acre farm and grew small grain, kept livestock, and had a big garden to help raise the big family.

As a little girl, Myrtle helped out by carrying in wood and water and doing the dishes. She admitted she got spoiled by her older brothers and sisters. When her older sister was married, Myrtle made such a fuss that they took her along on their honeymoon! "She was just like a mother to me," Myrtle said.

The young people used to walk to the dances at the White Rock Hall. Myrtle went there with her older brothers even before she was confirmed. She learned to dance at the age of ten or eleven. Sometimes the Irish and the Swedes got into fights. It happened only if someone drank a little too much home brew. Myrtle recalled many "*Olle i Skratthult*" shows. They were all in Swedish, but Myrtle had no trouble understanding the jokes. The older folks also came and enjoyed his shows.

"We couldn't go to church all the time, we had to live too," Myrtle said. The pastors did not tell us what to do. They did not come to visit either. "It was too hard for them to get around. I can't remember the pastor coming to see us," she said. Myrtle was confirmed in Vasa Lutheran Church. Driving a horse and buggy to confirmation class, she used to pick up two other girls along the way. It was six miles to the church from where she lived.

Myrtle was the first one in the family to attend high school. Her older siblings finished eight grade but they missed a lot of school because they had to help at home. Myrtle was boarded out in Cannon Falls while she attended high school. Before her last year in school, her parents retired and moved to Red Wing. Myrtle explained how she got a job at the Red Wing Shoe Company and finished school at the same time.

"When I moved to Red Wing, I only needed three credits, so I worked in the afternoon, and when I graduated they kept me, and I stayed right on until I was married. I liked it. I took care of all their mail and filing. That was kind of fun. I enjoyed it." She had taken two years of typing and shorthand in high school. Having graduated in 1928, she married in 1929.

Myrtle met her future husband Leonard Hilan, a Norwegian, at a private party. They were married in Vasa Lutheran Church and settled at once on a 280-acre farm in Belle Creek that they rented. She then joined the Norwegian Lutheran Church in Minneola. In the beginning they did not have a hired man. The threshing could last four to five days. "You had to bake ahead of the time. Make stuff ahead of the time and put it down in the basement on the floor to keep," she said. If it rained for several days and the threshing had to be delayed, she had to worry about all that food spoiling. Down the cistern it went. She also lowered the milk cans into the cistern. "Didn't hear much about food poisoning in those days," she said.

Some of the milk became yogurt which they ate with sugar and cinnamon. "I loved that," Myrtle said. She also liked mush, which she still made for herself. At Christmas, they had lutfisk, *pölsa*, ostkaka, lefse, and rice. (Mush was made with milk thickened with flour. *Lefse* is thin like tortillas. The main ingredient is potatoes. It was a Norwegian food tradition.) The Norwegians rolled up their potatoes and *lutfisk* in the *lefse*. "I never forget the first time I saw that," Myrtle said. She ate the *lutfisk* with mustard. Santa Claus always appeared after supper as soon as the dishes were done. The Norwegians and the Swedes used to tease each other by telling jokes about their countrymen.

Speaking of the Depression, Myrtle said that the years 1931-'34 were very difficult, but they managed. After 15 years they were able to buy their own farm. Myrtle's daughter Janice, born in 1935, was ten years old when they moved to the new farm. Janice recalled that even before that, she and her sister would do chores. "Phyllis and I would split and chop wood and take care of the chickens, gather the eggs, and go and get the cows, drive the horses for the threshing team and the hayfork rope for haying. No one said anything about that it could be dangerous. When the threshers came, all the food got put in this basket and we carried it out for lunch, and my job was to stand there and swat the flies to keep them off the seven-minute frosting," Janice said.

Ferdie Martenson, Myrtle's brother, ran the Belle Creek hotel and grocery-variety store, and Ferdie's son Alden and his wife, Lydia, helped them. Ferdie Martenson died of cancer at the age of 45 or 46 when his youngest daughter was only six weeks old. The Belle Creek store sold beer and delivered groceries with a truck. Myrtle used to sell eggs for as little as eight cents a dozen. It was referred to as "Mother's egg money."

On Sunday afternoon, the hired man, Bill, accompanied the children to the Belle Creek store, where they could buy ice cream. They paid a nickel and got to scoop up as much ice cream as they could get into the cone. Janice recalled reaching so far down in the coolers that she got ice cream in her hair! Both Janice and her mother remembered the slot machines in the Belle Creek store at the time.

Most of Myrtle's brothers and sisters became farmers. Her brother Alvin took over the parents' farm at first; then Marvin farmed it until it was sold. All were married and had children. Myrtle and Leonard Hilan had three daughters and one son. The daughters married German Americans and the son married an Irish American. "They couldn't have picked better,' their mother said.

In the 1950s, Myrtle's husband, Leonard, went to school and got a Master Electrician license. Their son, Roger, also became an electrician. He took over the farm. He had his own electric business until sometime before the time of this interview. Being actively involved with the ELCA Mission of the Evangelical Lutheran Church in America, he had been to Haiti a couple of times in that capacity. He operated his farm with less livestock than his father did. Janice belonged to the Sons of Norway and believed that the Norwegians were more into their heritage than the Swedes. She had started to trace her family and planned to visit both Sweden and Norway. When her children were home for Christmas, they were treated to a Norwegian dish called *rommegröt*. (In Norway, the main ingredient is sour cream.)

Myrtle visited Skåne in 1957 and saw the *trollasten*. At that time she did not know that her grandfather, Pehr Martenson, was born in Trolle Ljungby; only that her mother was from Villands Vånga. She knew the Swedish table prayer and the Lord's Prayer in Swedish. The interviewer was Lennart Setterdahl.

> Myrtle Hilan was born Oct. 29, 1909 in Vasa Township, the daughter of Nels Martenson, b. Jan. 5, 1858 in Moline, Ill., and Hannah Carlson Wennblom, b. Nov. 12, 1864 in Villands Vånga. Nels was the son of blacksmith Pehr Mårtenson, b. Nov. 7, 1823 in Trolle Ljungby and Karna Petersdotter b. Apr. 16, 1824 in Vånga. The couple emigrated from Trolle Ljungby in 1855 with their son Carl b. 1850 in Ivetofta. They stayed in Moline for three years. When Nels was 6-months old, they moved to Vasa, settling near White Rock and joined the Vasa Lutheran Church. A daughter named Selma was born in Vasa in 1860. Carl (Charles) and Selma moved to Oregon and Washington states. Myrtle Hilan passed away July 11, 1966 in Goodhue County. She had three daughters and one son.

Hyllengren, Helen

The immigrants never talked about their lives

March 8, 1993

When asked if her grandmother told her about Sweden, Helen said, "She never told anything. You know in those days we weren't interested. And they never talked about their life."

Helen Hyllengren

While Helen grew taller, her grandmother was 'growing shorter.' Grandma Anna knit stockings and mittens. She always wore dark dresses with dark prints. "They never wore bright prints like they do nowadays. So people looked old years ago when they weren't really that old," Helen said. Her grandmother used to get letters from a sister in Sweden. The old people read *Svenska Amerikanska Posten*, published in Minneapolis.

Helen's grandparents, Peter N. and Anna Martinson, owned a farm in Section 27 of Vasa Township. The acreage increased from 80 in the 1870s, to 120 by 1895, and in 1914, the Maple Glenn Farm consisted of 160 acres. Peter and Anna had seven children, and all of them had spouses of Swedish or partly Swedish descent. Peter died in 1924 and Anna in 1947. Anna was a widow for 23 years. In her later years, she rented out her farm and lived alone in Red Wing.

They may have kept geese on the farm because they stuffed their pillows with goose feathers, Helen said. The women made wine from grapes, elderberries, or dandelions. The men sometimes put brandy in their coffee in the morning before going to work, especially if they had colds. They used to grow oats and barley, as well as some wheat, corn, and lots of potatoes, Helen said.

Her grandfather did not own a car. "I often wonder how they got to church. They must have walked. Or maybe there was a city bus that they could ride," Helen said. They socialized with their closest neighbors, and the children used to come and visit them.

"Times were hard. They didn't have much. They didn't get much rent from their farm when they rented it out. I don't know really how my grandmother lived. She never had any pension. Living alone in her house on East 7th Street in Red Wing, she didn't have any boarders and she did not take in any washing or ironing. I don't know if she had money saved up. She just got a little rent from the farm that kept her going. And then I suppose, when my folks came in from the farm, they'd bring her milk and cream and eggs and help her. And I remember she had a little old wood stove, and that's all she ever had in town," Helen said.

Helen's Uncle Elof took over the Martinson farm for a while. When her father Arthur married, he moved to the neighboring farm which was his wife's family farm, and that was where Helen grew up. She recalled that her mother churned butter. They took some of their cream to the creamery, but they would keep so much at home and make their own butter. She also made *ostkaka*, *kalvdans*, and liver sausage. (*Kalvdans* was made from the second and third milking after a calf had been born.) "We often wonder how our mothers could do all the things they did without modern conveniences," Helen said. Before electricity, there were washing machines powered by gas. Helen's father wanted to buy one, but her mother did not want it. She said, "I can wash better than the machine can." Helen explained that her mother had a big wash boiler that heated the water. "In the summertime, she'd stand outside and rub." They collected soft rainwater in a cistern, and if it didn't rain, they had to use the hard water winched up by the windmill.

In the summers, Helen attended Swede School in Vasa. "I remember I had a Swedish *läsebok* [reader] and the teacher taught me how to read Swedish." Helen can still help her friends translating letters from Sweden. The pastor's name at the time was Arthur Benson.

Having finished country school near her home, Helen entered high school in Cannon Falls, where she stayed with her maternal grandparents, who had moved into town. After four years of high school, she took one year of teacher's training and taught school for eight years. "I got fifty dollars a month for two years. I stayed at home and drove to school as long as I could, and then when the winter came I had to stay at a farm place. There, I paid $12.50 a month for board. Things weren't expensive at the time, and my mother was a seamstress, so she sewed my clothes. I drove Dad's car. I had to put in the gas," Helen said. At one time, she had the measles just before Christmas, but she still had to teach. "I was getting ready for my Christmas school program. I couldn't take off. There were no subs [substitute teachers]. They didn't have subs in those days," she said. When her uncle died, she wanted to take a day off for the funeral, but the school board said no.

When asked what she did for entertainment, Helen said, "We had to make our own fun. We didn't have much money to spend, so we didn't go to shows very often. We went to ball games on Sundays, and we'd have picnics. We had community club in Vasa at that time, and we'd go there once a month for meetings. I met him [Arthur] there, and then one day, I went out with him on a blind date. We went to an auto show in the city. And that continued on for eleven years until we got married. We didn't feel we could get married sooner because there wasn't any money to get married on. After we did get married, we worked for a farmer for three years, and the two of us got $125 a month, and it was during the war, so this farmer had Arthur deferred from service. I was the housekeeper. We worked for two bachelors. So my husband was the hired man and I was the cook. Then after the war was over, we moved over to my folk's place, and they moved to Red Wing. We farmed there until our son got married and took over the farm," Helen said.

Helen and her husband bought the farm on contract for deed. "We paid so much a year. And we paid five percent interest, and oh dear, we thought that was terrible. A lot of money, so we paid as much as we could every year, so we could get it paid up and get rid of paying interest." They farmed for 32 years from 1945 until 1977. The Martinson farm was not in the family at the time of the interview, but the Johnson farm still was.

Helen's Uncle Bert served on the Town Board, but he was the only one she could remember who took an active part in government. She had famous people in her family tree. Miss America 1989, Gretchen Carlson, has her roots in Vasa. Her grandfather, Rev. William Hyllengren was the brother of Helen's husband. Helen's uncle on her mother's side was a well-known contractor. He owned the Al Johnson Construction Company and built dams all over the United States during the Second World War. He also built an airstrip in Newfoundland. The interviewer was Lilly Setterdahl.

> Helen Hyllengren was born July 5, 1915 in Vasa, the daughter of Arthur Gerhard Martinson and Hulda Johnson. Her father was the son of Anna Johnson, b. 1859 in Trolle Ljungby. Anna came to Vasa with her mother, Pernilla Persdotter, in 1870. Her father Sven Jönsson had emigrated in 1869. Besides Anna, they had an older daughter, Chersti, b. in Trolle Ljungby, and three younger ones, Sissa b. 1862 in Trolle Ljungby, Amanda Evelina b. 1871 in Featherstone, and Fredrik Leonard b. 1875 in Vasa. Sven Jönsson (Swan Johnson) owned 80 acres in Sections 10 and 11, Vasa Township, in 1877. Anna married Peter Martinson, b. 1849 in Önnestad, who arrived in 1868. The Martinsons had the following children: Arthur b. 1878, Emil b. 1882, Lillie b. 1883, Harry b. 1886, George Elmer b. 1889, Harvey Lawrence b. 1891 or '92, Willy Clifford b. 1894, and Victor Milton b. 1896. Helen Hyllengren passed away June 2, 1995 in Red Wing.

Ingeman, Stella

The Irish wanted to take over

September 20, 1992

The young people in Vasa had barn dances with hired bands of two or three players. Stella recalled dancing the schottische and the polka. "They'd fight at the dances sometimes. The Irish wanted to take over and the Swedes weren't going to let them," she said.

Stella is a Trolle Ljungby descendant on both sides of her family. Her paternal grandparents Swanson had died before she was born, but she remembered her material grandparents, the Johnsons. They had five children.

Stella described her grandmother, saying, "She always wore a long black skirt. She also wore an apron. When she went to church she usually wore a bonnet. It was three miles to the Vasa Lutheran Church. They went by horse and single buggy. They were farmers, Stella said. Their stature was average. The children spoke in Swedish to them. They spoke about Sweden, but Stella could not recall what they said.

Stella Ingeman

Her aunt, Emma Johnson, stayed at home and took care of her parents. They were in pretty good health until they died, Stella said. Her uncles, John and Amon, became farmers. John was married and had four children, but Amon was single. Sigrid Amanda (Stella's mother) married another Trolle Ljungby descendant, John Nelson, and they had nine children, one of them being Stella. Her eldest brother married a girl from Sweden. "She came over here to this country. One brother married a Danish girl, and one married a Czechoslovakian," Stella said. The only surviving sibling, Marvin, lived in Ft. Myers, Florida at the time of the interview. "He worked on the railroad. He started to work for a company that furnished crushed rock for the road, and then he worked himself up so he got to be president of the company," Stella said.

"At Christmas time we had Swedish dishes always, she said. She mentioned *ostkaka* and *lutfisk*. They made dandelion wine. It was usually served before dinner at parties. The young people about 14-15 years old could get a little taste of it, she said. Grapes were also used for wine and Stella liked that better. They never raised geese, but some of the neighbors did, she said. When they had butchered they cured the meat in brine.

Stella never had a male teacher. She attended a country school for eight years. The children walked to school. In the wintertime they wore buckled rubber boots and in the summertime the boots were made of cloth. When she was 18 years old she went to Minneapolis and took a business course. Having secured a job as a stenographer at Andrews Hotel in Minneapolis, she worked there until 1939 when she married Harry Ingeman, who also hailed from Skåne.

Since they had relatives in Hallock they went there on their honeymoon. Stella had no comments about the choice of honeymoon, but she said, "I was used to the big city." The newly-wed couple took over Stella's maternal grandparents' farm. She described the original house. It had a summer kitchen and a regular kitchen, a living room and two little bedrooms. There were two rooms upstairs. "We built on to it, so we got a good kitchen with cupboards and that," she said. The farm was 80 acres and located in Section 27 of Vasa Township. The farm crops were corn, oats, and beans. They had four horses and eight cows. Her husband helped her with the milking. The milk was picked up in 9-gallon cans and taken to the creamery in Vasa. "It was a nice little town," Stella said.

During her first years as a farmwife, Stella canned her meat and vegetables, but later she froze them. Her mother-in-law, Hanna Jeppson Ingeman, taught her how to make *sylta* from the hog's head. She mixed the pork with chicken. When lady friends visited, coffee was a must, she said. She served homemade coffee bread, and for Christmas especially, she baked *pepparkakor*, *sprits*, and *smörbakelser* (baked in small tins).

Her husband died in 1962 but Stella continued to live on the farm. "I'm not a lonesome person," she said. She had no children. At the time of the interview she was a resident at the Seminary Nursing Home in Red Wing. She was 88 years old. The interview was in Swedish and English. She spoke good Swedish. Stella remembered Dr. Norelius. "I heard him preach many times," she said. He always preached in Swedish. About the orphanage, she said, "Anybody that didn't have a home, they were welcome." At one time, 45 to 50 children were cared for at the orphanage. The interviewer was Lilly Setterdahl.

> Stella Ingeman was born Oct. 21, 1904 in Vasa, the daughter of John (Jöns) Andrew Nelson, b 1858 in Vasa, and his wife, Sigrid Amanda Johnson, b. 1871 in Vasa. John Andrew was the son of Anders Nilsson, b. 1815 in Viby, who arrived from Trolle Ljungby in 1855 with his wife, Kersti Månsdotter, b. 1819 in Vanneberga, Trolle Ljungby, and their children, Karen b. 1845 and Nils b. 1843. John Andrew was the first child born in Vasa. He had a younger sister, Elna, b. 1861. Sigrid Amanda was the daughter of Ola Jönsson, b. 1833 in Trolle Ljungby (emigrated 1864), and his wife, Karna Jönsdotter, b. 1841 (emigrated 1866). Their other children were: Inga Maria b. 1867, Emma Christina b. 1869, and Minnie Phoebe b. 1873.

The Federal Census for 1880 lists two additional children: John 12, and Amon 1. In 1914, Ola Johnson still owned the 80-acre farm in Section 27, Vasa Township. He died in 1919. Stella Ingeman passed away July 13, 1994 in Goodhue County.

Johnson, Donald

They needed a team of horses so he sold 40 acres of land

April 13, 1993

Donald and Doris Johnson

The records show that Donald was a Trolle Ljungby descendant on both the Johnson and the Bengtson sides of the family. Moreover, at the time of the interview, he owned the farms that these families acquired when they came from Sweden. His grandfather Lars Jönsson arrived in 1856 and took a claim in Section 14. His grandfather Bengt Bengtson arrived ten years later and took a homestead in Section 1 in Vasa Township. Originally, the Johnson farm consisted of 160 acres, "but before 1877, Grandpa needed a team of horses, so he sold 40 acres of land to get the team," Donald said.

Donald's great-grandparents passed away before he was born, but he remembered his grandmother Hilma, who lived with his parents. His grandfather Olof died in 1925, when Donald was two years old. He had only fond memories of his grandmother. "She liked to speak Swedish, and I used to think it was so much fun to hear my grandma and the

older Swedes talk, because I had heard enough of it so I could understand what they were saying. I used to enjoy that very much," Donald
said. He described his grandmother as a large woman, who always
wore long dresses. His mother was born in Väröbacka, Halland, so
Donald's Swedish was quite good.

About the Bengtson homestead in Section 1, Donald said, "It wasn't
much open land there. It's good for dairying. They had a lot of pasture
land. There wasn't enough open land to make a living for the family,
so that's why my great-granddad worked out." Two of Bengtson sons,
Theodore and Sigfrid, owned the farm jointly for a while. Donald
bought it from them. When he farmed he farmed only the land that was
open. When he rented it out, he gave permission to many of his friends
to hunt for deer in the woods.

Theodore Bengtson married Anna Anderson, who was related to
Bernard Anderson. Theodore was a good carpenter, who built houses.
After they got electricity, he took a course in wiring, and wired their
house and many other buildings. Sigfrid Bengtson, who was a railroad
man, moved to Plenty Wood, Montana.

Speaking of electricity, Donald said, "That was a great boon to everybody and to agriculture. They weren't used to more than a lantern to
see with in the barn, and to turn on electricity, I thought that was really
something. And then, of course, they gradually got their heavier equipment and bigger motors."

Asked if he had heard about Lasseli, the hill named after his ancestor
Lasse Pehrson, Donald said, "Sure have. We have gone up and down
Lasseli and even been stuck in Lasseli a few times. It was a real quag-
mire there until the new highway came through." On the Johnson side,
Donald remembered his Uncle John, who was a bachelor and lived
with them on the home farm. Donald's father was a livestock farmer.
When Donald was 14-years old, he started to drive a truck for him and
helping him on the farm.

"Dad was quite a large man and he, no doubt, didn't have the best
eating habits. Well, he had a heart attack," Donald said. He blamed his
father's heart attack on all the cholesterol and salt he consumed, bacon
and eggs, cream and lard. The food was always tasty but very rich.
Donald's wife, Doris, spoke of the *palt* (blood pudding) that her
mother used to fry and let simmer in milk. "I grew up on it, she said.

Donald didn't like it. He didn't eat *kalvdans* either, but he had plenty of food. "I can never remember going to bed hungry," he said. He mentioned that sometimes they had herring, but that, too, was fried.

About his own life, Donald said, "I trucked livestock for a few years and farmed, but then I saw that there wasn't any future in livestock hauling, so I more or less took over the farm. When Dad passed away, I bought the farm from Mother." Donald tried sheep farming. He bought thin sheep from the stockyard. "I fed as many as 1000 head a year of lambs. Oh yes! I was a big sheep feeder. You feed them for so long, and then you get rid of that batch and you get another batch," Donald said. He usually had three batches a year. Then when it was time to shear the wool, the wool clipper would come around and clip and bag the wool, he said. Donald fed the sheep with corn and special protein feed and fattened them before sending them to the market. They were confined to a yard. He also had dairy cows and hogs.

After farming for a few years, Donald decided to rent out the farm. He then began to work for Meyer Industries in Cannon Falls, Having retired after 25 years he took a part-time job, driving large trucks for Fil-Mor Express. It turned out to be a full-time job that he had kept for five years. At the time of this interview, the 70-year old man started his day at 2 a. m and worked 60 hours a week. Donald and Doris had three daughters who all liked *lutfisk*. Doris's mother was from Värmland.

In 1993, I found distant relatives of the Johnsons in Trolle Ljungby. The interviewer was Lilly Setterdahl.

> Donald Johnson was born June 26, 1923. His parents, Willie L. Johnson, b. Oct. 6, 1898, and Hannah N. Johnson, b. Feb. 27, 1899 in Halland Sweden, lived in Vasa. Willie was the son of Olof Johnson (1857-1925) and Hilma Bengtson (1871-1955), both born in Vasa. Olof was the son of the former Åbo Lars Jönsson, b. 1822 in Trolle Ljungby and his wife Olu Larsdotter, b. 1827 in the same parish. They emigrated in 1856 and were among the first Swedish settlers in Vasa. Olu was the daughter of Lasse Pehrson. Hilma Bengtson was the daughter of Bengt Bengtson, b. 1838 in Trolle Ljungby and his wife Elna Nilsdoter, b. 1849. They emigrated from Trolle Ljungby in 1866. Lars and Olu's other children were: Anna b. 1860, Carry b. 1862, and Johan b. 1867. Bengt and Elna Bengtson's other children were: Carrie, b. 1869, Albertina, b. 1874, Anton Louis b. 1876, Theodor Oscar b. 1878, and William Sigrid b. 1881. In 2008, Donald and Doris Johnson lived in Red Wing.

Lamberg, Donley

It was easier to read writing than to write reading

April 12, 1993

Donley Lamberg

Donley told us how he became interested in the Lamberg ancestry. Some years ago a relative in Sweden, Lars Lamberg of Sölvesborg, wrote to the Vasa Lutheran Church and inquired whether there were any relatives in the area. The church forwarded the letter to Donley's cousin, Sharon Nelson. Sharon in turn forwarded the letter to Donley. Since then, Donley has done quite a bit of research about members of the family after they came to America.

"It's been fun. I enjoy it. The letter from Sweden is what got me stated. I've been at it slow. I have our family [traced] without too much trouble," he said. Lately, he has been working on the Emil Lamberg family. Emil was a brother of Nels Lamberg, Donley's grandfather. It gave Donley a reason to visit Emil's sons, whom he had not seen for years.

From cemetery records and walking around the cemeteries, Donley learned that Anders Lamberg died in 1898, and that three of the children died young. Hilda died at the age of 11. Arthur was 24 when he passed away, and John was 29. This left only Nels and Emil to carry on the family line. Donley was puzzled about why Kersti Pearson was buried in the family plot. She died in 1894 at the age of 76. When I was in Sweden in 1993, I found out from Lars Lamberg that she was the mother of Anna Lamberg.

Donley pointed to the Lamberg farm in the plat book in Section 12, Vasa Township at the intersection of routes 19 and 118. "It was hilly, some of it was good, some of it had rock," he said. His dad pastured the rocky part. The farm was located below the Lasseli hill. The 1914 plat book shows that Nils Lamberg owned two parcels, one that was 100 acres and one that was 118. Later, the farm totaled 263 acres, Donley said. His father farmed the same land as Nils Lamberg. Donley grew up on the tractor, he said, but wasn't interested in becoming a farmer, so the farm was sold.

About the correspondence with Sweden, Donley remarked, "It's easier to read writing than to write reading." Thanks to his relative in Sweden, he has a family tree that goes back to the 1700s. It begins with the forefather, Anders Lamberg (1779-1873), who was a *carabinjär* and *torpare*. He joined *Skånska dragonregementet* (Cavalry) in 1805. His company was engaged in the "German War," 1813-14 (Napoleonic War). When Anders Lamberg's wife died in 1817, the probate records showed that the family owned silver, tin, and copper.

Some day, Donley hoped to visit Sweden. He was a maintenance worker for a company in Rochester, taking care of heating and vent-ilating equipment in county buildings. At the time of the interview, his mother, the former Mabel Blom, resided in a nursing home in Red Wing. His father had passed away. Donley married Carol Bekkelund off Swedish and Norwegian descent. They had three children. The interviewer was Lilly Setterdahl.

> Donley Lamberg was born June 30, 1937 in Vasa Township, the son of Virgil Lamberg, b. 1905 in Vasa Township, and grandson of Nils Lamberg, b. Jun. 14, 1874 in Trolle Ljungby, who emigrated with his family in 1880 from Trolle Ljungby. Nils's parents were Anders Lamberg, b. 1850, and his wife Anna Nelson b. 1845, both of Sölvesborg. Their other children were: Jöns (1877-1906), Hilda (1879-1890), Emil b. 1880, and Otto Arthur Sigfried (1885-1910). Anders Lamberg died in 1898 and his wife, Anna, in 1929.

Landon, Doris

They opened up the parlor for Christmas

September 18, 1992

Doris Landon

Doris spoke of their Swedish Christmas traditions, her sister becoming a Catholic, her mother's Norwegian heritage, and how it all worked out. Her great-grandparents, the Andersons, came from Sweden in 1869. According to the 1870 Federal Census, they lived in the northeastern part of Vasa (the Skåne Ward) with their eight children. Their neighbors were Nels Johnson and Ole W. Peterson, also from Trolle Ljungby. In the 1880 Federal Census, they were still listed as farmers in Vasa Township. Anderson died in 1883. He probably rented the farm, because he is not listed in the plat book for 1877. In the census for 1910, we found their son Ola Anderson and his wife Alma Olson listed as farmers in Cannon Falls Township. Ola's mother, Margareta, lived with them and their seven children. Ola owned the farm mortgage-free. The 160-acre farm in Section 24 was listed in the names of O. O. and A. O. Anderson (Plat book for 1914).

Most of the Anderson children settled around Cannon Falls, Doris said. Some settled in other counties in Minnesota. She remembered her grandparents on her father's side. "My mom and dad lived with them for a while on the farm until they moved to town, but then we'd go into town and visit them. We'd hitch up the horses and go in and see them. It was like ten miles. They could speak English," Doris said, but she could also understand Swedish. "I can understand almost everything.

Being I'm the oldest child, I'm the only one that can. I can speak very little of it," she said. Her father, Winfred, married Annie Aslaksen of Norwegian descent. "They talked a little bit of Swedish and Norwegian between themselves until I was about six years old," she added.

Doris grew up on a farm. "My dad's brother farmed with us. We had a milk separator and separated the milk from the cream. Mother made butter. And we'd butcher every year, a pig, and a cow. W canned the meat, put it in the basement," she said. When they had slaughtered a pig, her mother made blood sausage. Doris thought her mother added barley to the meat when she made the sausage. Swedish traditions were mixed with Norwegians in Doris's home. Her mother was a Norwegian from Wanamingo Township. The in-laws got along even though one was Republican and one Democrat. "They just kept it to themselves," Doris said.

At Christmas, my mother made *lefse*, so we had *lefse* and mashed potatoes and butter and put *lutfisk* on that, and then we rolled it up. That was the way we ate it," Doris said. She liked *lefse*. Her dad always put white sauce and mustard on the *lutfisk*. For a treat, they would have it a couple of times during the year, maybe at the New Year's holiday. They had live candles on the Christmas tree, and they were lit only once. They had the tree in the parlor. "They opened up the parlor for Christmas and took the tree down 21 days later," Doris said. Santa came on Christmas Eve. On Christmas morning, they went to julotta at the Vasa Lutheran Church.

Doris's confirmation classes in Vasa were in the English language. When she went to Cannon Falls High School, she didn't have any relatives there to board with, so she lived with three or four other girls. "Mother would make the meals for the week, and then each one of us had to take turns serving for a week. We had to pack our lunch and go to school. We didn't work. We'd just get hand-me-downs, maybe wore one dress all week," Doris said. About half of the young people did not go to high school at all. "They didn't' have any money."

After high school, Doris took a job helping a neighbor. One of their sisters married a German Catholic and had ten children. "They worked on the farm and everything was made from scratch. One child pretty near every year, but she had those children in church every Sunday morning. Had them all dressed up perfect and their hair curled, and she was a very good Catholic," Doris said. When asked what their mother thought about that marriage, Doris said, "She was a little prejudiced at first, but the man that she [my sister] married was so nice, and this made a lot of difference, so Mother kind of overlooked it. Going to church, I think, was the main thing." When the tenth child was born, she died. Only one of the sister's children is a Catholic today, Doris said.

When Doris was 21 years old she married a farmer. His mother was half Norwegian and his father English. None of their children married farmers. At the time of the interview, people in the area were unable to start out farming unless they inherited farms, Doris said. She and Paul did not butcher on the farm. "We did raise our own animals and took them into town and had them butchered, so we had our own meat." The meat was kept in a freezer locker in town. They took the milk to the creamery in Vasa. Their children attended grade school in Vasa up to the third grade. After that, they were bused to Cannon Falls.

When Doris's mother died she had 63 grandchildren and 45 grandchildren. Doris had no contact with Sweden. The interviewer was Lilly Setterdahl.

> Doris Landon was born July 6, 1926 in Red Wing, the daughter of Winfred Anderson, b. 1902 in Vasa. He was the grandson of Ola Anderson, b. 1823 in Kiaby and Margareta Olsdotter, b. 1832 in Trolle Ljungby (sister of Swen Olson). They came to Vasa with six children in 1869: Karna, b. 1853, Anders b. 1856, Marta or Mathilda b. 1858, Carl b. 1861, Ola b. 1863, Johanna b. 1866, Nils Alex, b. 1869. Two more children, Alice and Selma, were born in Vasa. Their daughter, Annika, b. 1852, arrived in 1868 with Alfred Johansson. Ola Jr. married Alma Olson, and they also had many children: Arthur Oliver b. 1891, Lillie Emelia b. 1893, Ethel Rosalia b. 1895, Pearl Mildred b. 1899, Winfred b. 1902, Irene b. 1905, and Delmar b. 1907. Doris had two brothers and two sisters. Doris Anderson married Paul Landon, b. 1922 in Draper, South Dakota. They had to sons and three daughters. In 1998, Doris Landon lived in Cannon Falls.

Lersch, Elsie Mae

The wages were ten cents an hour

September 18, 1992

Elsie Mae Lersch

From this interview we learn what it was like to be a small farmer in Wisconsin during the Depression, but first, Elsie Mae told us what she knew about her grandparents. "Mother would talk about when they were children and went to visit Grandpa and Grandma Truedson. They would lay down straw mattresses, and they would all sleep in a row." The Truedsons were Elsie Mae's great-grandparents, who lived in Spring Garden, Featherstone Township. About the landscape, Elsie Mae said, "Oh, it's hilly and there is a little creek that runs through the farm area. There are patches of field and then there is pasture, and then there is a patch of wood, a little mixture of everything."

Her grandmother Kjersti, called Carrie in America, had long hair that she would put up in a pug on the back of her head. "Sometimes she would speak Swedish, especially if she wanted to be funny and didn't want us to understand. She always wore an apron. I can remember she always wore a kerchief and she called it a *klut*. Grandma was a great shopper. She'd go downtown and she'd check into the second-hand store, and it seemed like she was always trading the 'kitchen sink' for something new, and they weren't always new. Sometimes it was somebody else's that they had traded in, but it was something better than she had."

Elsie Mae went to grade school in Wisconsin. "My parents moved to Wisconsin to take care of my father's mother and father when I was six. I had just started school here in Red Wing when we moved out to the country." They lived near Hager City, Wisconsin. "Dad still worked in town and would come home weekends. It's only ten miles and we did have a car," Elsie Mae said. During the Depression, her father lost his job in Red Wing. Their 30-acre farm was not large enough to live on, so he worked for farmers with larger farms. In the wintertime, he cut wood for one farmer. The wages were 10 cents an hour and one meal. He would eat breakfast and supper at home. Mother always had a big garden and we had fruit trees and berries. We always had food. We had one or two cows, and one horse." Elsie Mae explained that they did not expect to get anything new except perhaps in the spring or in the fall before school started.

They grew potatoes, corn, and hay with the help of one horse. They didn't have much machinery, so they had to have somebody come and help with the harvest. "I remember the potato digging and the corn husking. We did most of that by hand. Mother always helped out. I remember working in the garden, picking the berries, helping with the canning. Mother always canned at least 50 quarts of sweet corn. And we always had our own potatoes and our own apples. We had a few pigs, so in the fall we butchered the pig. If it was cold we'd freeze the meat, because we didn't have refrigeration," Elsie Mae said.

Her mother made headcheese from the head of the hog. She would can some of the meat and then they would salt down the pork. Her mother would also make meatballs, and of course, the ham would be smoked. Sometimes, fishermen came around and sold carp from a bucket with ice, Elsie Mae said.

In the wintertime, Elsie Mae's dad did the shopping. "In the summertime, this little grocery had a truck and they came around and picked up the eggs and would bring groceries and you would call your order in the morning and they would bring it. In the fall they would buy 100 pounds of sugar to last through the winter. We lived out in the country. The car would be put up on blocks in November and you didn't drive that car until the snow went in the spring," Elsie Mae said.

When she was old enough to go to high school, she came back to Red Wing and worked for room and board while attending school. "There were some young folks, especially girls, who did light housekeeping. They had a room and would sweep and cook. I stayed with one family, and that's where I met my husband because he was working at the tannery here in Red Wing and lived there [with the same family]. I stayed my last two years with a different family," Elsie Mae said.

She was married before her parents moved back to Red Wing. Then the Sewer Pipe Company opened, so her dad could go back to work there. He received a small pension. It wasn't much more than forty dollars a month. "They bought my grandmother's home after Grandma died," she said. It was the big house that Gladys Eckholm described.

When the United States became involved in World War II, Elsie Mae's older brother volunteered for the Air Corps and her younger brother was drafted and served in the Navy in Europe and in the Pacific. The one who served in the Air Force was injured and died in Italy, but the younger brother came home after the war with Japan was over.

Elsie Mae worked as caterer and in a school cafeteria. "I worked for a lot of wedding receptions, and we made lots of fancy sandwiches and fruit breads. I also went into the homes, and the lady of the house had already prepared most of the food, so I came in at the last minute to make the gravy and serve the dinner and wash the dishes," Elsie Mae said. She still has her mother's sprits maker and meat grinder.

"My husband liked coffee, and my mother always liked afternoon coffee, so as long she lived with us, we always had afternoon coffee when my husband came home from work," Elsie Mae said, adding that they had *skorpor* (rusks) with their coffee. Her husband, Robert, was an engineer at the tannery. He died in 1974.

Elsie Mae's mother never corresponded with relatives in Sweden, but Aunt Lillian (her mother's older sister), did. "After we had the reunion up north a year ago, I think my daughter was really intrigued with going to Sweden to visit these folks who were there from Sweden. There were ten people that came from Sweden." Elsie Mae said, and explained the relationship. "My mother's father was Nels Anderson here, and he would be listed as Nils Åkesson over there. He took the name of Anderson." The Åkessons were from Västra Vemmenhög in Skåne. In 1974, Elsie Mae, her husband, Robert, and two of their children went to Germany to visit her husband's sister's family, but they did not go to Sweden. The interviewer was Lilly Setterdahl.

- Elsie Mae Lersch was born July 23, 1916 in Red Wing, the daughter of Louis Larson and Mae Anderson. Mae, b. June 13, 1899 in Hallock, was the daughter of Kjersti Truedson, b. Sep. 9, 1866 in Trolle Ljungby, married to Nels Anderson, b. in Östra Vemmenhög, Skåne. They were the parents of Gladys Eckholm, who was also interviewed. Kjersti arrived in 1869 together with her parents Åbo Pehr Truedson, b. 1842 in Trolle Ljungby and Margareta Pehrsdotter, b. 1846, and brother Nils, b. 1859. Six more children were born in Featherstone Township: Lina in 1872, Theodor in 1877, Arthur Sigfrid in 1880, Eric Wendel in 1881, and Hilma in 1885. Elsie Mae had two brothers and four children. She married Robert Lersch of German heritage. In 2008, Elsie Mae lived in Red Wing.

Nelson, Everal

His ancestors lived at the Trollasten Farm

September 17, 1993

Everal Nelson

Everal said that his great-grandfather (Nils Pehrson) rented the Trollasten Farm (Magletorp) from the Count of Trolle Ljungby, and that his portrait can be found in a framed picture together with some 90 other tenant farmers photographed in 1892. Being interested in his heritage, Everal learned to read Swedish late in life. He thought one of the reasons his grandfather Jöns Nelson emigrated was that he had married out of his class. *"Han var dräng* (He was a farmhand), but his wife was of higher rank, so it didn't go very good. [Her name was Hemmelin.] My grandfather's father was a small businessman in Nymö. He made cigars and he installed and probably built pipe organs in the churches around there. They [Jöns and Elna Nilson] traveled via England, probably to New York. They came here by train. We already had a railroad in Red Wing. They stayed with somebody else they knew. Their name was

Johnson, and it was in the Welch valley not too far from the river [Cannon River]. They stayed the first winter with them and they had a little house, a little attic up overhead. They climbed up on a ladder and that's where they stayed with their children the first year they were here," Everal said. Asked about the first farm buildings, he said, "They were very low barns usually, not very high, and had just dirt floors in them."

"When I was born in 1914, they [the grandparents Nelson] purchased the first farm they owned. The oldest boy never married and he worked at the Red Wing Pottery and they got together enough money to purchase a farm, not very far from here," Everal said. Later, when the state had bought the property for a school for delinquent boys, the Nelsons purchased the farm in Welch. It was a large farm on top of the hills from Cannon River.

"The big drawback was there was no well on the place. A great many of the immigrants at that time drank water out of the cistern and that's what they used for drinking water, but that wasn't enough water to supply their cattle, so every day, they had to drive the cattle down to the Cannon River, which was a long steep drive into the valley, and in the wintertime, they had to cut a hole in the ice so that the cattle could drink," Everal said.

At one time the sheriff came out and put a padlock on the granary so they wouldn't sell the grain. "They had it mortgaged, I suppose," Everal said. They stayed on the farm until they were quite old and then moved in with a daughter in Red Wing. Jöns Nelson died in 1938 when he was 92 years old. He had nine children (See also interview with Mildred Peterson).

"Only Swedish people lived around here. There was a lot of noise in that house with all of them talking *Skånesvensk* [Scanian Swedish] all at the same time," Everal said. He recalled visiting his grandparents Nelson as a child. When his dad started school, he didn't know any English. "But they had a rule in school that they had to talk English even on the school grounds and they had some penalty for them if they didn't use English, so they had to use English right away then. After that time, my father really never used Swedish," Everal said. Therefore, he was surprised that his dad could speak Swedish when the two of them visited Sweden in 1973. "We left on this 80th birthday, so we were in Stockholm riding on the bus and a lady started to talk to my father. My father answered her in Swedish, and the lady said, *'Du är från Skåne.'* [You are from Skåne.] And his Swedish came back to him," Everal said.

He rented a car in Stockholm and they drove down to Skåne. Thanks to that trip, and Everal's research, the family knows where the ancestral place is located in Trolle Ljungby. It was farmed by a distant relative. "They lived right there at Trollasten farm," Everal said. Since then a descendant of Jöns Nelson's sister has also been to Sweden and become acquainted with relatives and places over there (See interview with Betty Jane Withers).

Growing up in a Swedish-Norwegian home, Everal noticed that his father would not eat *lefse* and that he wanted a white sauce with his *lutfisk* instead of the melted butter, which was the Norwegian way. Everal's parents were farmers. As soon as Everal was old enough, he struck out on his own. At first he worked for farmers in the neighborhood. Between 1930 and 1935, he clerked in a grocery store in Vasa and learned enough Swedish so he could wait on the Swedish-speaking customers. "We had a number of Swedish families that didn't talk English at that time," Everal explained. It was during the Depression, and Everal was paid only 30 dollars a month, plus room and board. After that he got a job at the Shoe Factory, where he earned twelve dollars a week for 40 hours of work. In 1946, he started to work for the Northern States Power Company as a mechanic, taking care of trucks, cars, and machinery. "I worked for them for 31 years. That was a very, very good job," he said.

Everal belonged to the Swedish Singers in Red Wing, organized in the Bicentennial year of 1976. The singing club had between 40 and 50 members. He also belonged to a small Swedish group of about ten to twelve people who studied Swedish twice a month. The interviewer was Lennart Setterdahl.

> Everal Nelson was born July 28, 1914 in Red Wing, the son of Philip Nelson, b. 1886 or 1887 in Welch and Anna Eidem b. 1894 in Wisconsin. Philip was the son of Jöns Nelson b. 1846 in Trolle Ljungby and his wife Elna Hamline, b. 1852, also in Trolle Ljungby. Jöns was the son of åbo Nils Pehrsson and his wife Lena Jönsdotter, V. Ljungby 4. Jöns and Elna emigrated from Nymö in 1875 with two children, both born in Trolle Ljungby, August in 1871 and Anna

Maria in 1874. The children born in Welch were; Selma in 1876, Nils William in 1879, Oscar Emil in 1881, Hulda Angelina in 1884, and Manfred Philip in 1886. Everal had two sons and one daughter from a previous marriage. Everal Nelson passed way Mar. 10, 2005 in Red Wing.

Nelson, Harriet

Her father could play any instrument there was

September 9, 1992

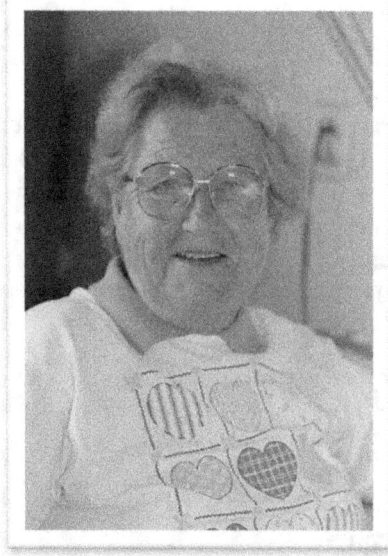

Harriet Nelson

Harriet's father Clarence played in the old river cornet band in Hallock. "He was very musical. Then they had the new Red River Cornet Band, and my dad was the band leader," Harriet said.

Reminiscing about farming in the Hallock area, Harriet said they grew wheat, rye, barley, and potatoes, but no corn. "The hay was raked and shocked by hand with a pitchfork. I even remember that they used to have some of these old wooden rakes, and they'd rake it in a pile. Many of the farmers in the Red River area hauled the grain to North Dakota. They would take it over on the ferry with the wagons and two horses and some with four. The grain was hauled to Bismarck, North Dakota. I think the prices probably were better there. A lot of other horses and buggies were going across and they had to pay, sometimes ten cents for one horse and buggy and sometimes 15 cents for two horses, and 25 cents for a load of grain, but when they'd take the threshing machine, why it came to around two dollars. They would go back and forth by ferry across the river," she said, adding that quite a few Swedish people moved to North Dakota. Harried recalled the large threshing crews that had big engines, separators, bundle teams, and sometimes a cook car.

Clarence Truedson worked as a mail carrier for a while before buying a farm in Hallock. "Then the Depression came, so he lost the farm and that's when they decided to move to Red Wing," Harriet said. In Red Wing, he worked at the Tannery until he retired.

About her mother, Harriet said she was a very good seamstress. Her mother's sister, Hilma, also did sewing for the women at that time. "They spoke Swedish all the time, and my sister and brother could speak it. I could understand everything because I used to stay with the Ingemans. I went to first grade in the country school ... and I stayed with my grandmother and my uncles on the farm and went to first grade here," she said. Her parents had bought a place in Red Wing.

Harriet recalled some Swedish foods like *kalvdans, ostkaka, pölsa, palt*, and *lutfisk*. "They served everything so beautifully," she said. "First they would come with a tiny glass of wine with a real Swedish tiny cookie or else a little hard piece of candy with it." Harriet was also familiar with *kaffehalv*, which she called *snaps*. Midsummer was celebrated with picnics. Christmas ended with *Tjugondedag* Knut, the last day of Christmas (the 20th day). "We'd always kind of celebrate that," she said.

The Swedes liked to settle together out in the countryside, she said. "They used to try and settle pretty close to where there was a river or where there was water and transportation. There were an awful lot of Swedes that moved into Red Wing, and the people would go to town on Saturday nights or when the stores were open, and they'd always be standing and talking Swedish," she said.

Many moved to Red Wing upon retirement, but Harriet believed that new immigrants from Sweden also settled there. She had a written family story that traced the immigrants back to Sweden. Harriet and her husband traveled widely, but the only place they visited in Sweden was Stockholm and that was only for a couple of hours. The interviewer was Lilly Setterdahl.

> Harriet Nelson was born Jan. 13, 1918 in Hallock, Minn., the daughter of Clarence Julius Truedson, b. June 3, 1882 in Welch, and Ida Ingeman, b. Oct. 3, 1881 in Vasa. Clarence was the son of Nils Truedson, b. 1844 in Trolle Ljungby, who emigrated in 1869 and

Nilla Månsdotter b. 1856 in Trolle Ljungby, emigrating in 1871. They moved to Hallock in 1892. Nils and Nellie had three children: Theodore Wilhelm b. 1875 in Welch, Hilma Maria b. 1878 in Svea, Wisc., and Clarence Jules b. 1882 in Welch. Harriet's parents moved to Red Wing when she was five years old. She married Earl Nelson and lived in Goodhue. She had three children from a previous marriage. Nellie Harriet Peper Nelson passed away June 23, 2009 in Minnesota at the age of 91.

Nelson, Lawrence

They got three cents a dozen for the eggs

October 5, 1992

Lawrence Nelson.

Lawrence talked about the 'good old days' when it was difficult to make ends meet, but they had more fun. He remembered his Swedish-born grandparents. "I think my grandmother could talk a little English, but my grandfather couldn't talk English at all. We talked Swedish. My dad didn't talk Swedish too much, but when I was with my grandfather, I used to talk Swedish quite a bit," he said. Lawrence was baptized and confirmed in the Cannon River Lutheran Church. "I was confirmed in Swedish. I could talk Swedish, but when I married a German I forgot all about the Swedish," he said.

The 1880 Federal Census shows that Lawrence's grandfather, Per Nelson, worked as a farm laborer for Lewis (Lars) Johnson in Vasa, who was also from Trolle Ljungby. According to the plat book for 1894, Per owned 40 acres in Section 28 in Welch Township. In 1910, he owned the farm mortgage-free.

"Father died when I was pretty young. I think I was only 15," Lawrence said. The father was 43 years old when he died of cancer. After that tragic event, Lawrence and his brother Arthur, 17, took care of the farm. The hills didn't bother them. They didn't plow up and down, but along the hills. "It's easier on the horses. We had droughts. They were bad years," he said.

Lawrence started to farm on his own in 1928. He inherited the farm, so he didn't have to take out a mortgage. "We didn't need much money. We got along. Winter wheat was a good crop. I hit the worst part of it. We sold eggs at three cents a dozen. You bought groceries for it. Eggs were for groceries," he said. They had between 100 and 150 chickens that ran wild.

During the Depression the milk prices went down to two dollars per hundred pounds. A bushel of corn was 15 cents. "In them days, they cut most of the corn and fed it to the cattle, and the pigs. I spent most of my time along that creek, fishing trout. I liked to hunt too. I did a lot of hunting in my days, some ducks and squirrels and rabbits, and pheasants for a while. I was deer hunting. There were lots of deer around here," he said.

About the time the farmers were supposed to burn the little pigs to get better prices, Lawrence said, "It did not seem right. All the people were hungry and then take all of them pigs out and burn them up!" He admitted that Roosevelt did some good, "but they didn't have to keep it up. Look where we are now. In ten or 15 years, our country is going to go bankrupt. If they get more money, they spend more money. They don't care about the debt," he said.

Lawrence's son farmed part of the land at the time of the interview, and rented out the rest. He also sold crop insurance. "You could make a living on 160 [acres] if you wanted to do it, if you aren't going to have expensive machinery. A combine costs close to $100,000. It was more fun in the old days. They had threshing machines, and the neighbors used to go together and thresh from one farm to another, six to eight farmers went together. We worked more than they do now. Now everybody is by himself. It was more fun when you were a little more social years ago. Sometimes, they would walk a couple of miles to get together for a drink. They were all Swedish around Welch. That was a Swedish town for quite a few miles," Lawrence said. His dad used to walk to the town of Welch to get his mail. There was no delivery service until Lawrence was about five or six years old. "We didn't have any light out here before 1960. They could have had electricity earlier, but the farmers thought it was too expensive," he said.

Lawrence wasn't interested in politics, but he served on the school board for a couple of years. He also served on the church council. "I never was a trustee, but I was a deacon for a while," he said.

About the changes that had taken place since he was young, he said, "It's been an awful change in my lifetime. It wasn't even a car on the road when I was born. I think the first car was about 1910 or 11. If they needed a doctor they took the horse and drove for him. When the river was frozen, it was only between six and seven miles to Vasa, but it did not always freeze. It was running fast," he said.

Asked about what he thought of the future, he said, "You know as well as I do, how it's going downhill." The interviewer was Lennart Setterdahl.

> Lawrence Nelson was born May 5, 1901 in Welch, the son of Andrew Nelson, b. 1873, and Anna Johnson, born in Halland. Andrew was the son of Bengta Larson, b. 1847 in Trolle Ljungby, and Per Nilson, b. 1847 in Hörröd. They arrived in 1879 with two sons, Anders (Andrew), b. 1873, and Nils, b. 1875. Four more children were born in Welch, Ola in 1880, Alice Amelia in 1883, William David in 1885, and Manfred Emanuel in 1888. Lawrence was married twice, both times to women of German ancestry. He had two sons and one daughter. Lawrence Nelson passed away Apr. 19, 1995 in Goodhue County.

Nelson, Lola

She had to work like a hired man

December 2, 1992

There was a shortage of men in Lola's family, so she had to do men's work. Both of Lola's grandparents on her father's side were from Trolle Ljungby. Per and Bengta Weberg settled at first in Spring Garden. Despite many hardships they persevered. Four of their children died in 1892, but eventually they had five more that lived.

Lola Nelson

In the Federal Census for 1880, Weberg is listed as a farmer in Welch Township. In 1900, he worked as day laborer in Cannon Falls Township. In 1895, the family lived in Vasa with P. J. Weberg listed as farmer. The plat books for 1894 and 1914 show that a Weberg owned about 108 acres in Section 18 of Vasa Township. In 1910, Christ Weberg, Lola's father, was listed as a farm renter in Cannon Falls Township.

When asked about her aunts and uncles, Lola began to talk about Aunt Augusta. "She was the one that moved around a lot after she was married. She married a man by the name of Fleming Smith from Pennsylvania, and they had one son. I have cards here and the postmarks are from all around the United States. I have no idea what they were doing traveling around the country. Aunt Della married a farmer, and they lived maybe five miles southeast of here. His name was Edward Haines. Nettie married a policeman from Montana by the name of Smothers, and they lived in Cannon Falls." About the youngest, John, named after the oldest who died, Lola said he lived in St. Paul. Lola didn't believe that anyone of them attended high school.

Lola had no memory of her grandfather Weberg as he died before she was born. She was six-years old when her grandmother died. Grandma Weberg had a house in Cannon Falls. "My mother told me that my great-grandfather had a brewery over there [in Sweden] some place and this was a sore spot with them.... I guess they didn't approve of it. No one pursued the history of it," Lola said.

Lola's parents were farmers. When she was about five years old, her family moved from Cannon Falls to a dairy farm just outside town. Her father always rented farms and did not own them. Her parents used to get up at 3:30 in the morning to get the cows milked. "He didn't have a tractor. He always farmed with horses. When my brothers left home I graduated to hired man. I milked cows, up at 5 o'clock in the morning.

I helped him plant corn. I helped him hay, and that was with the fork and driving the horses. There were a lot of long hours," she said. Her father delivered cream in half-pint bottles, coffee cream, milk, chocolate milk, and he disinfected the bottles when they came back.

"We had a generator hooked up to the windmill because my dad had to have milking machines and there was no electricity on that farm when we moved there." She said she studied by a lantern. "Then he got this generator so then we had electricity in the house, just one bare ceiling bulb, but that was really something. You'd push a button, and you had light!" It was a gasoline engine. But on the smaller farms, her father did not have a generator, so she had to milk the cows by hand, which she hated.

Lola recalled the sausage making and sometimes they smoked hams. They would cut the Christmas tree from the pasture. "We always celebrated *Tjugondedag Knut* [the 20th day of Christmas]. Some of the relatives would come and we'd have the last *lutfisk* supper. My father was a great one for *lutefisk* [Norwegian spelling], and that was always served on Christmas Eve, New Year's Eve, and *Tjugondedag Knut*. Santa Claus came on Christmas Eve. It was usually one of my older brothers. And we had sleigh bells for the horses, of course. One of them would go down to the end of the driveway and then they would ring the bells as they came up, because my younger brother and I were a lot younger and they were going to make it fun for us. But we didn't get much in Christmas gifts. We probably would get something to wear and maybe there would be one toy or something. It was the Depression. There was no money to buy gifts with," Lola said.

"We had one of those old crank phones, you know, where 120 people were listening in on your conversation. If they didn't answer, they were listening for sure." Lola says that in 1955 when she moved to Vasa, they still had about 10 to 15 people on the party line. The family farmed in Hay Creek for a couple of years. The year Lola started high school her father had an auction and sold out. "They owned a home in Red Wing that they had bought before they left the countryside. Then he [her father] bought another three-apartment rental house, so they had the rents from that," Lola said. He also worked at the undertaker parlor, picking up bodies and doing janitor work.

In Red Wing the family joined a Baptist Church, "because we only lived a block and half from there," Lola said, explaining that it was good to live close the church, especially during the war when gasoline was rationed. Another reason for joining the Baptists was that they knew the pastor from the time he used to come and preach on the street corner in Cannon Falls. "They liked him so well they visited his church [in Hastings] once in awhile even though they were members of St. Ansgar [Lutheran Church]. The young people had a very active society. I didn't leave the Baptist Church until my second husband and I moved out here, and then I transferred my membership to the Lutheran Church," Lola said.

Asked whether she noticed any difference when she joined Vasa Lutheran Church, she said, "They were just totally different from what I grew up with. They were much more formal. They had a liturgy. They weren't lively, like the music we had in church." It took her about 15 years to be accepted. She recalled being at a sewing circle meeting at one of the neighbor ladies' homes at one time. "She said to me, 'Well, Lola, I think you finally belong.' And I had been in all the activities and served on the committees," Lola said.

Lola's mother was of Irish, English, and French descent, but learned from her mother-in-law how to prepare Swedish food for Christmas. She also joined the Lutheran Church. Lola's father died in 1958, but her mother lived until the age of 101 in 1991.

Speaking of the Depression, Lola said, "There wasn't any money. Everybody considered the farmers real lucky because they at least were able to eat. They had their gardens and they had their livestock, but it was a bad time. People living in town were worse off," she said.

When Lola went to school, she had one dress for school, one for in between, like Saturday night, and one for Sunday. "That's all you had. You didn't have a closet full of clothes as they have now," she said. Lola graduated from high school in 1943. She then worked at various jobs—at the shoe factory for 18 cents an hour, for an advertising company, clerked in the Ben Franklin store, and worked in the art department at the pottery, hand-painting the dishes. After she had worked for several years at the pottery, she earned 28 cents an hour. It was not difficult getting a job. "Pearl Harbor had happened, and the shoe factory was making army boots and shoes for servicemen," Lola said.

After she had married her first husband, they lived in St. Paul for a short time before coming back to Red Wing, where they took care of the Isaac Walton League House, a wildlife club, down by the river. "We could get the house rent-free and Lee worked at the Swanson Hardware besides, and I think I remember that he was getting maybe 20 dollars a week," Lola said.

Her second husband, Merle Nelson, served in the Navy for six years. Having returned home, he began to work at the tannery and worked there for 35 years and farmed at the same time. "We only had 68 acres on this place. There was no land on it for farming. It's mostly pasture. That's why he could have the job at the tannery. We did have some cattle the first years we lived here. While the kids were growing up we had cattle, and we had sheep and we had some chickens. You needed to have a little something to supplement your income because wages still weren't real great," Lola said.

She started the Weberg reunions in 1969 as described by Virginia Fanslow. Paul Smith, the son of Lola's Aunt Augusta, went to Sweden a few years ago to try to find relatives and trace the ancestry, but was unsuccessful, because the old records had been moved. At the time of the interview, Lola lived on the farm in Vasa. The interviewer was Lennart Setterdahl.

> Lola Nelson was born July 1, 1925 in Cannon Falls, the daughter of Christ Weberg (1885-1958) baptized Peter Palmquist, and called Quist as a child, and Denise Campbell. Weberg was the son of Peter Wiberg (Åbo Per Jönsson), b. 1845 in Trolle Ljungby and his wife Bengta Westeson, b. 1850 also in Trolle Ljungby. They arrived in 1869. Four of their children were born in Spring Garden: John (1872-1892), Anette (Smothers) b. 1873, Hilda (Peterson) b. 1875, Emma (1877-1892). The other children were born in Welch: Augusta in 1879, Maria (died in 1892), Quist or Christ b. 1885, George Sigfried (1887-1892), Delia b. 1890, and John b. 1892. Lola's second husband, Merle Warren Nelson, also a Trolle Ljungby descendant, died in 1989. Lola had two children, one son, and one daughter, with her first husband from whom she was divorced. Lola Nelson passed away July 1, 2010 in Goodhue County, Minnesota.

Nelson, Norris

They dug into the hillside the first winter

April 20, 1993

Norris Nelson was a Trolle Ljungby descendant on both his mother's and father's side. His grandparents Nelson settled in Section 32 in Welch Township. His father told him they had a dugout in the hillside and then they built a house on top of the hill. Norris said they had 80 acres in one place and 20 acres in another, apparently in different sections. He recalled the prank of walking out on the bluff and rolling stones down the railroad track. "We'd get a stone rolling, and it hit a bigger one, and it rolled down the railroad track. Then the section man had to come out and roll the stones off the railroad track before the train would come in the morning, he said.

Norris Nelson

When the Nelson boys were grown, they were tired of the hills, so they moved down to Stanton and rented a farm, which they later purchased. "My grandmother, Alma, Ed, my dad, and Richard moved out here and farmed all this land in the Stanton flats. Before that, it was mostly sheep farmers here. Then my dad decided he'd go into general merchandising business in Stanton, and he became the postmaster up there [In about 1906]. Then they split up the farm. Uncle Ed took the farm south of the township road. My dad took this farm and some of the buildings and moved them here. They paid off my Uncle Richard, and he went over the hill and bought a farm. The other three brothers moved to Cannon Falls. They farmed for about three years. When they had saved enough money, they bought a house in Cannon Falls," Norris said.

The farm in Welch was sold to the daughter Emma and her husband, John Hagberg. "It must have been a good place to raise that many children. They had an apple orchard. But now you go there, it's so thick with cedar trees, you can't even get out there by crawling underneath the cedar trees," he said.

Norris explained that reforestation has taken place. "Back in the early days when the Indians had control of the country, the fires would get started and they just burned this area all off, so there was no trees or anything. It's just prairie, even the hillsides up here, no trees. But when the settlers came and built roads, stopped the fires, and plowed up the grass, the trees started growing on the hillside. The wildlife has also come back," he said.

About the soil, Norris said there had been much erosion in some places. "I can remember being out at my cousins, the Prinks out east of Cannon Falls—there was some top soil still left on top of those hills, but now today, with row-crop farming and so forth, it's all clay. You can see it by just driving. It's kind of a brownish color. But here we don't have much of any erosion. It's all flat here. They say it used to be a lake here, many, many hundred years ago," Norris said.

"We have about 12 inches of top soil and about 30 inches of clay and 60 feet of gravel underneath here. That's why these big seed corn companies like this area. There is a four million or five-million dollar research center over here, Northrop King, and we have another down the road here, Holden Foundation Seeds out of Iowa. We hardly ever had a crop failure until about three years ago, in about '88 we didn't get any rain whatsoever," he said.

Diverting to his own childhood, Norris said, "We played with anything. We'd make our own ski slides." He explained that since the land was flat, they made their own hills from banana crates. "When they were about 25-30 feet high, the kids waited for the snow to drift over the crates. They also went ice skating on the creek. "We had a lot of fun," he said.

When Norris attended Cannon Falls High School he boarded with relatives in the wintertime and drove with some other students when the weather allowed. Having graduated from high school, Norris continued his education at St. Olaf College in Northfield commuting from home. He studied as much mathematics, chemistry, zoology, and botany he could. He related how he earned money to pay his tuition. "It was kind of tough in those days to get money to get to college. It was only $75.00 we had to pay for a semester, so I had about half an acre carrots on the farm here that I raised, and we put them down in the basement in the store buildings and covered them up with sand, and then I'd dig up a few sacks of those once in a while, and when the treasurer over at St. Olaf College wanted some money, I'd bring them down to the cafeteria and that would help me pay for my tuition," Norris said.

Having graduated from college in 1940, Norris obtained a job at Mayo Clinic as research technician. He made only 80 dollars a month, so when the Lockheed Aircraft Company needed workers, he signed up with them and went to California to work. During the Second World War, Norris served as a radio operator aboard a ship. His service took him around the globe. He mentioned places in South America, Africa, China, India, Europe, and the Azores. He served for five years and never had a furlough. "But I didn't want to take the chance either. I was afraid to lose the outfit I was assigned to," he said.

After the war he built the house in Stanton in which he still lived at the time of the interview, and worked as an electrician in various places, and then married in 1948 and settled down on the farm. His wife was born in New Jersey and had no farm background. She said, "I grew up in a cemented backyard in New Jersey. We didn't even have a garden."

Norris kept dairy cows from the beginning and a few chickens. He bought a tractor on credit. After a few years, his knees began to trouble him, a common problem among dairy farmers. "The milk machines were bumping me in the legs all the time, so then I decided to build a milking parlor so I could stand up and milk the cows," he said. With that and other improvements, the expenses got so high that he had to have more cows, which in turn made it necessary to hire help. Norris said that with all the paperwork and insurance he had to pay, it wasn't worth it. He sold the cattle in 1990.

His wife worked as a nurse for several years. Finally, she retired and stayed home and raised calves. Her husband said, "We had to fill out an I-9 even for kids that she had slapped on the hind end when they were born. When you get only two dollars a bushel for corn and five dollars for the soybeans, it doesn't pay," Norris said. He got more for the corn when he started out than he was getting 42 years later.

Norris was related to Ted Norelius on his mother's side. The Youngberg side of the family have reunions he said, but not for the last two years. The Interviewer was Lennart Setterdahl.

> Norris Nelson was born Dec. 3, 1916 in Stanton, the son of Henry William Nelson, b. 1874 in Welch and Amelia, nee Youngberg. Henry was the son of Andrew Nelson, b. 1832 in Trolle Ljungby, who emigrated in 1865, and his wife Lisa Sara Håkansdotter, b. 1839 in Ivetofta. Amelia was the daughter of Nils Youngberg, b. 1870 in Trolle Ljungby. For more information about the Andrew Nelson family, see the interview with Helen Fredrickson, who is related to Norris Nelson. Norris married Kate Maria Zimmerman, b. 1921 in New Jersey. They had one son and one daughter. Norris Nelson passed away Aug. 8, 2010 in Cannon Falls.

Nelson, Sharon and Janet Larson

It was definitely hard work

April 17, 1993

Sharon Nelson

Janet Larson

Sharon and her sister Janet used to help their mother with the milking of 14 cows before they went to school in the morning. The family farm was located in Section 12, Vasa Township. Their father was not well, so their mother went back to school to get a 4-year degree to become a teacher. She then taught sixth grade in Burnside. One brother attended school for the deaf in the Twin Cities nine months of the year.

"It was definitely hard work," Janet said. "All of us had to help. Our mother went back to teaching school when my younger brother was only four. Father's health wasn't what it should have been, so he was limited as to how much physical labor he could do. The two older boys helped out with the field work, and Sharon and I ended helping out with the work around the barn. We milked cows. We took care of the pigs. We took care of the horses, the chickens, everything, all the livestock that was there. Mom and Sharon and I would get up and do a lot of the in-barn chores, and the boys were in charge of the field work."

Sharon added, "There was the old hand method of cleaning the barn, which we girls had to help with, too."

Both girls started their schooling in the one-room schoolhouse in Vasa. Janet was in the second grade when the schools consolidated. Sharon said their brother Lyle went directly from the country school to Red Wing High School. At the time of the interview, Lyle lived in Galesburg, Illinois, where he was the director of the head-start program for the schools. He and his wife also had a bed & breakfast establishment in Galesburg.

Sharon, the oldest of the sisters, barely remembered her grandparents Nels and Adelina. "They lived on Highway 19 east of Vasa on the original homestead in the Småland Ward. The farm place burned down," she said. Both sisters remembered their uncle and aunt, Virgil and Virginia, who were twins. Virginia was a teacher. She taught in California. They lived in California during the school year and in Vasa in the summertime. When asked, "Why California," Sharon answered, "Because that's where the good salaries were for teachers at the time. Virginia's husband had a farm accident before they were married and lost one arm, so she was basically the breadwinner. He would still farm. He would come back early and farm some land that they had. They lived here when the children were little. They went out to Battle Creek, Michigan, for a couple of years to teach. Their daughter also moved all over the country. Right now she lives in Naperville, Illinois," Sharon said. Virginia's twin brother Virgil was the father of

Donley Lamberg, who was also interviewed. Donley had contacts with relatives in Sweden.

Both Janet and Sharon went to college and became teachers. Sharon's first teaching job was in Vanamingo Township, which was primarily populated by Norwegians. She noticed the Norwegian heritage where she was teaching. It was as noticeable as the Swedish heritage in Spring Garden where she lived. She was the secretary at the Spring Garden Lutheran Church, her home church.

Sharon married Tom Nelson, a progressive farmer of non-Scandinavian heritage. The Nelsons owned 200 acres of the 1,000 acres they farmed in Leon Township. They needed to rent 800 acres to make a profit, Sharon said. Having discontinued their dairy production, they grew corn and soybeans that they sold. They had eight tractors, and during the busy season, Sharon drove one of them.

Janet and her husband, Merle Larson of Swedish and Norwegian background, raised Arabian horses on a ten-acre tract. Janet taught school in the Cannon Falls school district. The school children were of mixed heritage, she said.

Neither sister prepared *lutfisk*. They always went to the Edgewood Restaurant to eat it at Christmas time. The interviewer was Lilly Setterdahl.

> Sharon Nelson was born Feb. 11, 1942 in Vasa, the daughter of Arnold Johnson, b. Aug. 24, 1905 in Vasa and his wife Nina Lamberg, b. Feb. 5, 1908 in Vasa. Nina was the daughter of Nels Lamberg, b. 1874 in Trolle Ljungby, the son of Anders Lamberg and his wife Anna, who emigrated from Trolle Ljungby in 1880 with their children born in Trolle Ljungby: Nils, b. 1874, Jöns (1874-1890), Hilda (1879-1890). Two more children were born in Vasa, Emil in 1880, and Otto Arthur Sigrid (1885-1910). Sharon married Tom Nelson and at the time of the interview they were farmers in Spring Garden, Leon Township. They had no children, but Sharon's sister Janet had three children. She lived in Cannon Falls with her husband Merle Larson.

Nelson, Sterling

He is still a *lutfisk* fan

December 3, 1992

The Swedish tradition that seems to have survived the longest is eating *lutfisk* at Christmas time. Sterling loved *lutfisk*. The families, especially on Sterling's mother's side, used to get together at Christmas. His grandmother Elna was born in Trolle Ljungby and his grandfather John G. Nelson was born in Oppmanna and emigrated from Ivö. They had eight children. One of them, Bennet, became Sterling's father. Elna apparently died before 1904. Sterling recalled that his step-grandmother lived on the home farm for a while. There were two houses on the farm on Highway 19, he said. Eventually, the farm was sold.

"My folks never talked much about Sweden. In fact, I can't even speak Swedish. The only time they'd talk Swede was when they didn't want

Sterling Nelson

us to understand something. We said the Swedish table prayer. That's the only Swede we ever learned. It was the same with all four children in the family," Sterling said. Asked whether his grandparents visited Sweden, he said, "They just never thought of going back there. But, of course, we were awful poor in this country too at that time, during the Great Depression, you know, and that was the prime time of their lives. It would have been impossible. There were very few that ever went back anyhow. They were so glad to get over here. They never said much about anything at all. They were just so satisfied to be here, and we never could realize why until we went over there and saw how farming conditions were over there compared to what they are here," Sterling said. His great-grandparents Persson came from Tosteberga, along the sea, the only area in Trolle Ljungby which is rocky. "It was terribly rocky. No room for the younger generation to expand or anything like that. Around here, if you wanted to go farming, you can go out and buy land, but you couldn't really do that, it seemed like, over there," he said.

Sterling said that he was really surprised that the crops were as good as they were over there. They visited Skåne in the latter part of the summer when the crops were still in the field and Sterling noticed that farming around Ljungby was "pretty good."

Explaining that his grandparents started out farming in Lindstrom, Minnesota, Sterling said, "They were there for a few years, but the land wasn't very good up there either, so then they moved down this way—that was my grandfather's place on my dad's side. They settled there after they came from Lindstrom. The area was real sandy and that is why they have to have irrigation there, he said.

His father lived on the home farm for a while after he was married and his uncles bought their own farms. The eldest son went out to North Dakota. "They were offered land by the government out there. Up by Devil's Lake, it was dry. They had the government crop insurance and that's really what they lived on more than anything. The government must have supported them because the crops were so poor," said Sterling, who visited them several times. "It was pretty level, and in the wintertime when I was up there, we had a rope from the house to the barn because the wind and blizzard was that bad. You couldn't see the barn from the house. They had a few cattle." When his Uncle Willy visited Vasa, he used to say, 'How can you live on the small patches that you have?' They had big fields up there. You couldn't see the end. We had 15-20 acre fields, sometimes smaller than that. Pretty much like Sweden has," Sterling said.

In North Dakota, they grew wheat and it could look golden. "Then the hot wind would suck the thing right out of there and it would be all white," Sterling said. The relatives moved there in the 1920s and came back in the 1950s and bought a farm in Vasa. About his own experience of the Depression, Sterling said, "We were never hungry. We always had plenty to eat, nothing fancy, but we always had food. We had a garden and things like that." He said that people in town did not have enough food.

Sterling received all his formal education in a one-room school house in District 13. His wife went to high school and became a teacher. "They were a little better off than we were. We were really kind of poor. My sister is the only one that went to high school, and she stayed with my grandparents. I suppose we could have gone, but education didn't look like anything necessary at that time. School wasn't pushed then like it is now. As far as I'm concerned, I think I've done just as good as anybody that got an education. We've been to Europe nine times. And we went to China now this last fall," he said.

About his mother's parents, Sterling said, "When we butchered they came out and got meat and I imagine they got it at a pretty good price. It was two or three cents at that time. We butchered a beef and a pig. We made our own sausage and smoked it. We saved the blood from the pig, not from the beef. We would have what they called our blood pancakes and *blodpalt*. Oh, that was good with milk on in the frying pan. Oh, I can still taste it yet today," Sterling said.

Sterling was one of the few who could recall geese on the farm. "Yes, we had ducks and geese," he said. "We were pretty close to the river, so they would walk down to the river, or we'd chase them down to the river. We would clip their wings, of course. That was a good job for us to chase them down the river and let them swim for a while and come back again with them."

The children made their own fun, he said. They learned to swim in the river. "The neighbors would come down there with us. Now they don't know what their own fun is." In the wintertime, they used to go ice fishing on the Cannon River. "We got tubs of fish, carp and suckers, no game fish, smoked the fish, or fed it to the chickens," he said.

Before they had electricity on his father's farm, they had a 32-volt generator in the basement. An uncle wired the barn and the house. As long as Sterling could remember they had a phone. The wires were strung along the fence posts.

About politics, Sterling said, "They were never very politically minded as I remember it, but they were staunch Republicans. Since that I have changed. I'm pretty much a liberal. Well, the unions helped us out an awful lot. But then the unions got too strong, too," he said. His father was on the church board.

In 1944, Sterling was drafted. "I could have got out of it, but all the boys I knew was in the service, so I decided no more deferments." He took basic training in Little Rock, Arkansas, and was shipped out to the Philippine Islands. After the atomic bomb was dropped, his outfit went to Japan to take part in the occupation. "We went up into Hiroshima to clean up after the bomb was dropped. That was maybe a month after, but there was still a lot of stuff there." He also went to Nagasaki. In October 1946, he had served for about a year and a half and went home. All three brothers were in the Pacific during the war. "We survived it. There were quite a few killed from our area. One good real close friend of mine was killed. I went to school with the guy," Sterling said.

After the war, Sterling helped his dad on the farm for a while. They built a water supply tank, so they could have water in the barn. In 1947, Sterling married Grace Miller, also of Swedish descent. Having lived in Spring Green, Wisconsin, and in Red Wing for a while, they bought a farm in Vasa Township. They purchased 80 acres to begin with, and when a neighbor sold out, they bought another 90. "I paid $20,000 for that eighty and that was about 1970, just before farm prices really started to go up," he said. He raised beef cows and weaning pigs.

Sterling also worked in the tannery until retirement. The tannery employees have always been union organized, he said. A lot of the leather went to the Shoe Company in Red Wing. They also sold leather to the Florsheim Shoe Company and to the automobile industry. "We started out in '47 at 85 cents an hour, but we always worked more than 40 hours a week," he said. Saturdays they usually worked six hours getting time and half. "We started at 5 o'clock in the morning in the tannery, and got off at 2:30 and that was nine hours with half an hour break for noon and come home and do your chores," he said.

"I retired at 62 because we were far enough ahead. Got all five kids through the college and that was one of our main goals. They all got good jobs. One of the twin boys is interested in the Swedish heritage. They haven't been across the pond yet [overseas]. We drove to Alaska one time with a truck with a camper on. We've been to just about every state in the union, I guess," Sterling said.

The biggest thrill about visiting Sweden, said Sterling, was to hear the little children talk Swedish. We could understand a little Swedish. We went to some places where they were singing—Midsummer Day. There were some celebrations, and I really enjoyed that."

In Vasa they never had a maypole, only picnics at Midsummer. There was also a good picnic ground at the Belle Creek. "That's where we had Midsummer. We used to have the Training School band come out, and Andresen, the congressman, would come down there and speak."

Sterling's wife had good records of the family tree on both sides. The interviewer was Lennart Setterdahl.

> Sterling Nelson was born Apr. 11, 1924 in Cannon Falls, the son of Bennet Nelson, b. 1888 and Myrtle, nee Johnson. Bennet was the son of John G. Nelson and his wife Elna Person. Elna was born in 1854 in Trolle Ljungby, the daughter of Per Person of Tosteberga, Trolle Ljungby, who emigrated with his family in 1869. His first wife was Anna Svensdotter, b. 1831. Their children were: Nilla (1852-1881), Elna b. 1854, Nils b. 1856, Johanna b. 1859, Anna b. 1861, Christina b. 1863, and Per (Peter 1865-1920). Sterling enlisted Feb. 13, 1945. He married Grace Miller who was also of Swedish ancestry. They had four sons and one daughter and at the time of the interview they lived on their farm on Smoland Road in Vasa.

Olson, Janice

They didn't need all the things we need now

September 5, 1992

Janice Olson with family artifacts

Farming has never been easy on the hillsides north of the Cannon River, but Janice's grandparents wanted their own land and it was more important than comforts. "They did mixed farming, dairying and cattle, and crops. They didn't need all the things we need today. When Grandma and Grandpa came, her brother helped them buy the farm. It was way back in the pasture. They had a small house, and three of the children were born there. When we were little kids it was great fun to go there. There were wild plum trees. Dad always told about how Grandma canned plums. Anyhow, we would find broken dishes and broken pots and this was fun. There's a hollow in the ground where that house stood," Janice said.

As the family grew, that house became too small. "Then Grandpa bought this other place over here. It just seems to me it was a Hokenstrom they bought it from. My dad, Ed, and Sister Hattie were born in this place. There was a small room off from the kitchen and Dad always said Grandma slept in there, so she could be close to the kitchen stove and start it early in the morning. Then there was another large room and that was the living room, I suppose. Then they added on a living room and bedrooms upstairs. When my mother and dad were married, they added on to the house again," Janice said. The grandparents then lived upstairs.

They always spoke Swedish as long as the grandparents lived. "Grandma and Grandpa wouldn't talk English to us. When we would ask Grandma about Sweden, she told us how she stood on the ship and waved until she couldn't see them [the relatives] any more," Janice said.

"Grandma didn't want curly hair. She wanted straight hair. Grandma's was curly and she put sugar water on it to straighten it. They had open porches, and they would sit out there a lot. One of her expressions was, "*Gu' bevara mej.*" (God help me.) Grandma and Grandpa read the Bible faithfully. They knew what the text was going to be the next Sunday in church. They never went to church before they had studied the text. They attended the Swedish services. The minister had more than one church. I think he had three parishes, and we alternated with Prairie Island. We only had church every other Sunday [in the Cannon River Lutheran Church]. Welch would have it in the morning, and we would have it in the afternoon. Nowadays, people wouldn't go to church at 2:30 on a Sunday afternoon. The Germans lived next to the Swedes in Welch. The Norwegians went to the Swedish church," Janice said.

About intermarriages, Janice said, "I don't think there was a big reaction if it was just the nationality, but when it came to religious faith, I bet there was a big reaction."

Janice's grandparents were very superstitious and talked about ghosts. Her grandmother used to do a lot of knitting. They bought the wool from some Germans, who lived nearby and used to have sheep. Janice recalled the black-bordered cards that were sent out when her grandmother died. About the Christmas tradition, she said, "We had lutfisk every year for Christmas, and the grandchildren hated it. They'd hide it under the potatoes." On his birthday, her father wanted to be treated to *kaffekrans* (coffee bread shaped in the form of a wreath) rather than cake.

About the area, Janice said, "It's always been hilly and rocky. We wish the Swedes had settled some other place. We wish they had settled over at Northfield [where it's], real nice and level." One difference is that they have more deer now, she said. About the farm that their son now farms, she said, "It's a hilly farm and it's hard to make a living on it." He's a dairy farmer.

Having attended the country school up on the hill through the eighth grade, Janice went to high school and took one year of teacher's training in Red Wing. She taught school for about four years. Her first teaching position was in Hay Creek, where they had all the grades in one school room. When her mother died suddenly in 1942, Janice quit teaching and moved home to help her father on the farm. "It was hard. It was easier to teach. In those days the kids were nice. Oh, the children were darling. The worst they ever did was to chew gum in school. I stayed home for nine years before I was married," Janice said. They did all the slaughtering on the farm, even the big cattle, and that was the hardest thing she had to do—take care of the meat.

Janice married a neighbor, Donald Olson, and they farmed for 41 years before building a home for their retirement on a piece of the land. Her brother has the Wahlen farm, which had been in the family for more than 100 years at the time of the interview. The 1877 plat book shows that the 160-acre farm was located in Section 31. In the 1900 Federal Census, Ola Wallin (Swedish spelling) was listed as the owner of a mortgage-free farm.

Janice had many heirlooms from the Olson and the Anderson families. Her mother was an Anderson. Having found some quilting blocks with a star pattern that her mother had sewn together from olds scraps of aprons, Janice had it made into a quilt. She had two relatives who had visited Sweden. They have a family tree that shows the great-grandparents in Trolle Ljungby, Sweden, Janice said. The interviewer was Lilly Setterdahl.

> Janice Olson was born Feb. 1, 1918 in Welch, the daughter of Arthur and Florence Wahlen (nee Anderson), b. 1893. Arthur was the son of Ola Swenson, b. Nov. 27, 1847 in Trolle Ljungby and his wife, Pernilla Trulsdotter, b. Dec. 12, 1849 in Trolle Ljungby. They arrived in 1869. The following children were born to them in Welch: Katarina Lovisa in 1875, Oscar Sigfrid in 1877, Selma Emelia in 1879, Arthur Gottfrid in 1886, and Hattie Clarinda in 1889. (See interview with Mildred Schultz). Janice was married to Donald

Olson and they had one son and one daughter. Janice Olson passed away June 7, 2000 in Goodhue County, Minnesota.

Peterson, Mildred

Grandpa Nelson would pray and sing

September 18, 1992

Mildred Peterson

Mildred spoke mostly in Swedish during the interview. In her younger days she was a musician. Her husband had his own orchestra, and they traveled around the area to play at dances. He was a drummer, and she played the piano and the piano accordion. "We were lucky if we made seven dollars a night," she said. They were six members in the band. It was often two o'clock in the morning before they had packed up their instruments. If they had to travel far, it would be four or five o'clock in the morning before they were home. Mildred then had to fix a meal for them.

Before marrying she played her music mostly at home. "I played with my grandfather and my father because they both played the violin and they played harmony. I wish you could have heard them," Mildred said. "They had an organ. Grandpa bought an organ, and it was a real nice one, too, a pump organ. Grandpa Nelson didn't care if we had 50 people, he'd pray and he'd sing, do all kinds of things to entertain them," Mildred said.

Her grandparents farmed as long as they had the strength. "Then they came to the city and lived with my mom and dad. Food was all that my mother thought about. We had so much company. I remember baking four to five dozens of cookies, *pepparkakor* or what they call it, every Saturday," Mildred said. She recalled that the old people talked about ghosts. Where they lived in Sweden, they said there was a ghost, who was out plowing in the night, but her grandmother did not believe it.

Up to the fifth grade, Mildred took music lessons from the Catholic sisters. "And then after I was grown up, I played with some of the Catholic people that had children. They all seemed to know me. I did not play one instrument. I played everything they had me do. And on the xylophone, you play with hammers, and I learned to play with two fingers, and then the upper registers. I read music just like I would the ABCs," Mildred said.

"I didn't get married until I was 24 or 25, because they told me that I had tuberculosis. Do you know how old I am now? 93, I'm going to be 94 the 28th of March. And there is no sign of tuberculosis. And in those days the medication wasn't like it is today. I helped at home and I did what I had to do. I thought nothing of it. It was just a matter of things. Mother said I talked Swedish and English both, one was as good as the other," Mildred said. One time, when a neighbor boy put the water hose on her, she hollered, "If you don't understand English, I talk Swede to you." Another time, she told her mother, "I certainly don't understand Swedish." That was in reference to a Swedish family with young children, the Monsons, who lived next door for a while. Showing a picture of her mother, Mildred said, "Everybody just loved her. If I do have to say so, she was a wonderful person."

"I lived in St. Paul for a while, but I never liked any of those bigger cities," she said. Her husband started out as a shoe salesman in St. Paul. Then they moved to Red wing. "We had the home up on [the hill]. It is a little old-fashioned place. It's got a porch on it and it wasn't anything elaborate. It was just an ordinary plain home, but we took one wall out. I was handy at paperhanging and doing all kinds of fixing like that. I could do better with a hammer and saw and nails than my husband could even. If Vernon couldn't do it, I'd do it. Buy George! I took the wall out and the room was 18 feet long. That's how big my living room was. And I loved old-fashioned furniture. I didn't get rid of one thing. I have two china closets. I still got them, but they are in storage," she said. (Mildred was staying at a convalescent home at the time of the interview.)

At one time Mildred's propensity for handyman work resulted in an accident. She was working with a torch when it exploded. 'I don't know what happened to it, but it exploded in my hand, and it hurt me way down. It hurt the whole side on me, and it hurt in my chest. I can't explain it. I never even lit it. I just tossed it. And I thought I had to see how bad it was, and when I opened my hand, all I had was a hole. The flesh was all gone. It went through me. The electric shock went through me. The doctors said, they could not see how I lived," she said.

Her husband sold shoes during the day and played in the orchestra at night. The interviewer was Lilly Setterdahl.

> Mildred Peterson was born Mar. 28, 1899 in Red Wing, the daughter of Ernest Gotthard Englund, born in Sundsvall, and his wife Anna Maria Nelson, b. Apr. 1, 1874 in Trolle Ljungby. Anna Maria arrived in 1875 as an infant with her parents Jöns Nilson and Elna Maria Hamline, and one brother, August. Jöns's father rented the Trollasten farm in Trolle Ljungby. For more information, see the interview with Everal Nelson. Mildred married Vernon and was a widow at the time of the interview. Mildred Peterson passed away Nov. 17, 1996 in Red Wing.

Pladsen, Phyllis

Her great-grandmother was a "capitalist"

September 22, 1995

This interview was recorded after my first *Minnesota Swedes* manuscript was finished and has not been published until now.

Phyllis's grandmother, born in 1877 in Cannon Falls, did not carry on the Swedish traditions, but Phyllis has rekindled them by reading books and finding

Phyllis Pladsen

out how the Swedes celebrate Christmas Eve. She belonged to the American Swedish Institute in Minneapolis.

Her family did not like *lutfisk*, but they did like meatballs and rice pudding. She and her husband Vernon liked the Swedish sausage. Vernon, an engineer, was of Swedish-Norwegian and German heritage. They have two sons and one daughter, Glenn, Karen, and Eric. Eric had married that summer in 1995 in California, but the family had yet to meet his wife, the daughter of émigrés from Cuba. Glenn served six years in the Navy. While he was stationed in Spain and Scotland, he took a three-month leave one summer and traveled all over Norway and Sweden. After his service concluded, he traveled across Europe and Scandinavia for six months. Eric, a computer technician, also lived in California. The daughter Karen earned a Master's degree in textile arts from the University of Minnesota.

Phyllis said she was born out of wedlock. Her biological father was French Canadian, Scot, and English. Her stepfather was Bohemian, but his marriage to her mother was not a happy one, and Phyllis did not have a happy childhood. "I look back on it as an extremely lonely childhood. I didn't see my grandmother. My grandfather had died before I was born. I knew just one cousin on my mother's side. We were very poor and we moved from one part of the country to the other. I think I attended four different schools before I was even in high school, and I was the only child. The way the family circumstances were, I spent most of my time reading. Living in my imagination was the way I survived my childhood."

Phyllis said she started family research because there had been so many tragedies in her family. Her grandmother Emma was very erratic, and her great-grandmother Olu was probably difficult to live with since she divorced. Phyllis found a court case that Olu had filed against a neighbor because he had called her a scandalous name. When Olu and her husband Ole divorced, he transferred land to her. She sold that land and bought a house in Red Wing and evidently also a house in Brainerd. She was able to rent out those houses and support herself on that. In one census her occupation was listed as "capitalist." Toward the end of her life, Olu was committed to the State Hospital in Rochester. Phyllis thought she had Alzheimer disease. She was behaving in such a way she couldn't find her way in the neighborhood.

Phyllis said she had visited Sweden with her husband earlier in the summer of 1995. Lennart Olsson in Gualöv helped her with her research. He had found the tombstone for Ola Svenson and his wife Karna. "That's the only tombstone I know of in Sweden of my entire family," Phyllis said. There are no buildings left at their farm, Vestra Ljungby No. 4, but Lennart Olsson showed her where it had been located. She also got to see where her great-grandfather's sister Elsa, a schoolteacher, had lived, but that place was also gone.

On the day after the interview, Phyllis and her husband were headed for northern Minnesota. They were going to Grand Marais and Grand Portage by Lake Superior.

Phyllis has compiled a book with the English translation of old Swedish words that one may encounter when researching old parish records. The interviewer was Lilly Setterdahl.

> Phyllis's great-grandparents on her mother's side were Ole Daun and Olu Swenson, who emigrated in 1868 from Trolle Ljungby, where both were born, Ole in 1832 and Olu in 1840. Listed under Daun, Ola Peterson in my Minnesota Swedes, Volume II. The plat book for 1877 shows that they owned 40 acres in Cannon Falls Township, Section 33, but not in 1894. They had nine children, one of whom was Emma, who became Phyllis's grandmother. Emma's husband was from Värmskog, Värmland. Ole and Olu divorced in 1882 or 1883. Phyllis was born September 15, 1932 in Owatonna, Minnesota to Joseph William Larocque, born in Prairie Du Chein, Wisconsin, and Marie Elvira Anderson, in West Concord, Minnesota. The parents were not married, and Phyllis grew up with a stepfather. Phyllis died April 11, 2004 in Ramsey County, Minnesota.

Risberg, Arnold

When he was little he could speak more Swedish than English

October 14, 1992

Since Arnold was the only child in his family, he spent much of his time with adults, listening and learning from them. His first language was Swedish. All four of his grandparents were from Trolle Ljungby. Arnold's grandfather, *Jeppa* (John) Risberg, was a farm laborer in

Vasa Township. His children grew up in Vasa. Ola became a farmer in Welch Township.

Arnold described where the farm was located. "It was a little ways from the river. There is a place they call the Hidden Valley Campground, and that was the place where my grandparents lived at the time, and then they moved from there to here, the Upper Burnside. Just a little north of here, out on the road before you get to 19. There used to be farm there," Arnold said.

According to the records of Cannon River Lutheran Church, Ola and Betsey Risberg lived in Welch Township when their older children were born. The 1900 Federal Census lists Ola Risberg as a farmer of a mortgage-free farm in Burnside. In 1910, he was a general farmer in Vasa. "Down here below toward the river... is where my father said he plowed with a walking plow when he was younger. He grew up in that area. They lived pretty close to Red Wing for a while," Arnold said.

"My grandmother on my mother's side [Ellen Mattson] lived with us

Arnold Risberg and his daughter

all the time, so they had to speak Swedish. I could speak more Swedish than I could speak English when I started school, but I've kind of forgotten it now. I can understand some of it. I used to speak quite a bit. Of course, there was a mixture and blending of English and Swedish. Grandmother preferred to speak Swedish, but she could speak pretty good English too when she had to," Arnold said.

He remembered three of his grandparents, but not his grandfather on his mother's side (John E. Mattson) because he died in 1916. Arnold believed that Ola and Betsey Risberg sold their farm in 1923. They had an auction and then they moved to Red wing. Their daughter Ida moved in with them after her husband had died. They may also have been related to the Nelsons who were the parents of Emma Hagberg. One of the Betsey Nelson Risberg sisters married a Weberg, another member of the Trolle Ljungby group. One of Jeppa's sons, Albert, moved out to Big Sandy, Montana.

Recalling the Trulson Walberg family, also from Trolle Ljungby, Arnold said, "Swan Walberg married my grandmother Ellen's sister. John Walberg settled up around Webster, Wisconsin. He had about six or seven children." Arnold's mother corresponded with cousins in Sweden. One of them was Per Olsson in Rinkaby. Arnold thought that his mother had 36 cousins. "There was a whole bunch that was out in North Dakota, North and South Dakota, and then some in Chicago and even down in Florida, and in Michigan quite a few," he said.

Arnold also remembered Bengt Knutson from Trolle Ljungby. "He was about as old as my grandpa, but we'd see him. I wonder if there wasn't some relation or if it was just because they came from the same area in Sweden. Bengt had a farm between Cannon Falls and Northfield on Route 19 near Stanton. Anna Hokenstrom was a sister to my dad's mother. And then he, Weberg, married a Hokenstrom, so it's kind of a double relation," Arnold said. Andrew Nelson's children in Welch were familiar to Arnold. Edward Nelson and his wife were at the Risberg's the day Pearl Harbor was bombed, Arnold recalled.

Arnold grew up on a farm in Welch in the Cannon River area. "We farmed out there for quite a while until 1964. My mother died in 1963, and then we sold the places over there. We had two farms there. Some of the land touched the Cannon River. My father and I went fishing in the river pretty near every Sunday in the summertime when we didn't have anything else to do." Asked about winter sports, he said they used to go ice fishing and spearhead fish on the river when the ice was solid, but after the hydroelectric power plan was built, the river seldom froze, he said.

When Arnold moved to Wisconsin in 1964, his father moved with him. Arthur Risberg died in 1975. Arnold still lived on his farm in Wisconsin at the time of the interview, but rented out the land. He was one of the few descendants we have met who had heard of Trolle Ljungby. "I heard that when I was just a young child because they were always talking about it," he said. Since both sets of grandparents came from Trolle Ljungby, they had their birthplaces in common. "The story is that my ancestors, when they lived over there, used to park some of their machinery under the *trollasten....* It is a big stone there. We have a picture at home of the farm machinery parked by it. I learned a lot of things when I was younger because I didn't have any brothers and sisters. There was no television and not much radio when we grew up. I would stay with the older people and sit there and listen to them talking about all the old times and everything. I know a lot more about it than my cousins did because they didn't stick around so much and listened," Arnold said.

Asked whether most of the immigrants' children became farmers, Arnold said, "Some of them did, but not all." Arnold had a big selection of family photos. He had also looked up the ancestors' graves. For someone born in 1939, he had a remarkable recollection of what happened to the emigrants from Trolle Ljungby. The interviewer was Lennart Setterdahl.

> Arnold Risberg was born Apr. 1, 1929 in Red Wing, the son of Arthur Julius Risberg, b. 1889 in Welch and his wife Edna Adelia Mattson, b. 1889 in Welch. Both parents had roots in Trolle Ljungby. His father was the son of Ola Risberg, b. 1860 in Trolle Ljungby, and Betsey Nelson, b. 1856 in that parish. She was the sister of Jöns Nelson. Their children were: Ida Elenora b. 1886, Victor Cornelius b. 1887. Arthur Julius b. 1859, Edwin Emanuel b. 1891, Clarence Raymond b. 1896, and Frances Linnea b. 1899. The older children were born in Welch. Arnold's mother was the daughter of John E. Mattson, b. 1845 in Trolle Ljungby and Ellen Swenson, b. 1861 in the same parish. Ellen emigrated from Trolle Ljungby in 1880, and John E. may be identical with the farmhand Jöns Eriksson, b. Mar. 3, 1845, who emigrated from Trolle Ljungby in 1872. The Mattson children were: Edla Amanda, b. 1884 and Edna Adelia b. 1889, who emigrated from Trolle Ljungby in 1872. There may have been other

children. Arnold Risberg lived in Bay City, Wisconsin. He married Esther Villa Jakes, and they had three sons and one daughter.

Schultz, Mildred

One thousand Swedes were chased through the woods by one Norwegian

October 28, 1994

Mildred Schultz

This interview was recorded after my first Minnesota Swedes manuscript was finished and has not been published until now. I had searched for descendants of Bengt Knutson and was told that his daughter Hattie Swinton had settled in Charles City, Iowa. One day when my husband and I were on the way home from Minnesota, we took in at a motel in Charles City, and I began to call several people listed in the phonebook under the name of Swinton. On my sixth or seventh call, I was directed to Mildred Schultz, whose maiden name was Swinton. Her mother's name was Hattie. She said, "Come 'right over.'" Her son, Dick, was present during the interview.

Hattie had grown up in a Swedish-Norwegian neighborhood in Minnesota and was found of the saying, "One thousand Swedes were chased through the woods by one Norwegian." Mildred was the eldest of 14 children born to Hattie and Fred Swinton.

Her grandfather, Bengt Knutson was born in 1861 in Trolle Ljungby and emigrated from that parish as Bengt Persson in 1882 to Goodhue County. About him, Mildred said, "He was stocky-built, he wasn't a little man, but he wasn't fat either. I used to go up there in the summer and stay with Grandpa. He was not on the farm at that time, he lived in Cannon Falls. His house was on a hill and in those days you could have an animal on your lot. He had a little barn where he kept a cow that he milked. There was a wooded area where he'd take the cow, and

I'd walk with him. And there was a gate he'd open and that's where the cow would graze. Then he'd go and get it late in the afternoon and take it down to his little barn and milk it. They had a cellar door that opened from the floor in the living room, and Grandma used to put the milk in a crock in the basement. She used the cream for cooking and for coffee," Mildred said.

About her grandma (Bengta, born in Blekinge), Mildred said, "She was a sweet lady. I remember we'd go there and she'd have some summer sausage. We could only have one slice, because there were 14 of us, and they didn't have a lot of money. She made a lot of cottage cheese. She was a good cook." Mildred described how the cottage cheese was made. Her grandmother also made something she called "lip-dab" of milk, some eggs, and a thickening (*välling?*). "It was thin and we kids like that. We put sugar in it." She also made "grape pudding" of boiled grapes thickened with corn starch. For Christmas, a red coloring was added. This sounds like the Swedish *kräm*, but they called it pudding. Mildred said that Grandma Knutson talked about *lutefisk*, but never made it. Apparently, she never made any other typical Swedish Christmas food either.

Mildred's mother, Hattie Knutson, married a German-American and lived in a neighborhood settled by Germans. Mildred's son, Dick, said that Hattie had not learned to cook while growing up in Minnesota. When she tried to learn to bake, "more than one batch went out to the hogs. One chicken had to be enough for the whole family," Dick said.

Mildred grew up on a 240-acre dairy farm with Holstein cows. The children were born at home and delivered by a midwife. "Mama stayed in bed for 14 days after childbirth." They always had electricity, but at first it was generated from Delco batteries in the garage.

Mildred described her childhood: "We all had our jobs to do. I used to have to hang up the washing in the morning before I went to high school. Not every day, but when we washed. We girls had to peel the potatoes. Mama never worked outdoors. She never even worked in the garden. She was in the house. Dad had a hired man. Dad worked in the garden. Mama did the canning. We had a long table with chairs for everyone in the dining room. It was quite a big house. We all sat down together. We did not say grace. My father and mother didn't go to church regularly. Occasionally, they went. They belonged to the

Methodist Church in Nashua. We lived only three miles from Nashua, and that's where most of us graduated from high school. My dad bought a Chevy Coop and we drove to school. I remember how I learned to drive. A hired man taught us out in the field. The clothes we wore to school, we had to take off and put on older clothes. Mama never shopped. My dad would buy our clothes. We could pick out our dresses, and he paid for them. Mama never sewed. Dad took us to Shirley Temple movies in Nashua," Mildred said.

For fun they made little houses of sticks and twine and used orange crates for a pretend stove and davenport. Mama would give them old jar lids that they covered with mud for pretend-cakes. The boys would take corncobs and pretend they were animals. They played fox and geese, and one would be the fox and try to get the geese. They never got spanked, but had friends who got spankings and thought it was terrible. They lived in a four-bedroom house, three upstairs and one down, with a dining room, living room, a parlor with a fireplace, and a big kitchen with a back entrance. The bigger rooms upstairs had two beds. There was a register in the ceiling and that was the only heat upstairs. The children doubled up in the beds. They had a coal furnace in the basement. They had a bathtub, but no running water. They had a windmill and pumped up the water which had to be carried inside. Mother cooked on a woodstove and baked all the bread in the stove's oven. The stove had a reservoir for hot water.

Mildred said she took a lot of training in high school to prepare her for becoming a schoolteacher. After graduation, she was lucky to find a teaching job in 1938 that paid 40 dollars a month. She didn't know what she was going to do with all that money. She paid ten dollars for room and board with the family, but since she helped with housekeeping she only had to pay eight dollars a month. Her first purchase was a new coat for her mother. She was able to keep her teaching job after she married until her first child was born. When Dick was in fifth grade, Mildred applied to college and took her children with her to the University of Iowa at Cedar Falls. She said, "I'm not a brain, but I worked hard." She earned her degree in three years because she took classes during the summer. Her husband was a building contractor and paid for her education. She rented student housing, two small rooms with a kitchen, and drove home on week-ends. After her graduation, Mildred taught Math and Science in

Waterloo. She drove 100 miles back and forth every day until she retired.

Asked if anyone in the family ever visited Sweden, Mildred said that someone did. It might have been Muriel (a cousin?) or her daughter Judy. An article about the visit said they went to Rinkaby, where they located the grave where Bengt Knutson's father, Per Knutsson, was buried. They also went to Trolle Ljungby. They compared the castle farm to a southern plantation with a huge house and servant's quarters. They could understand why people had to leave with no land available and therefore no future. They also visited Mjellby in Blekinge where Betsey Knutson was born. The towns were located only five miles from the Baltic Sea, and described as quaint and the countryside as dotted with wooded areas.

Most of Mildred's 13 brothers and sisters lived in Iowa or other Midwestern states. They all got along, she said. At Christmas they gathered together in one of their homes. In the summertime, they had reunions in a rented building in Waverly and Hattie's 34 grandchildren were included.

Mildred's siblings were:

Harold, born in 1917, married Bernice Hurting from Dubuque (Their children were Dean, Wayne, and Jackie). **Doris**, born in 1919, raised adopted children, and lived in Emmetsburg. Her married name was White. **Willard**, born in 1920, was married but had no children. **Donald**, born in 1922, married Dorothy and they had children. **Bill** lived in Long Beach, Cal. **Dale**, born in 1923, was married. **Herbert**, born in 1924, was married. **Maurice**, born in 1925, married Alice and had one son, Michael. **Lois** lived in Waverly, Iowa (divorced). **Alfrida** lived in Springfield, Missouri. **Helen** lived in Iowa. The two youngest siblings were **Wilma** and **Roger**. Wilma lived in Gowrie, Iowa. **Roger** was born in 1938, the year Mildred graduated from high school in 1938.

Mildred also spoke of her uncles and aunts on the Knutson side. Uncle Herman had three children, two boys, and one girl (Irene, Laverne, and Wilton). Uncle Ferdinand married Alma Nelson, also a Trolle Ljungby descendant. They had one son, named Wilton (no other living children). Uncle Edgar was married to Esther Fox. Their daughter, Muriel, probably wrote the family history. There were two other daughters in that family. Uncle Alfred was in the war. His wife's name was Hazel, and they lived in either North or South Dakota. He died when his wife was pregnant with their second child. Uncle Manford died of cancer. He liked to play baseball, but his mother didn't want him to play on Sunday. He'd sneak out and play," Mildred said.

Mildred's mother Hattie died in Ft. Dodge, Iowa in 1992. She was a resident at the nursing home Friendship Haven, owned by the Methodist Church. The children took turns visiting her. Mildred had a picture in which she was photographed with her younger siblings standing in the order of size. It was taken when Mildred was 17 years old. The interviewer was Lilly Setterdahl.

> Mildred Schultz was born Apr. 24, 1916 in Riverton Township, Iowa, the daughter of Frederich B. Swinton, born in Bremer County, Iowa, and Hattie Clarinda Knutson, born in 1884 in Welch Township, Goodhue County. Hattie was the daughter of Bengt Knutson, b. 1861 in Trolle Ljungby, who emigrated from there in 1882 as Bengt Persson. He married Bengta, born in 1861 in Mellby, Blekinge. Mildred was the oldest of 14 children. She married Reyn Schultz, b. in 1911 in Iowa of German descent. Mildred lived in Charles City, Iowa, at the time of the interview. She passed away Apr. 12, 2007 in Floyd, Iowa.

Skog, Earl

The farmers brought eggs and butter to the store

May 26, 1993

Unlike most of the interviewed Trolle Ljungby descendants, Earl had no farming experience. He was a grocer and traveling salesman. Earl remembered how the farmers used to pay for their groceries with butter and eggs. About his grandfather, he knew that he changed his name. "As far as I know, Nels Skog, when he came over here, had the name of Nelson. Too many Nelsons, so he changed it." His wife, Elna, was from Trolle Ljungby. The 1875 State Census and the 1880 Federal Census show that Elna's mother, Olu Jönsdotter, lived with the Skog family in Leon Township. The plat book for 1894 lists an 80-acre farm in Section 13 in the name of Nels Skog. In 1900, he lived in Cannon Falls. All the children remained in Goodhue County.

Earl Skog

Earl was born in Cannon Falls where his father had a grocery store. "My father and his father had grocery stores. They called them bazaars in those days. It means groceries and novelties," Earl said. He thought that his father and his brother-in-law, C. E. Soderlund, were the last ones to have a bazaar. "Then my father went to California on account of his health for one year, and he came back and went as a grocery salesman for many, many years. I was probably about five-years old when he sold it because I remember the snuff and candy," Earl said.

Luther Skog, Earl's father, was born in Spring Garden. Describing him, Earl said, "He was a jolly guy, I'll tell you. He had to be a salesman. He went by car or train, mostly in Goodhue and Dodge counties. He had a circular route. He left on Monday or Tuesday morning. He didn't come back till Friday because the last town he made was Hastings, Minnesota. It was in the 1940s. The company, Friedrich and Kempe of Red Wing, helped him get a car. The brand name on the canned goods was Trillium. They roasted their own coffee in the basement of the plant. And they roasted their peanuts there, too."

The cans that his father had to bring with him were heavy, so his mother said, "Why do you carry that stuff? Why not eat it? We'll empty it and put the empty cans back." That lightened his load considerably. Earl recalled that his father lost only one account during all this years in business, and that was for less than ten dollars. "They charged a lot. They used to bring in butter in a jar for credit, and also eggs in them days. I remember once he bought a whole railroad car of apples. You know how big that is. The whole thing froze." Earl also recalled the bananas his father had strung up in the store.

During the Depression, Earl ran a filling station in Cannon Falls. "Some days we'd sell a hundred gallon, some days, only 25," he said. Mrs. Skog said the profit was 2 ½ cents per gallon. The customers usually wanted only a dollars worth. "A lot of times, we'd only sell one or two gallons," Earl said. When the boys took girls out, they wanted only one gallon. The wage was 35 cents an hour. "And then it went to 40 and I don't remember the year it went up to 40 cents for a carpenter." They had the filling station in Cannon Falls for two or three years. Then they had one in Sparta, Wisconsin. After that, they opened a variety store in Pine Island.

During World War II, Earl was called into the service, but did not have to go abroad. "The wife wrote and said the tires had gone to pieces, so she got them re-threaded. They peeled off. It was kind of dangerous for her driving a car," Earl said. She was alone with their three-year old daughter. They didn't have to have any rationing coupons in the store, Mrs. Skog said, because the only food item they sold was candy. When their dry goods store burned down, they built it up again.

Earl reminisced about the rice porridge his mother used to make on New Year's Eve. "She'd put in a nut, and the one who got it had good luck the rest of the year." He liked *lutfisk*, he said, but not sauerkraut that his wife's mother made. "*Grit worst*" must have been another German food. His wife recalled her mother-in-law's Swedish meatballs and the German potato salad from her own background. "We made our own wine once in awhile at home, not much. One time it was elder-berries, and a lot of times it was grape, wild grape wine," Earl said. He knew what Irish coffee was, but it was not served at any parties he could remember.

Earl used to fish for walleye, sunfish, and perch in the Mississippi River. "I never owned a boat, so I went with somebody else once in a while," he said. Earl also recalled that his aunt Nanny Carolina and her husband went out west. "He hauled a trailer out there and he took his wife's piano every time. She liked to play the piano."

Pine Island is in the southern part of Goodhue County, so they didn't get to go to Vasa and Spring Garden very often. Mrs. Skog remarked, "When we had our store here we were so busy we never could get away very much. On the weekends, I had the house to clean and little things you didn't get done during the week. As long as we could handle it ourselves, we had things pretty orderly, so when we had to get them [supplies] we knew just where to go and pick them up in a hurry when we'd run out on our shelves," she said. They carried stationery, cards, dry goods, threads, embroidery flosses, and table clothes to embroidery. "We sold a lot of school supplies," Earl said. They also carried china. "Nothing expensive, more for every day," his wife said. It was nothing like her mother-in-law's china. Earl's father sold china from England, "the stuff you could see through," Earl said.

Earl retired in 1962, and they sold the store one month earlier. After that, they went to California every winter to visit their daughter. Earl was a ham-radio operator, and sometimes he conversed with ham operators in Sweden. The interviewer was Lilly Setterdahl.

Earl Skog, Pine Island, was born May 26, 1913, the son of Luther Skog, b. Jan. 17, 1884 in Spring Garden and Tillie Adamson, b. 1885 in Stillwater. Her father was from Västergötland. Luther was the son of Nels Skog, b. 1846 in Vinslöv, and his wife, Elna Jönson, b. 1849 in Trolle Ljungby. They had the following children all born in Spring Garden: Emma Josephina (Soderlund), b. 1873, August Victor b. 1874, Nanny Caroline b. 1876, Selma Helena (Anderson), b. 1878, Nils Albin b. 1880, Jehander (Julius) Christopher b. 1881, Luther b. 1884, and Clara Olivia b. 1885. Elna's brother took the name of Weberg in this country. Elna emigrated in 1869 with her parents Jöns Person, b. 1822 in Vanneberga, Trolle Ljungby, and Olu Jönsdotter, b. 1821, a brother Nels, b. 1860, and a sister Else, b. 1855. Another brother, the farmhand Per emigrated the same year from Trolle Ljungby. For more information, see interviews with Lola Nelson, Virginia Fanslow, and Wallace Weberg. Earl married Luella Rittmann, b. 1916 and of German descent. They had one daughter who lived in California at the time of the interview. Earl Skog died Sep. 14, 2008 in Roseville, Placer County, California.

Swanson, Aurora

Her parents-in-law were diligent

March 8, 1993

Aurora remembered her Swedish-born parents-in-law as good workers. She was married to Hilding Swanson, who was the son of John W. and Alma Swanson. Asked whether she knew what her father-in-law, John W. Swenson, did for a living when he came from Sweden, Aurora said he hired out to farmers. In the wintertime, he worked as a lumberjack in Wisconsin. In Sweden, he was a shoemaker. As soon as he could, he bought his own farm. According to the 1877 plat book, his Pleasant View Farm in Section 11 in Vasa Township consisted of 200 acres at the time. Later, it consisted of 320 acres.

Aurora Swanson

Aurora related how John W. met his wife. A neighbor lady wanted her heating stove moved to another room, but could not do it herself, so she asked John to come and help. Alma Enberg happened to be there, so the two got acquainted. They were married in Red Wing by Pastor Rust. Alma lived with Aurora and Hilding on the farm for 25 years. John W. died in 1939 or 1940.

Aurora said, "They were very diligent" [*De var mycket flitiga*] John took care of the barn. They had nine horses and lots of cows and hogs. Alma took care of the chickens." Since the horses had to work so much during the week, they were allowed to rest on Sundays. The people then had to walk to church. "Grandma was so mad at that. She worked hard, too, she said." The shortest route cross-country to Vasa Lutheran Church was two miles. They always had farmhands. One of them, Alfred Nelson, was born in Trolle Ljungby in 1886 and arrived in 1903. Having entered military service, he died from the influenza in 1918 as he was on his way to England. Aurora still had Alfred's trunk that he brought form Sweden.

Hilding had an older sister, Helga, who married another member of the Trolle Ljungby group, Nels Brodd. She was 17 years older than Hilding. Aurora said her father-in-law John had a brother in Trolle Ljungby by the name of Nils, who had three sons, Olof, Victor, and Eric. Olof immigrated to Vasa in 1900 and worked for John as a farmhand for many years. "He was very big and strong," Aurora said.

On the dairy farm they grew hay, corn, wheat, oats, and potatoes. They milked the cows by hand until they got a generator about 1925. They did not get electricity until 1948 "because we were way behind times," Aurora said. She showed us an old kerosene lantern that stood in a corner and said it used to hang in the barn. Aurora also had John W. Swanson's small trunk from Skåne that she had painted so it looked nice, and a wooden 'lunch box' that her own father had brought from Sweden.

Her husband Hilding told her that his folk used to play dominos and tell ghost stories in the evening. Hilding thought the stories were scary. The Nels Rooth family and other families from Trolle Ljungby came to visit. The Rooth family didn't have a farm of their own. "They were poor," Aurora said. Their daughter Mildred married a Lind, and they had several children.

Recalling the Lasseli hill, Aurora said, "Years ago when they first got the Model T, Hilding said that when they drove up Lasseli they had to get off and walk. Hilding was so mad at that." They got the car as soon as Ford came out with one.

Asked about the food on the farm, Aurora said, "They had a cellar, and it was full of food." The hams hung from the ceiling and there was a lot of meat preserved in jars or salted down. She also recalled the cabbage heads that were stored in the basement and barrel upon barrel of apples. "They never bought any. They had everything on the farm."

When Hilding's mother came from Sweden, she worked as a maid in Spring Garden. "She was a very good cook. She had a large garden." She even saved the seeds so she could use them the following year. When they had butchered she made *wienerkorv*. It was not the ordinary sausage the Swedes usually made, but strings of tiny sausages usually made by professionals. Hilding's mother baked white bread and seldom rye bread. She also made a special drink during for Christmas they called *'juladricka'* and rhubarb wine.

Aurora met Hilding at a community club meeting in the Town Hall in Vasa. The entertainment consisted of song, music, and speeches. "It was fun to go the meetings with the youth club. We played outside. We had ball games. And then perhaps a boy came and asked if he could accompany you home," she said.

When Aurora and Evelyn were small, they were obligated to attend summer school at the Vasa church. "We hated it. We thought we should be free from school in the summer," Aurora said. She and her sister did not have to work very much on the farm when they grew up.

While Hilding did not get to attend high school, both Aurora and her sister, Evelyn, did. After graduation, they continued their studies at a teacher's college. Aurora then taught school for four years until she married, and Evelyn taught for 47 years. When Aurora began to teach in 1929, her salary was ninety dollars a month and then it went down to 75 due to the depression. She had deposited money in a savings account to be able to buy furniture later when she married. When the bank closed in 1933, she could retrieve only part of her funds. "But you could buy a beautiful bedroom set for 75 dollars," she said.

Aurora had visited Sweden four times—the first time in 1959 on the passenger liner *Stockholm* together with Hilding and their daughter Claudia. They met relatives in Skåne, among them Hilding's cousins Ebba and Eric. Ebba and her husband Göte Persson had many cattle that grazed near the Baltic Sea, Aurora said. The family also visited Vislanda, where Aurora's father came from, and finally Hassela, the home parish of Eric Norelius. Aurora said they exchanged gifts between the Hassela church and the Vasa church. She didn't remember what they brought, but the return gift was a pair of long candle sticks.

In 1968, Aurora was accompanied by her sister Evelyn to Sweden. They went to Trolle Ljungby and saw the *trollasten* and the castle with the horn and pipe. They were also inside the Trolle Ljungby church. In 1975, Aurora and Hilding visited Sweden. Her husband's Swedish was as good as the natives' she said.

Hilding and Aurora quit farming in 1972 and sold both farms. Hilding then built a house in Lake City overlooking Lake Pepin. He died in 1990. At the time of the interview, Aurora shared a home with her sister Evelyn. Through marriage, the Enberg family on their mother's side was related to the actor and singer Kris Kristofferson. The interviewer was Lilly Setterdahl.

> Aurora Swanson of Lake City was born May 22, 1909, the daughter of Sam Person, b. in Traryd parish, Småland, and his wife Anna Ryden, b. in Ryssby, Småland. They emigrated in 1898. In 1909, Aurora married Hilding Swanson, b. Jan. 11, 1909 in Vasa. He was the son of John W. Swanson, b. Mar. 1, 1854 in Trolle Ljungby, who emigrated in 1873, and his wife, Alma Enberg, b. in Vanskiva, Kristianstad län, who arrived in 1884. They had only two children, Helga and Hilding. Hilding was born in 1909 and Helga was 17 years older. She married Nels Brodd. Aurora, who was widowed, had one daughter. Aurora was interviewed because her husband was a Trolle Ljungby descendant, and she lived for many years with her father-in-law, who was born in Trolle Ljungby. Aurora Swanson died Sep. 10, 2005 in Lake City.

Swanson, Stanley

There was a good goose pond on the farm

November 30 1992

Vasa lacked open water so few farmers kept geese. When Stanley moved to a farm with a pond, he saw the opportunity. It was the farm his grandfather Swan Swanson had taken as a claim in Section 13, previously owned by a veteran of the war with Mexico. In 1861, the government issued the deed to Swan Swanson.

Across the road lived Swan Olson, who came with Grandpa in 1855, Stanley said. He remembered Swan Olson who lived until 1923. Stanley bought that farm from Bodelson for $8,000, he said. Before that, he had farmed the home place together with his brother Walter. There was a spring on the former Olson farm. "We just put a pipe down and as far as I know the water is still flowing," Stanley said. He kept geese on his farm. "It was a very good pond on the farm, so I got some geese....," he said. He had never heard of *Mårten Gås* Day that is celebrated in Skåne on November 11th, but said they usually had a

Stanley Swanson

goose dinner in November. He recalled that Midsummer was celebrated in Vasa on June 24th and that Fourth of July was celebrated in White Rock.

Asked about the Vasa Children's Home, he said, "Norelius was up in Minneapolis and St. Paul. There were five [children] who didn't have a home, so he took them down to Vasa, and that's how the home was founded. They had their own school," Stanley said.

About his parents, he said, "I hardly think they talked any English." Stanley learned Swedish in his home. His mother was born in Sweden. Certain things were always named in English, such as fence, barbed wire, stove pipe, and store. He recalled two stores in Vasa, Ackerson's *på backen* (on the hill) was the largest. The post office was in Julian's store.

Grandpa Swanson did not live long. "They had been out after corn, and when he came home, he had hurt his head, and he did not live long after that," Stanley said. Swan Swanson died in 1890 and his wife in 1897. Asked why they came here, Stanley said, "They thought it was better land here."

In 1870 everyone in Vasa was Swedish except one person, he said. The one exception was the German who built the Vasa Lutheran Church. "They made so many bricks they had enough left to build a house. Oscar Edstrom lived in that house over in Norrbotten." In reference to the preacher's pulpit shaped like an open Bible, Stanley said, "It was Norelius' dream." Speaking of the "shriek wagon" (*"skrikarkärra"*) in the Vasa Museum, Stanley said, "They had nothing to work with, so they went into the woods and cut down a large tree. They sawed it down, and then they cut off four [rounds] for wheels. Then they had to make a yoke for the oxen and steered the oxen with a pole. The Indians they had horses," he said.

Nicknames were common. Stanley remembered *Löddar*-Peter, who lived in Vasa on the road to Welch and went from farm to farm to fix pails and cans. He carried a soldering iron. (*"Lödda"* meant to solder in Swedish.) Lasse Pehrson was called Lasseli. His last name was never used. Then there was another hill named Rosali, but Stanley didn't know if it was named after a woman called Rosa or not. He knew that *li(d)* was Swedish for hill.

Part of a *"skrikarkärra"* (shriek wagon) on display at the Vasa Museum

Stanley learned to read a little Swedish as a child in "Swede School" which was held at the church during the summer months. Both he and his brother Walter played in the Vasa Band. "I started with the cornet and then I played the trombone, and later I bought a baritone," he said. The Swedes also had an orchestra with violins and piano, he said. In later years, Stanley sang with the Swedish Singers in Red Wing. The interviewer was Lennart Setterdahl.

Stanley Swanson of Red Wing was born Aug. 31, 1908 in Vasa, the son of Henry Swanson (1864-19420 and Anna Anderson, b. in Halland, Sweden, who emigrated in the 1890s. Henry was the son of Åbo Swen Swenson, b. 1821 in Vanneberga, Trolle Ljungby, and his wife Nilla Lassedotter, b. Nov. 27, 1824 in Trolle Ljungby. They immigrated to Vasa in 1855 with three children, Karna, b. 1849, Bengta b. 1857, and Swen b. 1854. Born in Vasa were: Anna in 1859, Hendric (Henry) in 1864, and Emelia in 1866. Stanley had four older brothers and sisters: Elin Alvina b. 1896, Nanny Rosi Sofie (Weberg) b. 1900, and Walter Henry Arnold b. 1906. Stanley married Verbena Dammann of German ancestry. Stanley Swanson died Aug. 31, 1998.

Swanson, Walter

The settlers got the land for almost nothing

September 2, 1992

Walter Swanson

About his paternal grandparents, Walter said, "Hans Mattson kind of steered them over here to Vasa, or kind of helped them come over. When they came here, they got the land for almost nothing. A section is 640 acres, but there was all timber on this end and prairie on the west, so instead of making four 160 acres one mile wide and one mile long, each one took half prairie and half timber. They had to grub," Walter said.

He explained that when they cut off the roots the trees would fall. He also knew how his parents met. "My mother lived at *Lassali* [Walter's pronunciation]. When you come from Red Wing, you go up that hill; that was *Lassali*. She lived about half-way up the hill. That's where she got acquainted with my father," Walter said.

From his own childhood, Walter related, "We had to drive with horses [to Red Wing and Cannon Falls]. It took one day back and forth. I broke my arm when I was eight years old. My dad took me down with horses, and they really ran—to Red Wing [to the doctor]. We generally went to Red Wing. Cannon Falls was a little bit further away," he said.

"When I went to school up here—I wasn't very old—all the kids around here talked Swedish, and the teacher clamped down and said, 'You can't say one word in Swedish on the school grounds.' Otherwise, during recess we would speak Swedish." Walter explained that one afternoon when he was going to say goodbye to the Samuelson children and others who lived to the south of the school, he was caught speaking Swedish by the teacher. "I had one foot on the school grounds, so I turned around and hollered to the kids *adjö*. She heard it and made me come in after school just because I said goodbye in Swedish."

Walter did not go to high school. He attended the Swedish summer school at the church. "I was confirmed in Swedish. That was the last year Lindgren was here. He was a pastor from Augustana. We'd go to school nine months and had to go back in the summer [four weeks]. I didn't like it. The kids were not in favor of it. I wasn't anyhow," he said.

Mr. and Mrs. Swen Swenson, *Vasa Illustrata*

Walter could read Swedish, but he was not very fluent, he said. His parents read the periodical *Augustana.* Walter's father was a deacon for many years in the Vasa Lutheran Church. Walter spoke mostly Swedish during the interview. After he was confirmed, he helped his father on the farm. He said his father died in 1942 and he did not remember his father's father. "He died before I was born, I think. He planted maple trees and other trees, some are still here today. My father took over and I was born here. My mother's mother stayed with us. She spoke only Swedish, no English. My mother came here from Sweden, and she did not attend school here, but she learned English. She could read English," Walter said. Bernard Anderson's and Walter's mothers were sisters. They were from Väröbacka, Halland. Walter remembered their two brothers, John and Henry Anderson.

During the Depression the farmers got between two and three dollars per hundredweight for milk. "And, by golly, it was just so we could barely get enough money to operate. If you hired somebody for a month, you paid 40 dollars a month. That's all you could pay. We had a fellow that worked for us, Anthony. He worked for different farms. He was so terribly strong." Anthony went through a box of snuff a day. He served in the Cavalry during World War I. Most of the farms were paid up before the Depression, Walter said. "This farm here, I paid $10,000 for it in the 20s. So it was pretty cheap. It didn't seem to take long before I paid it up," he said.

Walter's wife, Dorothy, never had to milk any cows. "No, they never did that," Walter said. "I was born in this house," he said, adding that his brother Stanley used to live on the farm across the road. One of Walter's sons owned the ancestral land, but he rented it out and worked in Red Wing for Northern States Power Company.

Walter and Dorothy visited Sweden about 1982. They belonged to the American Swedish Institute and went on one of its tours and had one week on their own. They visited Trolle Ljungby and Walter recalled the *trollasten.* About the landscape there, he said, "It's kind of the same as here." They visited Dorothy's relatives in Emmaboda, and they were surprised that he could talk Swedish so well.

Singing or humming a tune now and then, Walter said, he will never forget the first song he heard on the radio. The Julian store had the first radio in Vasa. Walter used to sing with the Swedish Singers, founded in Red Wing in 1976, but after his heart attack he wasn't able to attend the practices. The interviewer was Lennart Setterdahl.

> Walter Swanson, Vasa, was born Oct. 13, 1906, in Vasa, the son of Henry Swanson (1862-1942) and Anna Anderson, born in Halland, Sweden. Henry was born in Vasa, the son of Swen and Nilla Swenson, both born in Trolle Ljungby (See interview with Stanley Swanson). Walter married Dorothy Munson, b. Feb. 5, 1912 in Minneapolis, the daughter of Olof Monson and his wife Olga Bodilson. The Bodilsons were from the Villand district, which includes Trolle Ljungby. Dorothy's parents came from Sölvesborg and Nymö. Walter and Dorothy lived on the original homestead in Vasa, but rented out their land .Both are deceased. They had three sons and a daughter, Janet, who lived in the Twin Cities. Walter passed away in 1995.

Swenson, Milton

The pastors had to be able to preach for one hour

September 30, 1992

Milton Swanson

When the Swedish Lutherans hired a new pastor, the rule was, "If they couldn't preach for an hour, you wouldn't hire them. I remember, as kids you got pretty tired of sitting there. But you paid attention. If you didn't, you'd get a flip on your ear. I'll say that for the old-timers, they had their kids behaving pretty good in church," Milton said.

Speaking of the first pastor in Vasa, Eric Norelius, Milton said, "When Norelius had arrived in Vasa, the Swedes in Spring Garden brought three babies across the prairie to Vasa for baptism. Norelius baptized their children and then they asked him to come and preach in their locality in Spring Garden. But I don't think there was a bridge at White Rock where you drive across now. They had to ford the creek. The creek at that time was as big as Little Cannon River is now. In the spring when the ice broke up it flooded," Milton said. Later, Norelius and his wife lived near that creek. The pioneers built their homes near a creek because they wanted water nearby, so they didn't have to carry it very far. There were many springs in Spring Garden and good water.

Milton was president of the Brotherhood (a Lutheran church group) at the time they dedicated a plaque in White Rock to commemorate the site of the first home owned by Eric Norelius in America. The president of the Minnesota Synod attended the dedication ceremony. Milton said, "They pushed aside all the people who had worked with it. I had a good speech made up. There were 150 to 200 people at the banquet. We had to move the outhouse because they didn't want that in the picture," he said. The dedication was in 1958. Milton remembered a building on that site, but is not sure whether it was the original or not. The first house was just a hut, Milton said. The stone is placed flat on the ground, and is rather difficult to find in the brush by the roadside. A sign on the opposite side of the road points to the site.

About the white rock, *Vita stenen,* Milton remarked, "They say that years and years ago, you could see it at a distance. The Indians worshipped it. I went to school only a quarter of a mile from the white cliff. At recess we would walk over there and climb on it and scratch our initials on it. It's a very soft stone. Now, there's wooded hills all over. It's not going to be too long before there ain't anything left of it (the white rock). There was talk about putting a cover on it that would keep it from eroding, but it never got done," Milton said.

It used to have a natural protective cap of limestone. There is much limestone in the area and it was used for house foundations. Sometimes entire buildings were erected of limestone.

Growing up with various nationalities, Milton said, "In those days, you had your lines, and you respected them. You went across the line you had to be a little more polite. If you were up among the Irish you didn't talk Swedish, but otherwise you did. And in those days, the Irish and the Swedes didn't get along so good. In a business way, they were always okay, but when they had a dance down in White Rock, then they had some rough ones who came there and they'd have a fight. And then it was the Swedes against the Irish. Whether they were Germans or whatever, they were one or the other," Milton said.

The music at the dances was provided by local violin players and occasionally a band from Red Wing. Milton remembered when *Olle i Skratthult* entertained in White Rock. "He was down to White Rock in that hole mind you. But it didn't go so good for him because he had worked for a farmer by the name of Manne Benson years ago, so he brought this company down to show off a little bit. But the company didn't like it in a small community. They felt they were degrading themselves a little, so they sat out in the car until they had to go in and play a little bit, and then they'd go back out again. But here in Cannon Falls, in the hall, he was here many times and then went over big here. He even had a play at one time about a couple of farm families. He had about the same jokes every time, but we laughed anyway," Milton said. Other forms of entertainment included the Edvard Persson movies that were shown in Red Wing. Milton remembered the song, *Lite grann från ovan* (A little bit from above), basketball games, and boxing matches.

Living five miles from a pioneer cemetery, *gravbacken*, in the Jemtland Ward, Milton told us how it happened to be preserved. "Fergie Larson had looked up records in the courthouse and found that Civil War veterans were buried there, and then the government gave them some help to preserve it. There is a great big stone there now. It's fenced off," Milton said. Steven Hedeen told us that many small children were buried there as well.

Milton mentioned a Swedish businessman by the name of G. O. Miller, who operated in the White Rock area. "He was the one who had a telephone company, grocery store, creamery, and also shipped butter and eggs to St. Paul. He had ten teams of horses picking up milk all over." Milton was 15 years old when he drove one of the routes for him. He did deliveries and pick-ups at the same time. "They could call on the telephone and say what they wanted, and he delivered groceries and picked up the eggs and the cream at the same time. He [Miller] could do what he wanted. He was the only butter-maker, grocery man around," Milton said. The farmers thought he made too much money, so they started a co-op, but they had a hard time to compete with the Vasa Creamery. In Vasa they made high-quality butter from sweet cream. "In White Rock, when they picked up the cream only once a week, it could be pretty sour sometimes. I remember they said they had to go to the bank and borrow money so they could pay within five cents of what Vasa paid," Milton said.

In 1917, G. O. Miller and P. A. Peterson opened a bank. Milton was the first depositor. White Rock used to be a thriving place "when all of them teams were there," Milton said. Groceries were shipped in by railroad. Hundreds of kegs of ice were piled up for the summer to preserve the butter. "There was a chapel in White Rock. Children would go there to Sunday school for a while. I think the Baptists had built that chapel. The Baptist 'thing' had died out, so it stood vacant. The literary society met there," Milton said.

Talking about his family, he said he was two years old when his paternal grandfather died. He had taught Milton to sing *Gubben Noak*. "They lifted me up so I could see him in the casket. They said, 'He sleeps.' The funerals always began in the home before they went to the church. Refreshments were served at home."

Milton was not a Trolle Ljungby descendant himself, but his wife was. For health reasons, she was unable to participate in the interview. Milton's grandfather on his father's side came from Barkeryd in Småland, and his mother's ancestry went back to Västergötland. He grew up in White Rock, not far from Spring Garden in Leon Township, where the Trolle Ljungby native by the same last name, Mons Swenson, owned 240 acres in Section 23 in 1877. He had ten children, one of whom was Esther, who became Milton's mother-in-law.

About his mother's roots, Milton said, "Her father was seven years old when he came. The father could remember when they mixed bark with grain to survive the winter. They had to stretch it. My mother told me this. They used to grind up bark and mix it in. She said it was no food value in that, but it filled them up." (Barkeryd, Småland, was a rocky area, where people had a hard time surviving during a draught.) Milton's father-in-law was Svante Young. His father had changed his name from Anderson to Youngquist, "but then thought it was too long, so he cut the 'quist; and called himself Young." Svante Young married Vanberg's widow, who had three children. "He had farms for each of his sons when they started out." Milton said. Mons Swenson did the same for his sons. "They maybe had to pay a little bit and they took care of the parents." Svante Young spent the winters in Kentucky. "It meant you were rich. The other ones they stayed here and froze," Milton said.

Milton retired from farming when he was 65. Then he helped his son, who had taken over the farm, for twenty years. His son bought more land, had one-hundred cows to milk, two barns and silos. "The bank had to have so much. So he sold out last spring, but not the farm. He kept that and rented it out. Very few young ones start farming now, Milton said. The price for corn is not much higher than when he farmed himself. The prices don't meet the cost of the equipment, he said. The interviewer was Lennart Setterdahl.

> Milton Swenson of Cannon Falls was born Oct. 7, 1906 in White Rock, the son of Arthur Swenson and Selma Anderson. Milton married Luella Young, b. May 13, 1910, in Spring Garden. She was the granddaughter of Mons N. Swenson, b. 1844 in Trolle Ljungby. Mons was the son of Nils M. Swenson, b. 1815 in Trolle Ljungby, who emigrated with his wife Kjersti Persson, b. 1820 in Trolle Ljungby and their son, Mons. Their daughter Selma Adelia married Vernon Young, also of Swedish descent. There were ten children in the Mons N. Swenson family. See the interviews with Eldon Anderson and Arlan Banks. Milton Swenson passed away Oct. 10, 1996 in Goodhue County, His wife, Luella, who was a Trolle Ljungby descendant, died Feb. 2, 1994.

Terborch, Marian and Loraine Deden

They made a pudding called *sötost*

October 13, 1992 and June 14, 1994

Marian speaks longingly about one Swedish dish prepared in her home, *sötost*, which she had never been able to make herself. She is a direct descendant of one of the first settlers from Trolle Ljungby, Swan Olson, and Swedish on all sides of her family. She told us that the last farm owned by her great-grandfather Swan Olson was located south of the Vasa church in Section 35. "He was a good farmer. At least that's what my mother and father used to tell me... I mean prosperous, and with all those children, I suppose he had a lot of help," Marian said.

His eldest daughter, Martha, who was born in Sweden, lived in the Seattle area. "I know my sister and her folks were out to see her when

Marian Terborch

she was around 100 years old. She died shortly after she was 100. She lived in Bremerton, Washington. Martha Stromberg was the oldest."

Marian's grandparents Ellen and Charles Bennett had a farm in Featherstone Township. The 1914 plat book states that it was located in sections 8 and 18. "I remember my grandmother telling me that when she was little, like four years old, she'd be out helping with the herding of the sheep. She learned tatting while she was herding the sheep. Grandma Bennett was always busy with her hands while the men could sit down and talk and read. My dad worked hard though, I must say, on the farm, but when the men come in, they would rest." Marian said she feels guilty if she sits down without doing something and believes she has inherited that from the older generation.

Having retired from the farm, her grandparents Bennett lived on South Park Street in Red Wing. "And to me, the house was always like a big white castle because it was a bigger old house and it had these two stairways. It was fun for us little kids," Marian said, as she recalled running up and down and around inside the house. "We loved that. I remember Grandma in the kitchen, and she'd probably serve us some peach sauce with cheese. They always had a nice big chunk of those round cheeses. We would have cheese and bread and sauce, just a little treat in the afternoon. My grandfather would ask us if we wanted to run a race, and then we would go through the halls in the house and come back around, and he always let us win. Right inside the house! Grandma stayed in the kitchen." Both sets of grandparents spoke mostly Swedish. "That's what I remember from home too, More Swedish than English," Marian said.

Marian's father started out as a farmer in Featherstone, "but then," she said, "he went to Wisconsin, where I was born in Pierce County, and bought a farm there. It's between Red Wing and Ellsworth. We were out 7 ½ miles from Red Wing. We started out with 80 acres and then he bought another 40, so it was 120."

Her mother sewed all their clothes. "She would make probably five to six outfits for each child during winter, so they would have clothes to wear, and I think that even included our underclothing. She would sew everything. Then besides doing that kind of sewing, every winter she would make quilts. We had this big frame loom that we set up in the dining room. I think she crocheted some rugs. There wasn't anything that was wasted," Marian said.

The grains they grew on the farm in Wisconsin included barley, wheat, oats, and flax. Her mother churned butter. "I learned how to milk, but I really didn't have to milk. I did learn it in case I had to do it. I don't think Mother wanted us to do the heavy chores. We had milk cows and chickens and pigs. We had geese when I was little, and I'm sure we must have eaten them at Christmas or Thanksgiving time. But in later years, we always had turkey," Marian said.

The specialty foods for Christmas included *lutfisk, sylta,* and two kinds of sausages that her mother made. One of them had more beef in it, Marian said. "Mother used to make a pudding at Christmas. It was made out of the curds. We had this … caramel type pudding, *sötost.* And oh, I miss that one at Christmas. I could never learn to make that." At other times they would have *ostkaka* served with berry preserves from the farm, and the whole, fresh herring that her mother used to bake in the oven. The Johnsons, Marian's first husband's family, used the third milking after a calf was born for *kalvost,* also called *kalvdans,* and the blood from slaughtered pigs for various foods, Marian said. They also made hardtack *(knäckebröd)* and rice porridge. When Marian's daughters came home for Christmas, they looked for pickled pigs feet, Swedish meatballs, *lutfisk, lefse,* and Scandinavian cookies.

When it was time for Marian to go to high school, she lived in a house on College Hill in Red Wing that belonged to the family rather than going to high school in Ellsworth. Her mother thought the schools were better in Red Wing, and since she did not get to go to high school herself, she really wanted her children to finish it. After high school, Marian got a job as a telephone operator, and later she worked at Sears' catalog office.

She left the farm when she married at the age of 19. Her parents stayed in Wisconsin for a few more years. Then her brother farmed for a short time before he married. While her brother was in the service in Europe, Marian and Milton took care of the family farm in Wisconsin. Her brother, who is five years older, was captured by the Germans and interrogated after his plane went down, but survived and came home. The farm was sold in the late 1950s.

Marian's older sister, Lorraine, did not know any English when she started school at the age of seven. "My sister was so embarrassed that she decided she was never going to speak Swedish again," said Marian, who remembered some Swedish words from the time she was growing up. "We could understand what the folks were saying. We caught on to a few words. I did speak a little bit of it. My husband, Milton, would almost force me to say something in Swedish. I had to answer him in Swedish," Marian said. He joined the Swedish Singers and the Swedish language class in Red Wing in 1976. Having worked for Meyer Industries, he later became a purchasing agent and traffic manager. He passed away in 1983.

In 1994, we asked Marian's older sister, Loraine, whether she remembered Swan Olson. "Yes," she said. "He was small, very small. He was thin. He had that goatee." She goes on to say that there was a friendly feud going on between him and Grandpa Bennett (Swan's son-in-law Charles). Both invested in real estate. "Granddad Bennett had money in the tannery here in Red Wing. That was burning one day. When Swan Olson found out, he laughed and said, 'Oh, that's good. Charley is losing some money now.' If one could put something over on the other one, they thought that was great."

Loraine thought that each of Swan Olson's children inherited $10,000. The ones who had gotten farms may not have received that much. But Grandma Bennett did. She kept the money in her own name at the bank, so she could buy what she wanted like new furniture. Grandpa Bennett lent people money. "He was his own bank," Loraine said. When he built his house on the farm in Featherstone Township he built it with two stairways between the first and second floor. "You couldn't get from one end of the house to the other end [on the second floor]. You had to go down the steps and go around. He had separate quarters for the hired men; he didn't want them with his girls on the other side." When the Bennetts moved into Red Wing, they bought a big house that was built as a hospital. It had three stories and a huge porch all around. They had those big radiators, the real old-fashioned ones, and a coal furnace in the basement." Charles Bennett died in 1943. He was the brother of Swan Olson's second wife Anna Brita Berndtsdotter, born in Värö, Halland. Loraine said that Anna Brita became Swan Olson's housekeeper at the age of 16 after his first wife had died. She took care of a tiny baby as well as the older children. Later, she and Swan married, and she became the mother of 15 children.

Both Marian and Loraine remembered their great aunt, Agnes, who never married. She took care of her father, Swan Olson. "She was a flirt," Marian said. She had a boyfriend at the nursing home. Her hair was so thin, she had this little lace night cap on. She looked so cute. She always had a friend," Lorain said. "She had somebody living with her too."

Recalling her visit to Washington State on account of her great-aunt Martha's 100th birthday, Loraine said she also accompanied her parents to see Martha's younger brother, Fred Olson, who had a drug-store in Spokane. In 1957 Loraine and her German-American husband went on a tour of the Scandinavian countries, but did not visit Skåne. Prior to our visit, Loraine had not heard of either Trolle Ljungby or the legendary Ljungby Horn and Pipe. In 1993, we found a distant relative of the two sisters in Trolle Ljungby. Through their great-grandmother, Karna Andersdotter, they were related to Sven-Olof Mattsson in the village of Östra Ljungby. The interviewer was Lennart Setterdahl. On June 14, 1994, Lilly interviewed Marian's ten year older sister, Loraine Deden, born Dec. 17, 1916 in Featherstone Township.

> Marian Terborch of Red Wing was born Feb. 2, 1926 in Pierce County, Wisconsin, the daughter of George Bennett (1885-1968) and Edna Warn (1890-1966). George Bennett's mother was Ellen Olson, the daughter of Swan Olson of Trolle Ljungby in his first marriage. She married Charles Bennett (formerly Berndtsson), who was the brother of Swan Olson's second wife. For more information about the S. Olson family, see the chapter, "Goodhue County Swedes." Marian married Walfried Milton Johnson, with whom she had three daughters. He died in 1983, and Marian then married Leroy Terborch, b. 1924 in Lake City, Minn.

Thompson, Marlene and Dale

Flowers were brought to the cemetery

September 25, 1992

Most of the older relatives on Marlene's mother's side were deceased. As a result she didn't have any communication with the older generations. Members of Marlene's family are buried in Vasa. "We take care of the cemetery and put flowers on, she said." She had not heard of either Trolle Ljungby or Skåne, but she knew that her grandparents on her mother's side were from Sweden. "They were both dead when I was born. They lived in Vasa right by the bridge, not too farm from the church. That's where the farm was," Marlene said.

According to the plat book for 1914, Mary Troline owned 80 acres in Section 22, as well as 40 acres in the northeast part of the Vasa Township. Apparently, the Olanders worked the farm in Section 22 until it was sold. It was no longer in the family, Marlene said.

The interview concentrated on Marlene's many aunts and uncles. Her great-grandmother, Anna Troline Olander, had four stepchildren, all of whom moved to Scobey, Montana, and became ranchers. Marlene met two of them, Martin and Clara, when they came to visit. Nine children were born in Anna Trulen's marriage to Peter Olander. The next youngest daughter, Eleanor, became Marlene's mother. The children of this large family did not have many children themselves. Recounting what happened to her mother's brothers and sisters, Marlene mentioned Daniel, who was not listed in the church records. He farmed and died of a burst appendix after he was married, she said. He didn't have any children. The Federal Census for 1900 lists Dan as being born in January of 1896. The next oldest, Myrtle, married Ernie Stahl (no children). Margaret became the wife of Arthur Richter of Goodhue (one son). Ethel's husband was Al Barringer (sp?) of Red Wing (3 children). Clarence married Nancy Thompson (2 sons), Nellie married Marvin Sahlstrom and they lived in Milwaukee. John Elmer died young. Pauline (Mrs. Eugene Davis) lived in Burton, Alabama (1 daughter).

Marlene and Dale Thompson

Marlene's husband Dale said that Clarence, who was also related to him, lived in Burnside Township, which has since been consolidated with Red Wing. They had a little farm and Clarence worked on the farm, and then he worked for different companies, Dale said. "He worked for an ice plant in Red Wing, delivering ice. That would be back in the 40s before the refrigeration. He had a truck and delivered ice to houses." Dale believed that Clarence died of a heart attack. He had two sons, and one of them, Jerome, lived in Red Wing. The other named Bruce lived in California. One of Jerome's sons lived on the farm at the time of the interview. "It's a small farm, so it has been passed on, Dale said.

Peter J. Olander rented a farm in Belle Creek Township in 1900 and in 1910. At that time, Dan was listed as the oldest child living at home. The youngest was John. Peter Olander's son from a previous marriage, Theodor, was 30 years old and listed with the family as a farm laborer. The interviewer was Lennart Setterdahl See also the next interview with Donald Trulen who remembered more.

Marlene Thompson of Red Wing was born Mar. 14, 1936, the daughter of Nelson Sylvander and his wife Eleanor Olander, b. Feb. 22, 1913 in Goodhue County. Eleanor was the daughter of Anna Trulen Olander, b. Nov. 20, 1873 in Trolle Ljungby. Anna emigrated in 1880 with her parents, farmhand Sven Persson and his wife Maria Andersdotter, and two brothers, Alfred b. 1876 and August b. 1878. Anna became the second wife of Per Olander, b. 1850. He was the son of Per Ålander b. 1819 in Kiaby, who emigrated in 1869. Anna's husband had been married before and had four children with his first wife, all of whom moved to Scobey, Montana, and became ranchers. According to Vasa Lutheran Church records, Anna's first husband was Andreas Bäckstrom, and they had one daughter, Sofia Mathilda, b. 1894. Anna's children with Per Olander were: Dan b. 1896, Myrtle

b. 1898, Maggie, b. 1900, Ethel b. 1903, Clarence b. 1905, Nellie b. 1907, John b. 1910, Eleanor b. 1913, and Ruth Pauline. Marlene and her husband Dale Thompson, of Danish heritage, owned and operated the Sylvander Heating Company in Red Wing at the time of the interview. They had one son and one daughter.

Trulen, Donald

Neither God nor the devil will want you

September 20, 1992

Donald Trulen

Donald's grandparents had twelve children. One of them got the above reprimand from his mother, "Neither God nor the devil will want you," when he did not keep up his appearance after he had left home. The emigration records from Trolle Ljungby in 1880 show that Sven Persson was a hired man. Donald was the son of John A. born in Vasa in 1886. Donald had no memory of his grandfather Swen. "He died before I was born, but Grandma Trulen, I remember her. They lived on a farm close to Welch, and I remember her very well," Donald said. He was probably referring to the 40 aces in the north-eastern part of Vasa Township on the border to Welch that belonged to Mary S. Trolin in 1914.

Asked whether his grandmother spoke Swedish or English, Donald said, "She spoke both. We couldn't speak it. Then she would speak English, but when she was with her children, mostly Swedish. Mom and Dad talked it when they didn't want us to hear. Myself, I can only say a few words."

Donald's father never farmed. "My dad worked down at a place called the Red Wing Motor Company. They built boat motors. Emil Trulen took over the farm after Grandma and Grandpa died. He kept it up until he got so he couldn't take care of it, and then he sold that, and he got a little place just out here by the Cannon River, where he used to raise garden vegetables and sell to the stores in town. But he got rid of the home place," Donald said. Emil was not married.

Recalling family gatherings at Margaret Richter's, Donald said, "We have a whole bunch up in the Cities, too, that I haven't seen for years. That would be Arthur Trolen's children. The reunions were held about every third year. Margaret Richter was a Trulen. They lived between Red Wing and Goodhue, where they had a farm and a big yard which was suitable for picnics."

About his Uncle Richard, Donald said, "Richard was the one who went into the service in the First World War. He never married. He went around and helped everybody out. He would do this and do that." According to the Richter family, Richard would come home sporadically.

On the Trulen side they never said much about Sweden, but Donald's mother who was from Värmland and emigrated in 1903 talked a lot about Sweden. "She had all of her school books when she came over," Donald said. She never got a chance to visit her country of birth, and neither did her sisters.

About his childhood, Donald said, "I started to work on the farm when I was nine years old. I worked for my uncle, Dan Olander. They lived out in Vasa, and I went out there when the schools were over until I had to go back. I worked for 25 cents a day and then during the harvesting I got one dollar a day, threshing. I saved. When I came home in the fall, I had a few bucks and would get my sister something, so she had a little spending money. She's two years older. And then when I was 14, I started to work in a grocery store in Red Wing," he said. Later he became the manager of the store.

Donald was confirmed in English at the First Lutheran Church in Red Wing. All of the people who had come from Sweden that he used to know had died, he said. "The postmaster came from Sweden. They were the ones who changed their name to Nordholm. He was a Trulen," Donald said.

Asked if he knew any Swedish politicians, Donald said, "I was a politician for three years." He explained that he lived in Burnside in the 1970s when the Northern States Power Company wanted to build the nuclear plant on Prairie Island. Red Wing then wanted Burnside for a tax base. "I was on the Town Board, the council, and we fought them tooth and nail, because we didn't want to come in with Red Wing, but we lost. They got us. Red Wing got the longest city limits of any town in Minnesota. They extend way out to Prairie Island," Donald said. The Minnesota Municipal Commission overruled. They said that Red Wing could not have survived without Burnside. "That's the only place you could build. The Shoe Factory built a plant out here and the tire company." Donald didn't like politics and got out of it. He was satisfied with Red Wing. "We have a good council. I couldn't ask for a better place to live," he said.

During World War II Donald volunteered for the service. "We went from a unit they called National Guard in Red wing, an anti-aircraft unit. Then we got to California. I was assigned with the Air Force. We weren't really flying. We were in gliders, the heavy machine guns. We went in with the airborne troops and protected the airstrips when they were building them—with gliders. We never thought of death or worried about it," he said.

"When I was in the service I was all over the world, and I wanted to get to Norway and Sweden so bad, and that's the only place I didn't go. I got to Europe, North Africa, South Africa, India, Burma, China and the whole world, but I never got to Norway and Sweden. We still got cousins over there in Sweden [on his mother's side]. Mother got letters but they were in Swedish," he said.

Donald met his wife in Connecticut, where he trained as a mechanic and worked at the aircraft plant, Pratt & Whitney in Hartford. "After the war, everything slowed up and they started laying everybody off, so we thought we were going to go to California, but we got back to Red Wing. My mother was still alive, so we decided to stay. That was in 1958," he said. Donald's father had died in 1955, but his mother lived until 1982.

About his father, Donald said, "He used to love to fish. My dad was crippled. He had a foot cut off in a sawing accident, so he had a wooden leg, artificial leg, from a sawmill accident, so we used to fish a lot. We used to go out to this Prairie Island and we'd catch some fish and walleye—things were pretty rough then back there."

Asked whether his mother followed the Swedish customs, Donald said, "Absolutely, *lutefisk*, lefse, and *tyttebär* [lingon berries]. We started the *lutefisk* on my dad's birthday the 9th of December [to cure] and we had it through January, a good custom, too. I love it." Donald's wife of Italian descent also learned to love it. "My children didn't care for it, but she did, she liked it. She'd make it and fix it for Christmas. She was a Catholic and I was a Lutheran. We went each one to our church, and we brought the children up Catholic," Donald said. He explained that they lost a daughter when she was 16-years old, and after that they decided it would be best if they both went to the same church. "Then I converted to the Catholic religion, which is so much like ours. I couldn't see any difference," Donald said.

The interviewer was Lennart Setterdahl.

> Donald Trulen of Red Wing was born May 18, 1920, the son of John A. Trulen, b. Dec. 9, 1896 in Vasa, who died in 1953. Donald's mother was born in Värmland and emigrated in 1903 with her parents and siblings. Her father was a farmer in Wisconsin. John Albert was the son of Swen Persson Trolin, b. Feb. 4, 1850 in Trolle Ljungby and his wife Maria Anderson, b. Dec. 21, 1849 in Trolle Ljungby. They emigrated in 1880 with three children, Anna, b. 1873, Alfred b. 1876, and August b. 1878. The children born in Vasa were: Wilhelm in 1881, Emil in 1882, Arthur Sigfrid in 1884, Albert in 1886, Theodor Hjalmar in 1889, Elin Mathilda in 1892, Otto Richard in 1893, and John in 1896. For information about Anna, see interview with Marlene Thompson. Donald Trulen died Oct. 12, 1992.

Weberg, Hazel

Grandma just talked Swede

September 28, 1992

Asked if her grandfather spoke Swedish most of the time, Hazel said, "No. He could talk English quite a bit, but Grandma could not. She just talked Swede. I understood part of what she said, but I couldn't converse with her because I didn't know Swede that well. I suppose they talked Swede at home all the time, but then when the younger ones got out to work, they had to learn the English language. I don't know why she never picked it up because Grandpa did." There were no discussions about Sweden that Hazel could remember.

According to the censuses, John Hokenstrom lived in Welch Township in 1895, in Vasa Township in 1900, and in Leon Township in 1910. He was listed as farm renter in Welch and Vasa, and apparently, he did not own a farm in Leon Township either. Hazel said her grandfather had dairy cattle. They brought the milk into the kitchen and separated it. They used to let me turn the wheel, not too slow and not too fast. We kids wanted to go real fast, but it seemed the longer you kept on, the harder it was to make it go around," she said.

Hazel remembered all her uncles and aunts on the Hokenstrom side. John did not marry. He was quite old when he died. Ruth was also single. Nellie married a man by the last name of Sander. She had one son, Walter, who lived in the Cities (Minneapolis-St. Paul). Nancy was their stepsister. Hazel explained that her grandmother Anna had been married before and had a daughter, Nancy, who was born in Sweden. She married Emil Ingeman.

Recalling her grandfather's, John Hokenstrom, funeral, Hazel said, "The weather was real bad. They lived by Post Corner, south of Cannon Falls. In those days, the funerals were at the houses, so they took everybody to the house by wagon." The casket was in the house, "in the living room, and then when it was over, they had to take us back out to the highway where everybody had their cars parked." It was on January 3rd.

Hazel said her grandfather's name was Nelson when he came to this country. He changed it because there were so many with the same name in the same area. "To get the mail straight they had to do something." Hazel had many family photos. Her father worked for a photographer, she said, "and he took pictures by the hundreds."

Hazel was born on Midsummer Day. She recalled going to the Vasa Midsummer festivals, but had no memory of any *majstång* (pole decorated with green leaves and flowers). She was confirmed in English in the First Lutheran Church in Red Wing. The family lived on East 5th Street, so they had only five blocks to walk to church. The *Julotta* service was at 5 o'clock on Christmas morning. Both of her parents worked at the shoe factory. Their next-door neighbor worked at the milling company. Hazel thought there were three flour mills in Red Wing.

She talked about how the Mississippi River used to freeze over in the winter and how the young people tried to cross it. "When I was a teenager, I rode with some friends in a car from Pepin, Wisconsin, to Lake City across the ice. My folks never knew about that though. It was in the spring of the year, and when we came over to the Minnesota side, we had a hard time finding a place to get up on land because it was open along the edges." That was quite dangerous, she admitted.

At Christmas time they did not get together with the relatives in the countryside because the roads were too bad. "We lived in town, and we used to get together with the sister who lived in Vasa or the brother that lived in Red Wing, and we had the *lutefisk*, of course, and potatoes, and sweet potatoes. Another thing we had a lot of was rosettes (cookies fried in hot oil). That was always a treat at Christmas. My mother had one iron that was shell-shaped, and she would put creamed peas in it," Hazel said.

"After I graduated from high school, I worked at the Woolworth Company. I was a cashier there the last three years, and then after we married—we were married in '44—I worked that winter at Durke-Atwood during the war, and from then on, I was home. When we had the children, I stayed home until they were pretty big and we could trust them at home. He [her husband] was always around, so it wasn't too bad to leave them."

Her husband Wallace said that in his family they used to go over to Henry Swanson's in Vasa for Christmas. Birthdays were not celebrated in a big way. Hazel recalled one 50th wedding anniversary in the Risberg family. "That was unusual in those days," she said. Neither Hazel nor Wallace had heard of *spettkaka*. See also next interview with Wallace Weberg. The interviewer was Lennart Setterdahl.

> Hazel Weberg of Welch was born June 24, 1920 in Red Wing, the daughter of Swan Hokenstrom, b. 1885 in Welch and his wife Edith Rundquist born in Vasa. Swan Hokenstrom was the son of John Hokenstrom, formerly Jöns Nilsson, b. 1857 in Trolle Ljungby, who arrived from Sweden ca 1882, and his wife Anna Jönsson, who arrived in 1889. (She was the sister of another Jöns Nelson, see interview with Everal Nelson.) John and Anna had the following children: Jennie b. 1880 in Trolle Ljungby, Nellie Carolina b. 1883 in Vasa, Swen Sigfrid b. 1885 in Vasa, Ruth Elvira b. 1895 in Welch. Hazel married Wallace Weberg, b. Dec. 29, 1922 in Spring Garden. He died in 1992. See next interview. They had three sons and two daughters. Hazel Weberg passed away Aug. 24, 2009 in Goodhue County.

Weberg, Wallace

We all worked for nothing, just for food

September 28, 1992

Like so many others who lived through the Depression, Wallace said that times were hard also in the countryside, and his ancestors didn't have it easy either. His grandfather Nels raised eight children alone after his wife died in 1900. Nels was married to Betsey Risberg, another Trolle Ljungby descendant.

According to the Federal Census, Nels Weberg owned a mortgage-free farm in Leon Township in 1900. His wife was still living when the census was taken. There were eight children between the ages of one and 15. One of them was named Titus, and he became the father of Wallace. The plat books for 1894 and 1914 show that the farm in Leon Township consisted of 80 acres and was located in Section 13.

Wallace Weberg

Wallace's parents farmed in Jemtland from the time he was five years old until he was grown. His father had bought the farm, but lost it during the Depression. "Everybody just about lost the farms, something nobody could help. Then he rented it from this person he had bought it from. He was a good renter [landlord]. Can't think of his name—his last name was Pearson," Wallace said.

"He gave him a chance to rent it, and we rented it until the time we moved out of there. We stayed on the farm and worked out a little bit besides. I think I was 13-years old when I pitched bundles on the threshing gang. I followed the threshing rig. We all worked for nothing, just for food. Today, who would do that, I wonder? It's a different world... the dust, the heat.... You want to eat, and the family worked together and that's how they survived," Wallace said.

"Walter Swanson's dad had the old steam engine, and I used to go there as a kid, and I enjoyed the steam engines. I wasn't old enough to be working on the bundling team. At 5 o'clock, whatever time the engineers decided to quit, they pulled the whistle. Everybody raised grain at that time, and we had an excess of straw. Finally, they had so much straw they had to burn it," Wallace said.

Wallace cannot remember picking corn by hand. He said, "We used to go out and pick the best ears for seed corn, and then we dried it and then we shelled it by hand. You can use your own seed corn for one year, but then you go backwards instead of forward," he said.

Wallace grew up close to White Rock and the white cliff. "Us kids used to go there every time we went to school. It was fun to go up there. We'd grab the tree whips on the tops. We'd crawl up to the top, and going down we'd be swinging from it. We were up there just a few years ago, and the rock has deteriorated down to where it isn't the way I remember it at first. It has soft crumbling rock," he said.

About the Irish in the area, Wallace said, "I can remember out in White Rock—the Irish lived on the south side and the Swedes lived on the other side, and us kids used to get together every now and then in White Rock in the Town Hall to play basketball. We had boxing matches, and the Swedes were just as tough as the Irish were, and they were good friends of ours," he said. Wallace recalled that the Globetrotters put on a basketball show in the White Rock Town Hall at one time.

He mentioned a Swede by the name of Bodelson who lived in White Rock. "He had a way of getting along with people, and they predicted, "He won't last long out there with the Irish, but he did. He even died out there." Wallace went to school in Vasa Township, Districts 131 and 16. Some of the neighbor children went to school with Irish children.

One big Irishman with 12 or 13 kids trained a boxing team in White Rock, which Wallace belonged to. "He watched us pretty darn close. If it was getting out of hands, he just stopped it right there," Wallace said. His parents didn't mind as long as he didn't come home "too beat up." Being active in boxing for a couple of years in the 145-pound class, he had to run two miles a day to be in good condition. One of the guys went to the championships, Wallace said.

The family moved from Jemtland to a place near Red Wing and lived there for a number of years before moving to Welch. "We bought this place right down below here, and then about 1950, I moved in here and lived with a bachelor and provided him with a household. He furnished the house and we fed him. He was an elderly fellow. I think we bought this place in '63," he said.

Wallace married Hazel Hokenstrom in 1944. He has belonged to three different Swedish Lutheran churches, Spring Garden, Vasa, and Welch. He estimated it would have taken Norelius one whole day to walk from White Rock to the church in Welch. The town of Welch at one time was much bigger than Vasa. "They had sort of a hotel. There was a feed mill and sawmills and stockyards. They had passenger train service through here, so they could commute between Red Wing and

Cannon Falls, and any place they wanted to go. So it was really a thriving community down here—a post office and the stores, the hardware stores, and blacksmith shops," Wallace said. The town of Welch also had saloons. "That was a hot town with gamble under the table. It was safe until the sheriff went in there," Wallace said. White Rock also had a beer joint. Wallace suspected there was bootlegging in Spring Garden. "Everybody was making home brew," he said.

At the time of the interview, Wallace was still doing some work in his machine shop. "I've always done a lot of repair work. I got into becoming an inventor too, I guess. I got a patent on a great netting machine that put netting over grapes. There is this fellow over here that raised grapes, and they [the birds?] would make a mess of it. So I developed a machine—I showed it at the inventors' congress here at Redwood Falls," he said.

One day he sat down and drew a number of sketches. Finally, it looked like it was going to work. "It takes a 5,000 ft roll and it could be put on a tractor in ten minutes. It went over big." Wallace got his patent, but then he ran into a lot of problems. "If you try to enter the corporate field to produce something like that in this country, you are vulnerable before you even start. You can't buck these big corporate outfits. I went to a certain point and then I gave up," he said.

Wallace remembered family reunions in the Weberg family ever since he was a small child. "Even back in the Depression we had one right at our place," he said. Neither he nor his parents ever visited Sweden. The interviewer was Lennart Setterdahl.

> Wallace Weberg of Welch was born Dec. 29, 1922 in Spring Garden, the son of Titus Weberg, b. Oct. 13, 1890 in Spring Garden, and his wife Rose Swanson, b. 1900 in Vasa. Wallace was a Trolle Ljungby descendant on both his father's and his mother's side. His father was the son of Nils Weberg, b. 1860 in Trolle Ljungby, who emigrated from that parish in 1869 with his parents *Åbo* Jöns Persson and Olu Jönsdotter, and two other children, Elna and Else. Wallace had two brothers and two sisters, one of whom is Virginia Fanslow. He married Hazel Hokenstrom, a Trolle Ljungby descendant. See interviews with Virginia Fanslow and Hazel Weberg. Wallace Weberg died Dec. 29, 1992.

Withers, Betty Jane (Betts)

Her grandmother talked about Sweden all the time

September 19, 1992

Betty Jane's roots on her mother's side go back to Trolle Ljungby. In 1877, her great-grandparents, D. O. Swanson (Ola Svensson) and Pernilla Nilsdotter, both born in Trolle Ljungby, owned 120 acres in Section 32 of Welch Township. They had six children. One of them, Amanda, became Betts' grandmother. She married Ole Andrew Hanson, whose mother was Norwegian and father of Scotch and Irish heritage. Since Betts' ancestry on her father's side was not Swedish at all, one can say that she was only one quarter Swedish. That part of her roots, however, had captured her interest more than any of the other nationalities.

It was her grandmother Amanda who stimulated her interest in Sweden. Amanda was born in Welch and had never visited Sweden herself. But she had listened to her mother's stories about the old country, and she told Betts what she had learned.

Betty Jane Withers

"She was Grandma Hanson, and I loved her very much. We did not live in Red Wing when I was a young child, even though I was born here. We moved away, and I spent every summer vacation with her from the time I was three years old. Grandma Hanson and I were very close, and she—I could tell—just thought that Sweden was heaven because she just talked about it all the time. She would always tell me—'this is the way they do things in Sweden. Look here, Betty Jane, this came from Sweden. My mother brought it over here.' And I was supposed to just oh and ah, which I did. We would use a dish or a glass, and she would say, 'this came from Sweden.' I was so impressed, so I grew up thinking that Sweden was, oh, get down on your knees! Of course, I've been over there a few times, and I think it is just wonderful, just as wonderful as my grandma told me."

Evidently, Amanda had also stimulated her daughter Ruth's (Betts' mother) interest, because she went to Sweden twice in her lifetime. "That was before people knew a lot about tracing family trees, and she looked around over there. She went to some churches, but she didn't really know where to go, and so she came back very disappointed. Now that she is dead, and I have found relatives in Sweden, I just wish I could tell her," Betts said.

Betts has been to the Trollasten Farm in Trolle Ljungby, where her great-grandmother Pernilla was born. It was her relative, Everal Nelson in Red Wing, who put her on the right track. He had been to Sweden first, and found the home place. In 1980, Betts took her husband, three children, their spouses, and grandchildren on a trip to Sweden. There were eleven people in the party. They drove to Linköping, where they met Ingvar Svensson, whose grandfather was a half brother of Pernilla. From Linköping they drove to Skåne, where they visited relatives in Kristianstad and Trolle Ljungby. Betts visited Trolle Ljungby a fourth time after that. About the landscape in Trolle Ljungby, she said that it is "much more flat" than around Red Wing.

Among Betts' treasured family possessions is a pump organ that her mother received as a gift on her 16th birthday. "It's a beautiful little organ that I had repaired and refinished for my oldest daughter's wedding. She was married right here in the living room in our home," Betts said. One of the relatives played the wedding march on that little old pump organ. "Had to keep her feet moving all the time," Betts said.

Music brought Betts together with Seth Withers. He played the drums in a band that needed a piano player, and Betts was chosen for that position while she was a senior in high school. "So that's how we got acquainted and married later, after the war, because he went over to Europe during World War II and was over there from 1941 until 1945," Betts said.

After high school, Betts studied at Iowa State Teacher's College in Cedar Falls, Iowa, and later went to the Minneapolis Business College. During the war, she worked in an Air Force office in Miami, Florida. Three months after Seth Withers had returned from the war, they were married. Her husband went to school on the GI Bill and graduated from the University of Minnesota four years later. He was of English and German ancestry. He later served as mayor of Red Wing. The mayoral office was not a full-time position and it was not political, Betts said. Her husband was also the postmaster for about 25 years. A drive in Red Wing is named after him. Betts was a life-long Lutheran and a member of the American Swedish Institute in Minneapolis. She had three children. The interviewer was Lilly Setterdahl.

> Betty Jane Withers of Red Wing was born Oct. 26, 1921 in Red Wing, the daughter of Clarence Maetzold, a dentist of German heritage, and Ruth Hanson, b. in 1892. Ruth was the daughter of Amanda Swanson, b. in 1875 in Welch, whose father was Ola (D. O.) Swenson, b. 1844 in Trolle Ljungby and his wife Pernilla Nilsdotter, b. 1844 in Trolle Ljungby. They emigrated in 1868 and had the following children: Mathilda b. 1873 in Vasa (married Martin Lofgren and had children), Sven Adolf b. 1868 in Welch (married Selma Mattson and had one child), Amanda, see above, Nancy b. 1876 in Welch (married Alfred Norlin, 2 children), and Alma b. 1879 in Welch (married Elof Carlson, 2 sons). Betty Jane married Seth Withers, mayor and postmaster of Red Wing. He was deceased at the time of the interview.

Young, Richard

He knew the Swedish table grace

December 3, 1992

Richard was the youngest of our interviewees, but he remembered his grandparents Young. Grandpa Swan Young passed away in January 1953 at the age of 80. Grandma Young was a Sander and she was Swedish too. Like so many others of the third generation, Richard knew the Swedish table grace.

Swan Young farmed 40 acres located south of Cannon River, Richard said. In the 1910 Federal Census, Swan Young is listed as a general farmer in Cannon Falls Township. He rented the farm. Swan's brother, Andrew, rented a separate farm in Vasa Township. (His sister, Annie, born in Cannon Falls, was the housekeeper.) Their father rented another farm in Vasa Township in 1910.

Richard's father also became a farmer. "Dad's 40 acre—we rented that or ran that for them [the grandparents] when we lived with them, but then we moved over to another farm that we rented and bought finally, many years later," Richard said. They lived in Vasa Township, six miles from White Rock. Richard attended elementary school in Vasa and then the Cannon Falls High School. He always had the benefit of school buses. Farming was in his blood, he said. "I enjoyed that. I wasn't more than five or six years old—I was out in the barn helping

Richard Young

Dad cleaning the barn and stuff like that." They did general farming with dairy cows, but Richard never did any hand-milking.

About Andrew (Anders) Young, born in Sweden, Richard said, "That was my dad's uncle. He lived not too far from where my mother's folks lived. And then they auctioned off out here and moved out to North Dakota and homesteaded out there. In '75 my brother and I and Dad went out to the Black Hills… and we found cousins up there. That was Andy Young and Art Benson. They were my dad's cousins, and he had never met them before or seen them before in his life, so he got to visit them that time. And Andy is gone now, but Art is still living," Richard said.

"Young's Farm" was painted on the walls of an outbuilding. "They were glad to meet us and get to know us. They enjoyed that. They knew there were relations some place, but never had gotten, or seen each other in their life," Richard said.

Walter Swanson's wife, Dorothy, was related somehow to Art Benson, Richard said. "One year, when they were down here, they were staying at Walter's. And they came around and we got to meet them a little bit, and then we went out there afterwards to visit them." His uncle on his mother's side, Cyrus Lindell, lived out by the farm where Richard used to live. Asked whether many of the Swedes in Goodhue County were related, he answered, "You bet."

Richard was the eldest of three brothers. "I stayed on the farm. My brothers got five acres each, so they could build their houses when they got married. So they are living out there now on the farm, each one," Richard said. His brother, Kermit, has rheumatoid arthritis and is not working. Lyle is the manager of Barron's Oil Supply in Cannon Falls. Richard's diabetes was discovered when he was eleven years old. "I've been on insulin ever since then," he said. Ten years ago, he said, he lost his eye sight.

The old-timers spoke Swedish, Richard said. "I know if I go up to the Cannon River nursing home now, and run into my aunt, she will talk Swedish to me—Blanche Lindell. She likes to talk Swede with me because she knows I understand it. She can talk. I can answer her in English. I can't answer her too much in Swedish. As long as I lived up there at the Cannon River nursing home, I always said the prayer every meal before I ate my meal, I always said the prayer in Swede," Richard said.

His mother taught him the Swedish table prayer, and he could recite it. The table prayer was printed in a cookbook his mother used. "She was baking one day, and I was looking in there, and I found this [prayer] and I was going to learn it, so I learned that, about 10 or 12 years old. My mother told me how it was supposed to be said in Swede. I learned from her." The Swedish table grace was still used in the 1950s in his family. He recited the old version correctly: "*I Jesu namn går vi till bords, äta dricka på Guds ord. Gud till ära oss till gagn, så får vi mat i Jesu name. Amen.*"

Richard met his fiancée at the nursing home where he was staying after his legs had been amputated about six years earlier. "She was working there as an aide, and I got to know her. She said she'd figured out how she could get me transferred from a wheelchair into the car. She could take me to church, so we decided we are going to get married." He would like to get married in the Vasa Lutheran Church, where he was baptized and confirmed. The interviewer was Lennart Setterdahl.

> Richard Young was born Feb. 7, 1947 in Red Wing, the son of Mayland Young and his wife Marie Lindell, both born in Cannon Falls.

Mayland was the son of Sven Young, b. 1873 in Trolle Ljungby, who emigrated in 1880 with his parents, Soldier Per Nilsson Ljung, b. 1848 in Trolle Ljungby and Ingar Svensdotter, b. 1844 and four children: Sigrid b. 1868, Sven b. 1873, Nils b. 1876, and Anders b. 1879. Richard was handicapped from the complications of diabetes. He died Sep. 11, 1995.

Epilogue

In my first *Minnesota Swedes*, published in 1996, I reported on what the situation was for the leaseholds under the Trolle Ljungby Castle Farm in 1995. I asked Rune Persson in Ynde if he had been able to purchase his leasehold. At that time, his answer was "No." In 2014 when I asked the same question, he happily reported that he and his wife Lena are the proud owners of the manor and outbuildings, as well as part of the land that his forefathers had farmed for generations.

Rune Persson reminded me of the fact that the heads of the castle estates were not the owners of the land, but rather trustees or administrators, who were entitled to the income of the property. In the sources that I have quoted, the Count of Trolle Ljungby always referred to himself as the owner, and others did refer to him as such. Thus I have kept the quotes intact. However, to comply with the accepted practices of today, I have replaced the word "owner" in narratives with other descriptive words when it refers to the heads of noble estates.

The privileged castle farms in Sweden are decreasing in numbers. Less than 30 remain. The *fideikomiss* law prohibits sales of entire leaseholds unless the count agrees. No complete leaseholds have been sold so far in Trolle Ljungby. At the time of this writing, the head of the Trolle Ljungby estate was still Count Hans Gabriel Trolle Wachtmeister, born in 1923. According to a law of 1963, the Trolle Ljungby estate will cease to exist as a *fideikomiss* when the current count passes away. He and his wife Alice have no children. The heir, his brother's grandson, Carl-Fredrik Wachtmeister, born in 1984, will then be the owner of 50 percent, plus parts of the rest of the estate and will be richer than his predecessor, according to Rune Persson.

Bibliography

Books

Åkerman, Sune. *From Stockholm to San Francisco: The Development of the Historical Study of External Migration.* Uppsala: Preprint from Annales Academaie Regiae Scientiarum Upsaliensis 19/1975.

Anderson, Alexander P. *The Seventh Reader: Short Stories with Some Verse.* Caldwell, ID: n. p. The Caxton Printers, 1941.

Anderson, Ingvar and Jörgen Weibull. *Swedish History in Brief.* Södertälje: Svenska Institutet, 1980.

Barton, H. Arnold, ed. *Letters From the Promised Land: Swedes in America, 1840-1914.* Minneapolis: University of Minnesota Press for the Swedish Pioneer Historical Society, 1975.

Beijbom, Ulf. *Swedes in Chicago: a demographic and social study of the 1846-1880 immigration.* Studia Historica Upsaliensia nr 38. Stockholm: Läromedels-förlagen, 1971 (Växjö: Davidsons boktryckeri).

Bengtsson, Karl. "Blick på häradet." *Handlingar angående Villands härad.* Vol. XIII. Kristianstad: Villands härads hembygdsförening, 1955.

Benson Holmes, Dorothea. *Bittersweet.* Tuscon, AZ: Skyline Printing, ca. 1979.

Bergendoff, Conrad. *The Augustana Ministerium: A Study of the Careers of the 2,504 Pastors of Augustana Evangelical Lutheran Synod/Church, 1850-1962.* Rock Island: Augustana Historical Society, 1980.

Beskrifning Öfver Norra Still Hafs Banans Land i Minnesota. New York, 1873.

Bidrag till Sveriges Officiella Statistik, XVI: Statistiska Central-Byråns Underdåninga Berättelse För År 1874. Stockholm: P. A. Norstedt & Söner, 1875.

Bidrag till Sveriges Officiella Statistik. A) Befolknngsstatistik. XXII:1: Statistiska Centralbyråns Underdåninga Berättelse För År 1880, Första Avdelningen. Stockholm: P. A. Norstedt & Söner, 1882.

Bolin, Sture. *En Skånsk Prästson in Amerika.* Malmö: Gleerups, 1960.

Carlson, Sten. "Bonden och Industrialismen." *Bonden i Svensk Historia*, Del III. Stockholm: Lantbruksförbundets Tidskriftaktiebolag, 1956.

Carlson, Sten. "Bonden och Industrialismen." Bonden i Svensk Histoira. Del III.

Celebrating.... Our 125th Anniversary: Vasa Spring Garden Mutual Insurance Company (Cannon Falls, MN 1985).

Christianstads Läns Kongl. Hushålls-Sällskaps Förhandlingar jemte Berättelse. Kristianstad: 1859-67, 1869, 1871, 1891.

Curtis-Wedge, Franklyn, ed. *History of Goodhue County Minnesota Illustrated.* Chicago: H. C. Cooper, Jr. & Co., 1909.

Den Nya Svenska Kolonien I Minnesota—Nord-Amerika: Goda land förEmigranter, på de billigaste vilkor vid Lake Superior Jernbanan. Kristianstad: K. J. M. Möllersvärd, 1872, and Stockholm, Rediviva, 1970 (Facsimile).

En Smålandssocken Emigrerar: En bok om emigrationen till Amerika från Långasjö socken i Kronobergs län. Växjö: Långasjö Emigrantcirkel, 1967.

Frälsebönder Åbor Arrendatorer: Yttrande från Willands arrendatorförening. Särtyck med förord av Rune Persson, 1992.

Genrup, Kurt. "Skånsk Folkkultur." *Skåne.* Stockholm: Brevskolan, 1988.

Gjerde, Jon. *From Peasants to Farmers: The Migration From Balestrand, Norway to the Upper Middle West.* New York: Cambridge University Press, 1985.

Goodhue County's First Hundred Years: From Earliest Times as Recounted in the Centennial Edition of the Red Wing Daily Republican Eagle, July 7, 1954. Red Wing: Goodhue County Historical Society, 1972.

Guide to Swedish-American Archival and Manuscript Sources in the United States. Chicago: Swedish-American Historical Society, 1983.

Hedblom, Folke. *Swedish Speech in an English Setting: Some Observations on and Aspects of immigrant Environments in America.* Offprint: Leeds Studies of English, II, 1968. (Studies in honor of H. Olson).

Hembygdens Jul 1987. Kristianstad: Rinkaby IOGT-NTO, 1987.

Historiska Arrenden: förslag till friköpslag. Delbetänkande av 1990 års arrendekommitté. Statens offentliga utredningar 1991:85 Justiedepartment, Malmö: n. p. 1991.

Hofberg, Herman. "Ljungby Horn and Pipe," W. H. Myers, tr. Masterpieces From Swedish Literature II. Rock Island: Augustana Book Concern, 1908.

Ingers, E., ed. "Rutger Maclean." *Bonden i Svensk Historia,* Del II. Stockholm: Lantbruksförbundets Tidskriftsaktiebolag, 1948.

Johansson, Nils. "Till det stora landet i väster." *Handlingar angående Villansd härad*, Vol. XXIV. Kristianstad: Villands härad hembygdsförening, 1967.

Johansson, Nils. "Östskånsk emigrantforskning." *Handlingar angående Villands härad.* Vol. XXV. Kristianstad: Villands härads hembygdsförening, 1968.

Johansson, Nils. "Emigrantöde från Näsum." *Handlingar angående Villands härad.* Vol. XXV. Kristianstad: Villands härads hembygdsförening, 1969.

Johansson, Nils. "Utvandrare från Trolle Ljungby." *Handlingar angående Villands härad.* Vol. XXV. Kristianstad: Villands härads hembygdsförening, 1970.

Johnson, Niel and Lilly Setterdahl. *Rockford Swedes: American Stories.* East Moline, IL: American Friends of the Emigrant Institute of Sweden, Inc., 1993.

Jörberg, Lennart. *A History of Prices in Sweden 1732-1914.* Vol. I. Lund: CVK Gleerup, 1977.

Kastrup, Allan. *The Swedish Heritage in America: The Swedish Element in America and American-Swedish Relations in Their Historical Perspective.* St. Paul: Swedish Council of America, 1975.

Kämpe, Alfred. *Svenska Allmogens frihetsstrider.* Stockholm: LT's Förlag, 1974.

Krona, Hilding, ed. *Folkskollärare Ola Jönsson Lundbergs Krönika från Trolle Ljungby socken.* n.p. n.d.

Krona, Hilding, "Ola Jönsson Lundborg, en trotjänare i skolans tjänst." *Hembygdens Jul* 1987. Kristianstad: IOGT-NTO, 1987.

Ljungmark, Lars. *For Sale—Minnesota: Organized Promotion of Scandinavian Immigration 1866-1873.* Chicago: The Swedish Pioneer Historical Society, 1971.

Lund, Emil. *Minnesota-Konferenses och Dess Församlingars Historia.* Rock Island: Augustana Book Concern, 1926.

Map of Goodhue County Minnesota: Drawn From Actual Surveys and the County Records. Red Wing, MN: Warner & Foote, 1877 and Goodhue County Historical Society, 1991 (Facsimile).

Mattson, Hans. *Minnen.* Autobiography. Lund: Gleerups förlag, 1880.

Nelson, Helge. *The Swedes and the Swedish Settlements in North America,* New York: Arno Press, 1979.

Nelson, O. N. ed. *History of the Scandinavians in the United States*, Del I-II, revised edition. Minneapolis: O. N. Nelson & Company, 1900.

Noreen, Paul. *Emigrationen from Sundals härad i Dalsland, 1866-1895: Emigrationens orsaker och förlopp*. Faksimil från licentiatsavhandling 1967. Historiska institutionen, Amerikanska avdelningen. Uppsala unviversitet. Mellerud, Sweden: Logen nr 644 Melelrud. Vasa Orden of America, 1987.

Norelius, E. *De Svenska Luterska Församlingarnas och Svenskarnes Historia i Amerika.* Rock Island: Lutheran Augustana Book Concern, 1890.

Norelius, Eric. *The Pioneer Swedish Settlements and Swedish Lutheran Churches in America 1845-1860*. Conrad Bergendoff, tr. Rock Island, IL: Augustana Historical Society, 1984.

Norelius, Eric. *Vasa Illustrata: En borgerlig och kyrklig kulturbild.* Rock Island: Augustana Book Concern, 1905. Norman, Hans. *Från Bergslagen till Nordamerika: Studier i migrationsmönster, social rörlighet och demografisk struktur med utgångspunkt från Örebro län 1951-1915*. Studia Historica Upsaliensia: Historiska Institutionen vid Uppsala Universitet, 1974.

Olson, Ernst W. Ed. *History of the Swedes in Illinois*, Part 1. Chicago: The Engberg-Holmberg Publishing Company, 1908.

Ostergren, Robert, C. *A Community Transplanted: The Trans-Atlantic Experience of a Swedish Immigrant Settlement in the Upper Middle West, 1835-1915*. Madison: The University of Wisconsin Press, 1988.

Pearson, Trued Granville. *En Skånsk banbrytare i Amerika*. Autobiography edited and published by Arvid Bjerking, Kristianstad: Arvid Bjerking, Kristianstads Läns Tidning A-B:s Tryckeri, 1937.

Rasmussen, C. A. *A History of Goodhue County, Minnesota*. C. A. Rasmussen, 1935.

Report upon the Statistics of Agriculture, 1880: Compiled from Returns Received at the Tenth Census. Washington, DC: Government Printing Office, 1880.

Röndahl, Uno. Skåneland II: *På Jakt Efter Historien*. Karlshamn: n.p. Lagerblads Tryckeri AB, 1986.

Rosenberg, C. M. *Geografiskt-Statistlskt Handlexikon Öfver Sverige.* Faksimil-utgåva. Göteborg: Landsarkivet i Göteborg och Genealogisk Ungdom, 1982.

Rosenquist, Per. "30 kronor för 100 år sen." *Hembygdens Jul 1987*. Kristianstad: Rinkaby IOGT/NTO 1987.

Scott, Franklin D. *Sweden The Nation's History*. Carbondale and Edwardsville: Southern Illinois University, 1988.

Setterdahl, Lilly. *"Emigrationen från Frändefors: Ättlingar i Pennsylania."* Hembygden 1983. Åmål: Dalslands Hembygdsförbund, 1983.

Setterdahl, Lilly. "Emigrant Letters by Bishop Hill Colonists from Nora Parish." *Western Illinois Regional Studies*, Vol. 1, No. 2. Fall 1978. Macomb, IL: Western Illinois University, 1978.

Setterdahl, Lilly. *"Scandinavians in Alabama."* Memories Preserved, Vol. II. East Moline, IL: American Friends of the Emigrant Institute of Sweden, 1992.

Skarstedt, Ernst. *Våra Pennfäktare: Lefnads-och Karaktärsteckningar.* San Francisco: Eget Förlag, 1987.

Soderstrom, Alfred. *Blixtar på Tidnings-Horisonten: Samlade och Magasinerade.* Varrod, MN: Alfred Soderstrom, 1910.

Sundbärg, G. *Emigrationsutredningen: Jordstyckningen*, Bil. XII. Stockholm: Statistiska Centralbyrån, 1911.

Svenska Slott och Herresäten vid 1900-talets början. Stockholm: Nordisk familjeboks tryckeri, 1909.

Svensk Uppslagsbok. Andra omarbetade upplagan. Malmö: Förlagshuset Norden, AB, 1964.

Tynderfeldt, Bo. Ed. *Skåne.* Stockholm: Bervskolan, 1988.

Vecoli, Rudolph. "An Inter-Ethnic Perspective on American Immigration History." *Swedes in America: Intercultural and Interethnic perspectives on contemporary research. A report of the Symposium Swedes in America: New Perspectives.* America: New Perspectives. Ulf Beijbom, ed. Växjö: The Swedish Emigrant Institute Series, 6, 1993.

Wallentin, Hans. *Svenska folkets historia.* Lund: Prisma/Föreningen Vedandi, 1978.

Westman, Erik G., ed. *The Swedish Element in America.* Chicago: Swedish-American Biographical Society.

Wilson, Horace B. "History of Goodhue County." History of Goodhue County Including a Sketch of the Territory and State of Minnesota. Red Wing, MN: Wood, Alley & Co., 1978.

Newspapers

Gull, Judith. "A Pioneer's Retrospect." Clipping from an unidentified Red Wing newspaper, Sep. 1, 1915.

Johansson, Nils, ed. "Ett gammalt amerikabrev." *Kvällsstunden*, Västerås Sep. 18, 1987.

Kullberg, Emil Albert, "Memories of Years and Days Gone By" in "History lives in Vasa, Part II." *Cannon Falls Beacon*, Cannon Falls, MN Feb. 24, 1983.

Mattson, Hans, öfverste. "Bref från Sverige." *Svenska Amerikanaren*, Chicago Apr. 6, 1869.

"Bref från Amerika." *Svenska Nybyggaren*, St. Paul, Nov. 7, 1872.

"Bref från en 70-årig Skåne Bonde till en lärd Doktor." *Hemlandet*, Galesburg, IL Apr. 6 1869.

folkets hus, Borås, *No. 7, 1983.*

Kristianstad-Bladet, Kristianstad. 1856 (Vol. I), 1857, 1858, 1963, 1964, 1965, 1867, 1868, 1869.

Argus, Red Wing, MN Jan. 14, 1869.

Goodhue Co. Republican, Red Wing, MN Aug. 24, Sep. 21, 1866, Jul. 9, 1874.

Minnesota-Posten, Red Wing, MN 1857-58.

Svenska Amerikanaren, Chicago, Apr. 20, 1869.

Svenska Nybyggaren, St. Paul, Jan. 2, 1874.

Unpublished Manuscripts

Aminof, Sten. Excerpts of Swedes sailing from Hamburg. Handwritten manuscript. Svenska Emigrantinstitutet, Växjö.

Anderson, Glorian. "Stories my mother Alice Bodelson told me." Typed manuscript in English.

Bjerstedt, Edit. "Minnen från Tosteberga vid tiden för min uppväxt." Typed manuscript in Swedish.

Hellquist, Katherine. "D. O. Swanson." Typed manuscript.

Johansson, E. "Mina barndomsminnen." Typed manuscript in Swedish.

Johansson, Nils. "Utvandrare Från Önnestads Socken 1851-1920" Softbound photocopy containing excerpts from emigration records and newsclippings of Sam Rönnegård, "Höfdingen av Vasa: Berättelser från svenskarnas kolonisering av Minnesota." Published in *Svenska Amerikanaren Tribunen,* Chicago, 1972.

Johansson, Nils. Excerpts from Trolle Ljungby Household Rolls, 1854-60. Typed manuscript in Swedish.

Lundborg, Ola Jönsson. "Anteckningar" nedtecknade av Ola Jönsson Lundborg med dagboksanteckningar, 1882-1916. Typed manuscript in Swedish edited by Gunnar Christensen. Svenska Emigrantinstitutet, Växjö.

Malberg, John J. "Diary of John J. Malberg." Spring Garden, Leon Township, Goodhue County, MN. Jan. 1, 1869/ Oct. 2, 1903. Typed manuscript translated from the Swedish by Viola Young-Knutson.

Mattson, Hans. Family Papers. Two letters in Swedish to his wife. Minnesota Historical Society, St. Paul.

Nelson, Lucille. "Grandpa and Gradma Ingeman." Typed manuscript in English.

Peterson, Björn-Åke. Excerpts from Passenger Arrivals in New York, 1855-60. Computer printout. Svenska Emigrantinstitutet.

Rosenquist, Stephen. "Bengt Per Rosenquist: Pioneer of America." Typed booklet in English, 45 pp. Copyright, 1959.

Rosquist, Gunnar. "Ett 25-årigt statarliv." Typed manuscript in Swedish.

Young-Knutson, Viola. "Childhood Memories." Typed manuscript in English.

Other Unpublished Manuscripts

(Sweden)

Arrendekontrakt, Årup Goods, ca. 1850-1933. Landsarkivet, Lund.

Arrendekontrakt, Trolle Ljungby Goods, 1902.

Arrendekontrakt. Trolle Ljungby Gods, 1880. Svenska Emigrant-institutet, Växjö.

Household Examination Rolls and Exit Rolls, ca. 1850-1901. Microfiche. Svenska Emigrantinstitutet, Växjö.

Interviews made in Sweden 1993 by Lilly and Lennart Setterdahl. Trolle Ljungby Project consisting of 13 recordings. Originals held by the author.

"Landshövdingarnas femårsberättelser." 1951-55: 1871-75. Landsarkivet, Lund.

Passenger Lists. Copenhagen. The Danes Worldwide Archives, Aalborg, Denmark. Microfiche copies at Svenska Emigrantinstitutet, Växjö.

Passenger Lists, Gothenburg and Malmö. Svenska Emigrantinstitutet, Växjö.

"Utredning om arbetstorpens bärighet." (1908). Årup Gods 1875-1971 20:2 Landsarkivet, Lund.

(United States)

"A Town book for the Town of Featherstone Presented by William Fayberger July 28, 1858" Original Minute Book, Goodhue County Historical Society, Red Wing, MN.

"Book of Records," 1855-1860 and other land records. Goodhue County Courthouse, Red Wing, MN.

Birth, Marriage, and Death Records, Goodhue County Courthouse, Red Wing, MN.

Correspondence between Sweden and emigrants from Trolle Ljungby, 1856-1881. Copies of 15 letters deposited at Svenska Emigrantinstitutet, Växjö.

Genealogical records (family charts and sketches) received from descendants of Trolle Ljungby emigrants.

Interviews made in Minnesota by Lilly and Lennart Setterdahl with descendants of Trolle Ljungby emigrants, Originals housed at Svenska Emigrantinstitutet, Växjö. Copies held by the author.

Minutes of "The Leon Literary Debating Society," Jan. 24, 1896-Feb. 24, 1902.

Naturalizations Records, Minnesota Historical Society, St. Paul.

Original Deed, 1861. Privately owned.

Plat books, Goodhue County, 1894 and 1914. Goodhue County Historical Society, Red Wing, MN.

State of Minnesota Population censuses, 1865, 1875, 1885, 1895, 1905, 1915.

Swedish-American Church Records, Goodhue County, MN. Microfilm copies at Svenska Emigrantinstitutet, Växjö, and Swenson Swedish Immigration Research Center, Augustana College, Rock Island, IL.

"United States Land Office Receiver's Certificate." 1856. Privately owned.

United States Agricultural Census Manuscripts, 1860, 1870, 1880, 1900, 1910, 1920. Microfilm Copies. Minnesota Historical Society, St. Paul, Red Wing Public Library, Red Wing, MN and Svenska Emigrantinstitutet, Växjö, through 1910.

Endnotes

[i] **Swen Olson** (later Swan Olson) was born June 28, 1827 in Nymö. He was a hired man at the castle farm in Trolle Ljungby at the time of his emigration in 1855. His first wife was Karna Andersdotter b. Sep. 8, 1826 in Trolle Ljungby. Their daughter Märta (Martha) was born Oct. 9, 1853 in Trolle Ljungby. Before Karna died she bore three children in Vasa: Elna b. 1857, Anders b. 1860, Olof b. 1861. Martha married Charles Emil Strandberg and they moved to Seattle. Elna married Charles Bennet and stayed in the area. With his second wife, Anna Brita Berndtsdotter, b. 1845 in Värö, Halland, Olson had 15 children, but five died in childhood. The surviving children were: Carolina (Lena) b. 1864 (Mrs. Charles Axel Younggren), Oscar Bernard (1871-1906), Johanna Jublina b.1876 (Mrs. Frank F. Edstrom), Alma Matilda b. 1878 (Mrs. Victor N. Ramstedt), Peter Alfred b. 1880, Hilma Minerva b. 1882 (Mrs. Axel Peter Ramstedt), Agnes Amanda b. 1885, Minnie Emelia b. 1887 (Mrs. Herman A. Chinlund), Fred b. 1889, and Esther Larinda b. 1894. The sons, Peter, Alfred and Fred also married. Peter moved to Idaho and Fred to Spokane. All the married children of Swan Olson had children of their own. See more information about Swan Olson's children in the interviews with Marian Terborch, Betty Bender and Marian Terborch.

[ii] **Swen Swenson** (later Swan Swanson) was born Mar. 11 or 19, 1821 in Vanneberga, Trolle Ljungby, and his wife Nilla, Nov. 27 1824 in the same parish. The children born in Sweden were: Karna b. Feb. 7, 1849, Bengta b. June 12, 1851, and Swen b. Mar. 14, 1854. Bengta married John Johnson from Rogberga. Karna and Swen moved to Minneapolis. The following children were born in Vasa: Anna in 1859, Hendric in 1864, and Emelia in 1866. Hendric (Henry) took over the farm. He married Anna S. Anderson, b. 1870 in Väröbacka, Halland, and they had the following children: Fred Alvin b. 1895, Elina Alvina b. 1896, Nanny Rosie Sofie b. 1900, Walter Henry Arnold b. 1906, Stanley Winfred b. 1908. See interviews with Walter and Stanley Swanson, and Virginia Fanslow.

[iii] **Anders Nilson** (later Andrew Nelson) was born Aug. 13, 1815 in Viby and his wife Kjersti Månsdotter May 4, 1819 in Vanneberga,

Trolle Ljungby. Nilson was listed as *åbo* at the time of emigration. Two children were born in Vanneberga: Karna in 1845 and Nils in 1848. Karna married Peter Engberg. The children born in Vasa were: Jöns (John) in 1858 and Elna in 1861 (Mrs. Charlie Bergquist). John married and had 9 children. He took over the family farm. See interview with Stella Ingeman.

iv **Bengt Anderson** was born Mar. 11, 1829 in Trolle Ljungby. At the time of emigration he was listed as hired man. His wife Elna Larsdotter was born Sep. 23, 1825 in Fjelkestad. Their children born in Vasa were: Ingrid b. 1855 (Mrs. Pehr W. Peterson), Bengta b. 1859 (Mrs. Per Gustaf Anderson), Alfred b. 1861 (m. Anna Britta Back), Anna b. 1862 (Mrs. Swen Ackerson), Nellie (1864-68), and Esther b. 1868 (Mrs. John B. Back). See interview with Alfred's grandson, Bernard Anderson.

v Olof Swenson-Wallin was born in 1847 in Trolle Ljungby and arrived in 1869. His wife Pernilla Trulsdotter was born in 1949 in the same parish and arrived in 1873. They were the grandparents of Janice Olson, Welch.

vi Ola W. Swenson was born in 1838 in Trolle Ljungby and emigrated in 1866 with his wife, Elsa, born Feb. 16, 1846. Children born in Vasa: Hilma in 1866, (Betsey, died), Henry William in 1870, Swen Albert in 1872, and Emma in 1873. Children born in Welch: Bennet Olof in 1875, Carl Emil in 1877, Dorotea Adelia in 1882, and Ottelia S. in 1884. Mrs. Elsa Swenson died in Tustin, Michigan, Oct. 12, 1907, where she had lived for 15 years. She was survived by her husband and eight children.

vii Ola Swenson, later D. O. Swanson, was born in 1844 in Trolle Ljungby and his wife also in 1844. They arrived from Trolle Ljungby in 1868 and are ancestors of Betty Jane Withers.

viii Anders Nilson, b. 1832 in Trolle Ljungby arrived in 1865. His wife Lisa (also called Sarah or Sissa) Hokanson was born in 1839 in

Ivetofta. Their children were all born in Welch: Emma in 1869, Nils Edward in 1870, Henry William in 1874, Carl Richard in 1876, and Alma Victoria in 1883. Emma married J. F. Hagberg, b. in Dalsland, and they took over the farm. They were the grandparents of Helen Fredrickson. See interview with her.

[ix] Mons Person b. in 1824 in Tosteberga, Trolle Ljungby, arrived in 1868. He was married to Kersti Olsdotter, b. 1832 in Kiaby. Their sons, Ola and Pehr, were born in Trolle Ljungby in 1858 and 1860 and arrived with their mother in 1871. The daughter, Anna Oliva, was born in 1872.

[x] The wife of Swen Magnus Bloom, Johanna, was born in 1861 in Trolle Ljungby and arrived in 1881. Their children were Herman b. 1882, Godfrey b. 1884, Albert b. 1885, and Arthur b. 1898.

[xi] Anders Lamberg, b. 1850 in Sölvesborg emigrated from Trolle Ljungby in 1880 with his wife, Anna, nee Nilson, b. 1845 in Sölvesborg, and their children Nils b. 1874, Jöns b. 1877, and Hilda b. 1879. Two children were born in Vasa, Emil in 1880 and Arthur in 1885. All except Nels and Emil died young. In the 1900 Federal Census Nels Lamberg is listed as the head of the household renting a farm. His mother and two brothers, Emil and Arthur, lived with him. Anders Lamberg had died in 1898. In 1914, Nels owned 218 acres in Section 12, Vasa Township. He married Adelina Nelson, and they had three children: The twins Jeanette and Virgil b. ca 1905 and Nina b. 1908. Virgil's son Donley Lamberg lived in Rochester, Minnesota, when he was interviewed. Nina's daughters Janet Larson and Sharon Nelson lived in Goodhue County. Emil Lamberg became a farmer and married Esther Danielson and had four children.

[xii] Per Nilson Ljung b. 1848 in Fjelkinge emigrated from Trolle Ljungby in 1880 with his wife Ingar Svensdotter, b. 1844 in Trolle Ljungby, and their children Swen b. 1873, Nils b. 1876, and Anders b. 1879. A daughter, Annie Elise was born in Cannon Falls in 1881. In the 1900 Federal Census, Per Young was listed as farm renter in Vasa Township. In 1910, his sons Swan Young and Pete Young,

both of whom were married, rented separate farms. In the 1914 Plat Book, P. N. Young is listed as the owner of a small farm in Section 20. He died in 1913. There are many descendants in Goodhue County, one of whom was interviewed (Richard Young). Andrew (Anders) Young moved to North Dakota.

[xiii] Bengt Persson Rosenquist. B. 1848 in Rinkaby, emigrated from Trolle Ljungby in 1880 together with his wife Anna Olsdotter, b. 1846, and four sons: Per b. 1871, Ola b. 1872, Nils b. 1874, and Alfred b. 1878. The family came to Vasa from Iowa. Bengt worked on a farm 1880-86, where three additional children were born, Anna in 1880, Bennet in 1883, and Blenda in 1885. The Rosenquists moved to Hallock in Kittson County and bought land there. They later moved to Shickley, Nebraska, where Anna died. Rosenquist remarried and fathered five more children. A grandson, Stephan Rosenquist, lives in Bloomfield, Michigan. He was interviewed in Sweden.

[xiv] Per Svenson Wallin, b. 1850 or '51 in Trolle Ljungby, emigrated from that parish in 1880 together with wife Elna, nee Larsson, b. 1851 and their children Karna b. 1877 and Lars b. 1879. A daughter, Selma, was born in Vasa in 1883. In the 1900 Federal Census, Peter Wallin was listed as farm renter in Welch Township. He had remarried in 1889 and had seven more children. The son Lars (Louise) b. 1879 married Ida Malvina b. 1881 in Vasa.

[xv] Jöns Trulson Walberg, b. 1845 in Trolle Ljungby, emigrated from that parish in 1880 with his wife Anna Svensdotter b. 1853, and their children, Jöns b. 1875, Bengta b. 1877, and Sven b. 1879. He is the only one of the Trolle Ljungby migrants in Goodhue County who was a farm owner in Sweden. In the 1880 Federal Census, he is listed as laborer at Peter Swanson's a neighbor in Welch Township. His wife is living at the time, but when the family joined the Cannon River Church, the wife was not listed. John Walberg moved to Webster, Wisconsin. He had 6 or 7 children according to Arnold Risberg, who was a relative.

[xvi] Nils Nilson Rooth, b. 1854 in Vanneberga, Trolle Ljungby, emigrated from that parish in 1881 with his wife, Karna Anderson b. 1850 also in Trolle Ljungby, and their daughter Maria b. 1879. Another daughter, Alma, was born in Vasa in 1883. The 1900 Federal Census lists as a day laborer and renter of a house. In 1910, he was a hired man (farm laborer). He died in 1939. The daughter Maria married Leonard Albert Johnson and they had two daughters, Helen E. (Mrs. Glad) and Mildred L. (Mrs. Lind).

[xvii] Carl Anderson Ståhl (Steele), b. 1829 or 30 in Färlöv, emigrated from Trolle Ljungby in 1881 with his sons Anders b. 1863 and Per b. 1865. His wife, Anna Månsdotter, b. 1830, arrived from Trolle Ljungby in 1882 with daughter Maria Carlsdotter b. 1868. Another daughter, Hanna b. 1860 in Trolle Ljungby, is listed with the family in the Vasa Lutheran Church records as having arrived in 1882. Carl died in 1913. The son Anders (Andrew) married Anna Simonson and they had 8 children. The eldest, Maria Amalia, b. 1896, was the mother of Steven L. Hedeen, Vasa, who was interviewed. The 1910 Federal Census lists Andrew Steele as a carpenter and farm owner.

[xviii] Sven Olsson Brodd, b. 1862 in Trolle Ljungby, emigrated in 1903 from Nymö with his wife, Nellie Månsdotter b. 1862 in Nymö, and their children, Kersti b. 1888, Alfred Gustaf Adolph b. 1892, Anna Martha b. 1894, Ole b. 1898 and Esther Martina b. 1901. The two eldest sons, Nels b. 1884 and Sven b. 1886, had emigrated in 1901. The family settled at first in western Minnesota, where Mrs. Brodd had relatives. Having moved to Vasa in 1911, Nellie died in 1917. In 1920, the widower lived with his son Alfred in a rented house. The son Nels Brodd was a farmer. He married Helga Swanson and had two daughters, Mildred and Bertie. See interview with Ole Brodd, Kenyon, recorded in 1993. He had one daughter and three sons.

[xix] According to records in Trolle Ljungby, Sven Bengtsson, b. 1871 in Trolle Ljungby, emigrated in 1912 wit his family, but First Lutheran Church records in Red Wing states that he arrived in 1907. He may have left ahead of his family. His wife, Ingrid Andersson was born 1874 in V. Vram parish. She is listed as having arrived in 1912. The children born in Trolle Ljungby were: Berndt Anton in 1899, Nils Hilding in 1901, Knut Emil in 1902, Hanna Ingeborg in 1904, and Ragnar Sigvard in 1907. A daughter, Ebba Silvia, was born in 1913 in Belle Creek. Ragnar Sigvard was not listed when the family joined churches in Red Wing and Welch.